FIELDS
OF
FLYING

An Illustrated History

of Airports

in the Southwest

by

Robert P. Olislagers

Foreword

by

Brigadier General

Charles E. "Chuck" Yeager (USAF-Ret.)

Published by

Heritage Media Corp.

Encinitas, California

Heritage
p u b l i s h i n g
A Division of Heritage Media Corporation

AUTHOR: *Robert P. Olislagers*
PUBLISHER: *Charles E. Parks*
PHOTO EDITOR: *Robert P. Olislagers*
EDITOR: *Lori M. Parks*
ART DIRECTOR: *Lucia Lento, Art Dept.*

Aan mijn Ouders

TABLE OF CONTENTS

(Intro Photo on page 2)
Meadowlark Airport, near Huntington Beach,
closed forever in the 1980's
(Reprinted with permission from Roger Tonry)

INTRODUCTION

This book is in celebration of the 50th anniversary of the Southwest Chapter of the American Association of Airport Executives. As has been customary, the Association publishes, in one form or another, its proceedings every five years. In celebration of the 50th milestone, it was decided to expand the publication by including a history of airports, focusing primarily on the member states of Arizona, California, Nevada and Utah.

Although much has been written about the history of aviation, its primary focus has been on aircraft and their designers, yet little has been said about airports. The task of recording the history of airports has been largely left to the individual airports themselves, and in some cases, the communities in which they are located. In part, it speaks to their character as isolated entities, as if by analogy, they were islands in a vast ocean of humanity. It speaks to a secluded, yet wondrous world, where only the sacred surf, and where, with each wave that crashes upon the shore, just one more bit of warm beach is eroded. It is a place where the waters can churn with relentless energy, sometimes even with perilous deception or remorse. Yet, at other times, the waters are as calm as the blue skies above from which the view is like no other.

Aviation has always been an affair of the heart and so is this book. It was dreamed up along the beaches of the Pacific, just north of where the first flight in the United States took place. Having been born on a distant island along "the ring of fire", it seemed only natural to gravitate to where the air, surf and turf would meet. The analogy, however, is not too far from the truth and it seemed the best way to explain what is intrinsic. Fields of Flying is an illustrated history and only a cursory one at that. You will not find the tedious research generally required of a book with the lofty description "history" somewhere imbedded within its title. This is also not an academic work, although a "flash" or two are within the pages that follow. Last, this is no literary work; somebody else was supposed to write this book, but he ("bluestreak") got a job flying for an airline; imagine that!

This book is simply about how airfields came to be and about the legislative history that followed. Too many have vanished and "slipped the surly bonds of earth". One airfield a week now vanishes from the landscape forever, never to return other than in the minds of an occasional nostalgic aviator. The diligent research by Ed Leiser, Curator of the San Diego Aerospace Museum, demonstrates the sad legacy which has befallen much of the airport industry in America. Of the 140 some airfields he has documented in San Diego County alone, only a dozen or so remain today. It is just one such an example but it is by no means the exception. The sum total of airports represented in Fields of Flying, is only a fraction of the airports which still exist today. Let us all make sure that number does not get smaller still by the time the association celebrates its centennial in 2047.

ACKNOWLEDGMENTS

Fields of Flying is first and foremost in celebration of the 50th anniversary of "SWAAAE", as the association is affectionately known among its members. Many individuals have contributed to this book, but it would not have been possible without the generous support from the airports and companies featured in the profile section of this book. No greater compliment can be given, or measure of gratitude afforded, but to those who are featured. Thank you!

Personally, I owe a great debt of gratitude to many individuals who made this book possible. In no particular order, my thanks goes to the 1994-1995 Board of Directors of SWAAAE for supporting this effort in the first place; Bruce Mosley, Barclay Dick, Jim Bennett, Krys Bart, Margy Purdue, Robert Trimborn, Tracy Williams, Randy Berg, Brent Shiner, Jim Harris and Hal Bostic. To Chuck and Lori Parks at Heritage Publishing, for embracing the idea and breaking new ground. To General Chuck Yeager, not only for the Foreword, but for being my childhood hero along with other test pilots like Apt, White, Walker and Knight. They pushed the outside of the envelope and in doing so, each instilled in me a life long interest and passion for flight. To Jack Rowe and Joe Proctor, for giving me insight to John Montgomery, but above all, for showing me that the flame burns no matter how young you are. To Ed Leiser, Curator of the San Diego Aerospace Museum, and Dr. Tom Crouch, Chairman of the Aeronautics Department at the National Air & Space Museum at the Smithsonian Institution; not only for their time, but for their generosity in sharing with me some of their research in this book. To Melissa Keiser and the staff at the National Air & Space Museum Archives, for their tireless assistance while attempting to get their own work done. To Ray and Marion at the San Diego Aerospace Museum Archives for their great help with the photos. To Deborah Douglas at NASA, for introducing me to new and important academic work in airports, and for talking to me about esoteric points of interest, relevant to maybe a handful. To Colette McClaren, who made the contact in the first place. To the countless local contacts, like Pat Ware, Mark Hall-Patton, Linda Gray, Ethel Pattison and many of my colleagues and friends who made this job so much easier. Posthumously, to the late Maurice "Mo" (or less) Kimball, the former editor of *Western Flying* magazine (1926-1965). For his sense of humor and for donating the only complete collection of *Western Flying* magazines in existence, just five days before his death (not even Mo knew that day he would die so soon, or did he?) To Cynthia Price at Heritage Publishing, who worked so diligently to make this book happen and who deserves much of the credit. To the entire staff at Heritage for their help and to Lucia Lento for her outstanding creativity. To my beach neighbors for their support; Larry "nectar of the gods" and Ann "mother goose", and David, Susan, Tony "NY, NY", and Pat. To my friends and former colleagues at McClellan-Palomar Airport; Jack, Donna, Floyd and Joe, as well as the "gang" at the Airports Department in San Bernardino; Doris, Kathy, Robin, Glenn, Dick, Connie, Charles and Mary; thanks for your support. To Kate "Cash Register" and Tommy "Tailspin" at Barnstormers (1-800-SKY-LOOP) for the cover and a dogfight or two — yes, you too can fly this 1929 Travel Air. To Barbara Rustice for always making me laugh. To Hal and Carol Bostic; a great big thanks for providing the "glue", and for everything you have done in the last seven years; we could not have done it without you! To the late Roland Elder who left us all too soon. And last but not least, to Lorraine Townsend, who had to make too many sacrifices. To all, this is your book! In closing, I dedicate this book to my parents (Aan mijn Ouders), Peter A. Olislagers and Barbera Olislagers-Brouwer, who instilled in me a sense of wonder about a world without boundaries, and who encouraged me to dream and aspire. "Thanks" does not begin to describe it.

Robert P. Olislagers

FOREWORD

by

Charles E. "Chuck" Yeager

(Brig. Gen. USAF-Ret.)

In all my years of flying and testing aircraft, there have been a few times I was glad to see solid ground again. Most of the time it was forced by some event or another, such as right after we completed the first supersonic flight in the Bell X-1 and we prepared for the second supersonic flight. The electrical system failed and I dropped from the B-29 mothership with no power to ignite the engine, or radios to communicate what had happened. I bounced it in on Rogers Dry lake at Edwards, not knowing whether the gear was extended and more importantly, not knowing if all the rocket fuel had been jettisoned. There were a number of flights that followed where we experienced on-board fires and I had to abort the test flights and return to the lakebed at Muroc. And then there was the time when I brought the Bell X-1A back after it had knocked me out cold and I was barely

able to get the rocket back under control after regaining consciousness. Those are times when you count your lucky stars and really appreciate getting back down in one piece. But for the most part, I am happiest when I am up there flying and I suppose most pilots feel that way.

So, why write the foreword to *Fields of Flying*, a book about airports? I have been flying for the better part of 50 years now and logged more than 11,000 hours in over 180 types of aircraft. In all that time, I have never taken a single aspect of flying for granted. From beginning to end, a flight profile includes good planning, preflighting, knowing your equipment, route, weather and alternates. Flying is not just cranking an engine or lighting

the burners and taking off. Maybe that is why, along with experience and a good dose of luck, I am fortunate enough to still be flying. Bottom line is that an airfield or even a grass strip in the middle of nowhere is as critical to flying, as having enough fuel is, to getting there.

Over the years, I have taken off and landed from countless airstrips, aerodromes, airfields and a lakebed or two along the way. I learned to fly in the Ryan PT-21 monoplane in 1943. After I received my wings, I spent time training in the P-38 and the P-47 and became an ace in the P-51 Mustang during WWII. After the war and training at the test pilot school at Wright-Paterson, I went on to Muroc Army Air Field, now called Edwards Air Force Base in the high desert of Mojave in Southern California. There I became part of the XS-1 program. The XS-1 program was the beginning of a series of experimental flights to study supersonic flight. Until the XS-1 program, no aircraft had ever flown faster than the speed of sound.

The XS-1 program was started to study problems in loss of control and the severe buffeting experienced by pilots as their aircraft approached Mach 0.8 or eight/tenths the speed of sound. The Bell X-1 was the first research aircraft to be tested in this program and on October 14, 1947 I became the first pilot to go faster than the speed of sound. We did not just bust that "invisible wall". We inched toward the 1.0 Mach number with every flight and learned a lot about stability and control in the process. In supersonic flight we learned that a fully movable horizontal stabilizer was essential to control and stability. It was not the only thing we learned.

The flight tests with the "X" planes were not without difficulties, some predicted, some not. The large dry lakebeds below often served as the perfect emergency landing field and it was one of the main reasons that Muroc was chosen for flight testing in the first place. The two dry lakebeds, as well as a number of off-base lakebeds and small emergency landing strips, served as the perfect area for flight testing. Since the programs often involved one-of-a-kind vehicles, costing millions of dollars, it was essential that the greatest margin of safety be provided to pilot and aircraft in the event of an emergency. The lakebeds still do just that today. In addition, the Mojave Desert not only provides excellent visibility most of the time, it is also sparsely populated.

Rogers Dry Lake has approximately 60 miles of marked runways of which the longest runway is 12 1/2 miles long and five miles wide. Rosamond Dry Lake has eight miles of runway, including one which is five miles wide and five miles long. The ancient lake beds are composed of a clayey substance which re-compacts itself into a hard surface each year after the spring rains come and the water evaporates in the desert heat. When the rains come, it is the only time the lakebeds are neither dry nor usable for landing.

I have had to use those lakebeds on more than one occasion for less than a planned landing. On what turned out to be the last subsonic flight of the X-1, four days before going supersonic, the canopy froze over, forcing me to fly "blind". Chase pilots Bob Hoover and Dick Frost flying P-80's, flew along side of me and had to talk me all the way down to the lakebed. In situations like that it is good to know that you can concentrate on bringing the aircraft in and not whether you will come to a full stop before the end of the runway or whether 50 feet on each side is enough. Landing facilities are there for different purposes and reasons. Some are there to serve large urban centers, while others get picked because they are remote. But every airfield is important and part of flying.

Today, I continue to fly both military and civilian aircraft and whether I turn final over the desert skies of Edwards AFB or prepare to take off from runway 19 at a small general aviation airport in the Sierra's of Northern California, I always appreciate having a place that pilot and aircraft can call home.

Fly Safe...

Chuck Yeager

CHAPTER 1

THE FIRST FLYING FIELDS 1884-1903

THE FIRST FLYING FIELDS 1884-1903

John Joseph Montgomery —1858-1911.
(Courtesy: San Diego Aerospace Museum)

It was no coincidence that John Montgomery chose Otay Mesa as the testing ground for his glider experiments.

Blessed with abundant sunshine and cool ocean breezes, coastal Southern California has always been a place for dreamers. For many it has also been a place to make dreams come true, and in 1884, a young man set out to fulfill his dream.[1] Located just north of what is now the U.S.-Mexico border, and some 15 miles south of the city of San Diego, lies a vast plateau, punctuated by an occasional rise in terrain, known as Otay Mesa. For most of the year, this area is burnt golden yellow from the ever-present sun and tiny sprigs of grass sway gently in the steady breezes which almost always blow ashore from the nearby Pacific Ocean.

It was no different the day John Montgomery sought to fulfill his dream; a dream he had held since childhood, to fly effortlessly, like the birds he had watched so often and whose artistry he wanted to mimic. Holding on to the crossbars of the glider he had built out of wood, fabric and wire, John Montgomery, facing an eight to 12-mile-an-hour head wind, began his run down Wheeler Hill. The glider, complete with cambered wings and a movable tail, lifted from the ground, and like the birds he had observed, he floated in the air, seemingly held aloft by an invisible hand. The flight covered only a distance of 100 feet, but in doing so, John J. Montgomery became the first American to fly in a heavier-than-air vehicle and Wheeler Hill at Otay Mesa became the first flying field in the United States.

It was no coincidence that John Montgomery chose Otay Mesa as the testing ground for his glider experiments. The wide open expanses of this then sparsely populated area were perfect for his test flights. More importantly, the constant winds that originated from the Pacific Ocean blowing inland provided the critical platform for experimentation. Octave Chanute, the imminent engineer and scientist who corresponded with most of the aerial experimenters of the day and who would provide the synergy to make controlled flight a reality, commented to Wilbur Wright in a letter in 1900 that "the two most suitable locations for winter experiments, are near San Diego, California, and St. James City, Florida, on account of the steady sea breezes which I have found to blow there". [2]

Octave Chanute's observation was not an incidental remark about weather phenomena, but one which had piqued his intellect as an engineer and his curiosity as a scientist. As an engineer involved with the design of rail systems, bridges and other large structures, Chanute recognized the correlation between practical engineering and aerodynamic effect. About aeronautics Chanute would comment: "I gave some thought to the subject. I was more disposed to do this because I had been aware for years that there were a number of observed wind phenomena, such as the lifting of roofs, the blowing off of bridges, and the tipping over of locomotives, which the known velocity and pressure of the wind at the time was insufficient to account for." [3]

Octave Chanute —1832-1910.
(Courtesy: San Diego Aerospace Museum)

It is known however, that like many of his contemporary glider experimenters, much of what he knew about flying came from observing birds.

Thus, Chanute defined the classic problem which has been central to the field of aerodynamics. To this day, lift still dominates most facets of aerodynamic design. By nature of its effect on flight, lift in turn has dictated the basic layout of virtually every runway ever built. As such and what follows in an almost philosophical logical order, airfield layout and design, from airside to landside component, became and still is, highly dependent on the location and direction of its runways.

Whether John Montgomery understood this notion intuitively or intellectually, we will never know. It is known however, that like many of his contemporary glider experimenters, much of what he knew about flying came from observing birds; the characteristic camber of bird wings became the basis for his 1894 glider. Likewise, Otto Lilienthal, who flew some 2,000 flights between 1881 and 1886 near his home in

Berlin, Germany, also recognized this aerodynamic principle. In order to assure himself of the ability to always glide into the wind, Lilienthal constructed an artificial hill from which to launch his experimental gliders in the direction most advantageous to lift. Lilienthal's hill basically represented the first constructed "airfield" ever. In limited respect, the hill was an "all field" concept as well in that one could take off in any direction desired. True "all field" air fields would only become a reality later, when powered flight allowed controlled departures and returns from the same field and in the direction desired.

Orville and Wilbur Wright, who in 1903 would make history with the first powered flight ever, were also heavily involved with gliders and their selection of the Outer Banks at Kitty Hawk, North Carolina, was not merely a convenient area to conduct experiments, but a carefully selected site. The Wright Brothers understood the concept of lift empirically and were able to make mathematical calculations to produce a coefficient, correlating wing surface with expected lift. Their early research with kites had evolved to the degree that they were ready to experiment with gliders that could carry a person. Octave Chanute suggested either San Diego, California or St. James, Florida, as among the most suitable sites for glider experiments. History might have been recorded differently were it not for the Wright Brothers' well-documented penchant for discipline and methodology to the problem of flight. To find the ideal weather conditions for flight testing, they also wrote inquiries to the U.S. Weather Bureau and found that the Outer Banks at Kitty Hawk provided the most favorable wind conditions. From September 12, 1900, until that fateful day in 1903, Wilbur and Orville Wright experimented at Kitty Hawk. In the three years that followed, the Wrights would apply the knowledge gained from the glider flights to what the world has came to know as the *Wright Flyer*. With this truly marvelous, but delicate bit of engineering, Wilbur and Orville Wright defied all who said it could not be done. On December 17, 1903, as the *Flyer* lifted slowly from its 60 feet of track,

1902 Wright Glider.
(Courtesy: San Diego Aerospace Museum.)

The Outer Banks at Kitty Hawk, North Carolina, was not merely a convenient area to conduct experiments, but a carefully selected site.

Orville & Wilbur Wright. *(Courtesy: San Diego Aerospace Museum.)*

With this truly marvelous, but delicate bit of engineering, Wilbur and Orville Wright defied all who said it could not be done.

First Flight of the Wright Flyer. December 17, 1903. (Reprinted with permission from the Smithsonian Institution)

The Wright Flyer and the hangar at Kitty Hawk, North Carolina. 1903. *(Courtesy: San Diego Aerospace Museum.)*

Orville Wright became the first man to fly in a powered, heavier-than-air machine, covering virtually the same distance of 100 feet, as had Montgomery. The first flight took 12 seconds.

The Outer Banks at Kitty Hawk have since been known as the site of the first powered flight. However, overlooked by the sheer accomplishment of the Wright Brothers, is the fact that the Outer Banks not only became the first flying field for powered flight, more importantly, it was as critical to its success as Wheeler Hill had been to Montgomery's flight. One did not go without the other and the same applies today.

It was not until the late 1930s before the Wright Brothers were finally accorded their rightful place in history. [4] However, it has taken much longer for John Montgomery and his success at Wheeler Hill to be recognized. Montgomery himself is as much to blame for being such an elusive subject to historians. As a result, his contribution to American aeronautics has largely gone unrecognized. Following his initial success at Otay Mesa, John J. Montgomery abandoned his glider experiments in 1886, after succeeding attempts with different designs failed. He would not try again until well after the successful flight of the Wright Brothers, only to lose his life in 1911 in a crash of his glider the *Evergreen.*

Montgomery's contributions have been variously described as insignificant by some, and pioneering by others. His penchant for secrecy, ostensibly because he feared ridicule in the face of failure, failed to provide independent verification of his first flight generally accepted by most local historians as August 28, 1883. The date however, has to be viewed with great skepticism. It is an accepted fact that Montgomery did fly his glider at Otay Mesa. In the process, he became the first American to do so, making Wheeler Hill the first flying field in the U.S. But his own accounts to Octave Chanute in 1894 do not indicate when the flight took place. [5] His brother James however, recalled the "exact" date for the first time while in his 70s and local historians have accepted this date as given. Yet, the original account to Chanute stood uncorrected for nearly a decade after the flight took place and even Montgomery's own review of Chanute's notes at the time, did not cause him to change the account as originally presented to Chanute, including a definitive date. However, a newspaper article in the *San Francisco Examiner* in 1909, lists the flight as having taken place in 1884, as does a letter by his brother Richard Montgomery to the secretary of the Smithsonian Institution dated 1928.[6] Therefore, in all likelihood the first flight took place in 1884 and not in 1883.

On December 17,1903, as the Flyer lifted slowly from its 60 feet of track, Orville Wright became the first man to fly in a powered, heavier than air machine.

The Chanute account, considered highly reliable, also contains other material facts which differ with later accounts of the Montgomery flight at Wheeler Hill. Perhaps in an attempt at personal reconstructive history, Montgomery's own accounts of the flight appeared to gain in significance over the course of several years. With each successive account, the distance, altitude and duration increased in proportion, finally settling on an overall distance of 600 feet. While this is the distance accepted by local historians, and is repeated in virtually every modern account of Montgomery's flight, it is not supported by the record. The overall result has been that Montgomery's contribution has left many historians in a quandary. His successive failures at flight following his earlier success, and the secrecy which he maintained throughout his early flying career, did not contribute to creating a legacy upon which others might have built, as was the case with Lilienthal and the Wright Brothers. Some have viewed his flight as insignificant, even a fluke and at best only a semi-serious attempt no more important than preceding flights by Sir George Cayley, Louis Mouillard and Jean Marie Le Bris.

Montgomery and one of his gliders. *(Courtesy: San Diego Aerospace Museum.)*

It also places Wheeler Hill at Otay Mesa, like the Outer Banks at Kitty Hawk, as among the first fields of flying in the United States.

However, others have recognized the historical significance of the contribution made by John J. Montgomery, which he owes entirely to the integrity of Octave Chanute. Chanute's recognition of the flight, based on those conversations in 1894, has helped place John Montgomery in the venerable category of "first in flight" (non-powered/heavier than air) in the United States. It also places Wheeler Hill at Otay Mesa, like the Outer Banks at Kitty Hawk, as among the first fields of flying in the United States.

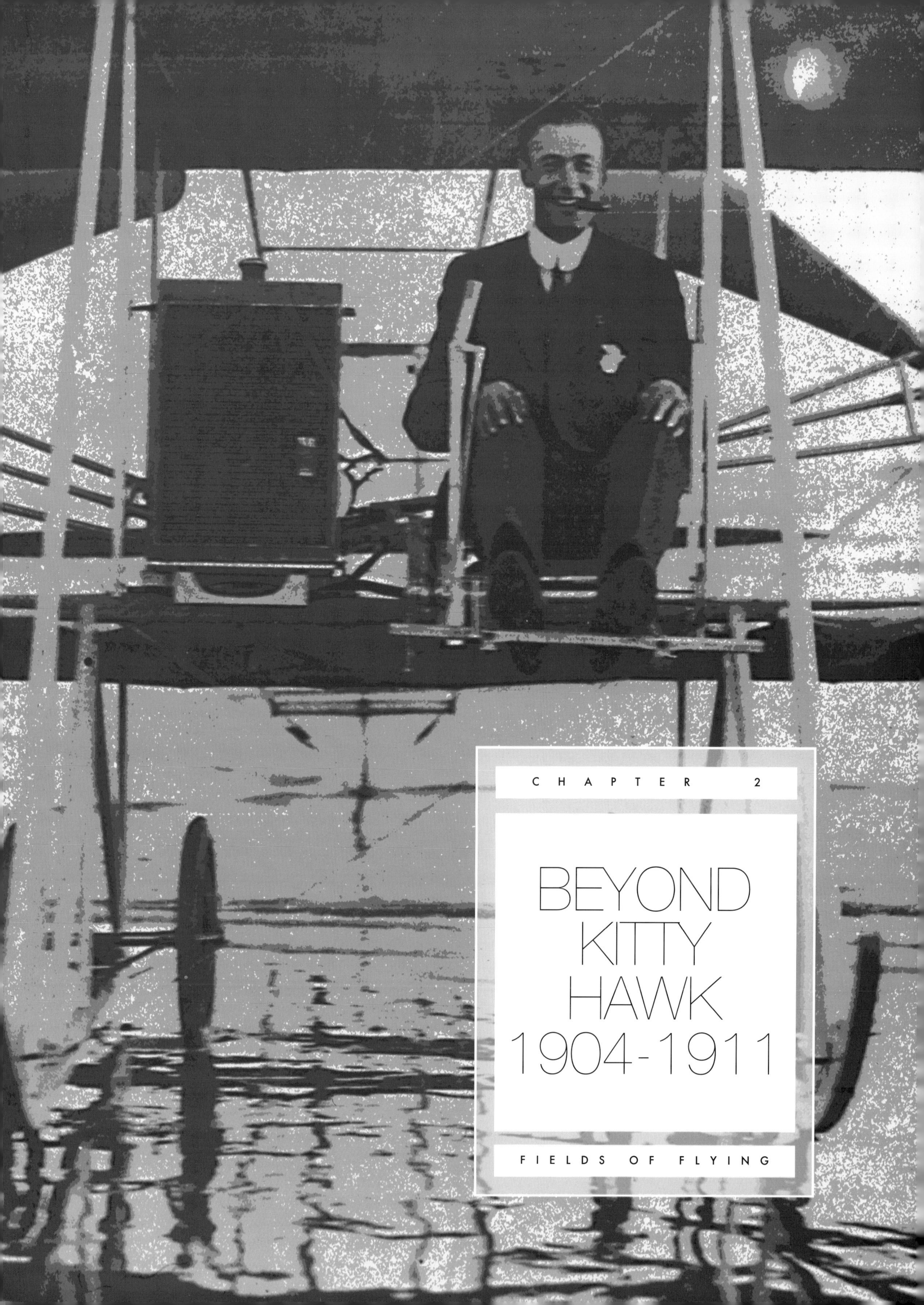

CHAPTER 2

BEYOND KITTY HAWK 1904-1911

FIELDS OF FLYING

BEYOND KITTY HAWK 1904-1911

The Wright IIB Flyer at Huffman Prairie.
(Reprinted with permission from the Smithsonian Institution)

Powered flight had finally been established and the "wing-warping" concept, developed by the Wright Brothers, allowed for greater control than was possible with gliders. Less dependent on wind and placing emphasis on increased control and powerplant design, Orville and Wilbur Wright spent the first half of 1904 getting ready for their next phase in flight. Since the original Flyer was badly damaged following a wind gust on the same day of the first flight, a new aircraft was built. Improvements were made to the wing camber in order to provide greater lift, and a new powerplant was developed to allow for longer running times. The old engine had a tendency to overheat after only a few minutes of operation, thus greatly curtailing total flight time.

Rather than returning to North Carolina, the Wright Brothers selected a cow pasture some eight miles outside of their hometown of Dayton, Ohio. The pasture was owned by a banker named Terrence Huffman and he allowed them the use of the field at no charge as long as they made sure that the cows and horses were chased away before starting their flight experiments. The site, known as Huffman Prairie, and the present site of Wright-Patterson Air Force Base, became the first airfield selected for its convenient location, wide open expanses, and relative flat terrain. While convenient, Huffman Prairie also "endeared" itself in other ways and became the subject of what must be the first-documented complaint concerning the conditions of an airfield. In a letter to Chanute, Wilbur wrote; "We are in a large meadow of about 100 acres. It is skirted on the west and north by trees. This not only shuts off the wind somewhat but also probably gives a slight downtrend. However, this matter we do not consider anything serious. The greater troubles are the facts that in addition to cattle there have been a dozen or more horses in the pasture and it is surrounded by barbwire fencing we have been at much trouble to get them safely away before making trials. Also the ground is old swamp and is filled with grassy hummocks some six inches high so that it resembles a prairie dog town. This makes the track laying slow work. While we are getting ready the favorable opportunities slip away, and we are usually up against a rainstorm, a dead calm, or a wind blowing at right angles to the track". [1]

1910 Race between an aeroplane and a car. Fresno, California.
(Courtesy: San Diego Aerospace Museum)

The Wright Brothers went on to make many short flights during the late summer of 1904 and further perfected their flying technique, including three flights in excess of 1,300 feet. With the successively longer flights, however, came a problem. Huffman Prairie was becoming all too small to accommodate the flights which essentially involved a relatively straight-line approach. Their first solution to the problem was characteristically ingenious. The Wrights developed a catapult launching system made of ropes and pulleys rigged to a weight, which would launch the aircraft into the air faster, thus allowing increased air time. But it was not until September 20, 1904, with Wilbur at the controls, that the first coordinated turn was executed. This particular flight was observed by I.R. Root, a bee keeper who edited *Gleanings in Bee Culture.* Amazed by what he saw, he wrote of his experience, making it the first independent written account of a powered aircraft (flying a pattern around a flying field). Root noted; "When it (the Wright Flyer) first turned that circle, and came near the starting point, I was right in front of it; and I said then, and I believe

1910 Flying Demonstration at the Coronado Polo Grounds. Coronado Island, San Diego, California.
(Courtesy: San Diego Aerospace Museum.)

still, it was one of the grandest sights, if not the grandest sight, of my life. Imagine a locomotive that has left its track, and is climbing up in the air toward you—a locomotive without any wheels, we will say, but with white wings instead..." [2]

The Wrights proceeded to fly for longer than one minute on a regular basis, something not achieved by anyone else until Henri Farman flew the *Voison-Farman I*

on Nov. 9, 1907 at Issy-les-Moulineaux in France. [3] In the United States, it would take until July 4, 1908 before Glen Curtiss flew the A.E.A. *June Bug* at Hammondsport, New York for longer than one minute. Several shorter flights had taken place earlier that year at Hammondsport as well, but no one had developed the art and mastery of aerial navigation like the Wrights had. Competition and legal battles over patent rights between the Wright Brothers and Curtiss slowed aeronautical development in the United States and Europe appeared to become the new Mecca of aeronautical activity. Aviators like Santos-Dumont, Voisin, Bleriot, Farman and others tested different designs, creating a truly experimental atmosphere. Although lagging behind the Wright Brothers in almost every respect, it appeared indeed that the focus in aeronautical development was about to shift geographically.

Having failed to convince the U.S. Army of the practical applications of the Wright Flyer III, the Wright Brothers too set out to pursue their interests in Europe in 1905. Although aerial experiments in Europe were punctuated by extremely short flights, the public's clamor for anything aeronautical was hardly dampened by flights lasting only seconds. Enthusiasm was high. It would reach a fever pitch after Wilbur Wright arrived in France and began a remarkable series of flight demonstrations. Wilbur Wright had first selected the racetrack at Le Mans because of the flat terrain and because the stands offered great viewing. The first demonstration, complete with a full turn, convinced everyone in the audience, including Bleriot, of the superiority attained by the Wrights. Wilbur however had become concerned with the size of the crowd and the relative small size of the track. Still lacking in engine reliability and concerned with safety, Wright moved the ensuing flight demonstrations to Auvours, a military facility with a large parade ground. There, having sufficient room to maneuver the Wright A, he would entertain the crowds with flights lasting more than one hour on several occasions and even taking up passengers. By the time Wilbur Wright completed his flight demonstrations in France, he would set

Program Cover of the 1910 Dominguez Field Air Races. *(Reprinted with permission from The Hatfield Collection, Museum of Flight.)*

new records for duration and distance (2 hours, 20 minutes and 23 seconds, and 78 miles) and; duration with a passenger (1 hour, 9 minutes and 45 seconds). [4] In doing so, the Wright Brothers had formally established that controlled flight was indeed possible and with more and more designs involved, interest began to develop to establish competition among them.

In 1907, *Scientific American* established a trophy for the first aircraft to be able to fly one kilometer, expecting the Wright Brothers to enter the event and win. Instead, Glenn Curtiss and the Aerial Experiment Association entered and won the prize with the A.E.A. *June Bug.* The Wrights showed no interest and did not partici-pate. For the next three years, a number of national and international trophy races were held, in addition to numerous individual flying experiments. The best known of the races was the Gordon Bennett Cup held at Rheims, France. Because of exhibi-tion potential, these races were held at racecourses and fairgrounds and people came from far and wide to see such events. Exhibition flying was to dominate the industry for a number of years, but the potential for prize money would become the driving force behind the advances made in aerodynamic design. It also created opportunity in air field development even although most flying was done at public places such as fairgrounds and racetracks like the Coronado Polo Grounds on Coronado Island, across the bay from San Diego and at Tanforan Racetrack in San Bruno, near San Francisco. Of course, cow pastures, unobstructed land sec-tions, and any other open areas suitable for landings and take-offs were fair game for the few pilots who wowed the crowds and demonstrated this new technology.

Changes were in the offing and scarcely six years after those first tentative flights in 1903 took place, a massive effort was underway to hold the first major aeronautical event in the United States. The site was Dominguez Field, near Los Angeles and it became the first airfield specially constructed in the United States for the purpose of exhibition flying. The event at Dominguez Field ultimately became a series of races and contests of skill spanning 10 days, from January 10 through January 20, 1910. Patterned after the Gordon Bennett Cup, held at Rheims, France the previous year, the races involved contests of speed, endurance, short field take-offs, precision landing and altitude competition. It also was one of the last events in which dirigibles and aircraft raced against each other in a respectable fashion.

1910 Dominguez Field Air Races:
View from the Grandstand.
(Courtesy: San Diego Aerospace Museum.)

Dominguez Field was located near where the City of Compton is today. Elliptical in shape and measuring about a mile and a half in circumference, some of the airplanes took three to four minutes to get around the track, while the dirigibles took five minutes to cover the same distance. One of the those dirigibles was flown by Lincoln Beachey who would later become one of the most famous of all barnstorming pilots. Glenn Curtiss took home money for winning a couple of speed and endurance contests and a Frenchman by the name of Louis Paulhan netted $19,000 in total prize money, including $10,000 for covering 45 miles in a cross-country flight from Dominguez Field to the Santa Anita racetrack and back. Hundreds of thousands of people watched the spectacle from the stands, including a young boy of 13 who was inspired by it all. Jimmy Doolittle would later recall the event in his biography, chronicling one of the most remarkable flying careers ever. [5]

1910 Dominguez Field Air Races: Airfield Hospital.
(Courtesy: San Diego Aerospace Museum.)

Prize money was now being offered for cross-country flights, pushing men and machine to even greater achievements.

Following the 1910 meeting at Dominguez Field, other contests of skill and endurance were proposed. Flying had evolved beyond mere short hops and flying the length of racetracks. Prize money was now being offered for cross-country flights, pushing man and machine to even greater achievements. A prize of $10,000 was offered to fly the length of the Hudson River, from Albany to New York. In England, the equivalent of $50,000 was offered for a cross-country flight from London to Manchester. Curtiss took the prize for the Hudson flight and also won the *Scientific American* trophy for the third time, allowing him to keep it.

Several newspapers offered additional prizes, as coverage of such flights became serious business. The *Times* offered $25,000 for the first cross-country flight between New York and Chicago, only to be topped by William Randolph Hearst's prize of $50,000 for the first cross-country, coast-to-coast flight, from New York to California.

Only six years after Wilbur Wright had even demonstrated the possibility of controlled and sustained flight, pilots were now considering flying great distances. Partially lured by big money and instant fame, these early aviators understood the enormous risks they took and it was this almost death-defiant attitude that earned the pilot's reputation. The aura of mysticism and daring, and the seeming incongruous melding of courage, madness and reckless abandon would become the hallmark of early aviators as much as the white scarf and leather flying jacket would, for those that followed. Possessing courage was not entirely without merit as emergencies were plentiful and the need to land quickly, essential. The early flying fields therefore had only two fundamental purposes, namely being able to launch and recover aircraft. These basic concepts, other than in scope and sophistication, have not changed. Back in the early days however, any open area would do just fine.

Louis Paulhan attempting to break the world's endurance record at the 1910 Dominguez Field Air Races. *(Reprinted with permission from The Hatfield Collection, Museum of Flight.)*

As such, the concept of flying cross-country in 1910 was a dual challenge. Not only were the wood and fabric aircraft delicate and unreliable (and had not been tested in diverse cross-country conditions), there were no airports or flying fields to speak of. Racetracks, fairgrounds and large open fields comprised the sum total of the facilities available to pilots and a system of fields connected by "airways" was to become a reality only years later. In fact, only about 20 "airfields" were known throughout the United States and most of those were privately owned for the purpose of teaching others how to fly. The major designers of the day, including the Wrights, Curtiss, Glenn Martin, Moisant and Benoist operated flying schools, alternating between their respective head-quarters in the summer and moving to Florida or California in the winter.

Under these circumstances, the flight that Calbraith Perry Rodgers undertook from the racetrack at Sheepshead Bay, Long Island New York on September 17, 1911, and concluded on December 10, 1911 on the beaches at Long Beach, California, is all the more remarkable and a testament to the difficulty of flying in those days. Attempting to win the Hearst prize of $50,000, for the first person to fly coast-to-coast in 30 days, Cal Rodgers, having learned to fly only months earlier, set out to defy the odds to become the first person to cover the 4,000-mile journey. Attesting to the extreme difficulty of the flight and the perseverance demonstrated by Rodgers, the aircraft he landed for the last time on his historic flight was hardly the same he took off with 84 days earlier. Undaunted by the fact that he had missed the 30-day window to claim the Hearst prize, Rodgers continued on, even although he seriously crashed the Wright EX Flyer on five separate occasions, necessitating the rebuilding of the airplane; had seven take-off and landing accidents, requiring major repairs and; his engine quit in mid-air six times. Only the rudder, drip pan and a few struts remained of the original aircraft upon landing on the beaches of the Pacific. [6] But along the way, Cal Rodgers forever linked cities and towns and inspired the people who populated them. Many of these communities, large and small, still enjoy a reputation among aviators today, often celebrated with fly-ins and other aviation events which are reminiscent of the indomitable spirit displayed by Rodgers.

Cal Rodgers and his Wright EX Flyer, the *Vin Fiz*, so named after the soft drink company that sponsored him, went on a southwesterly route from New York, Ohio, Indiana, Illinois, Missouri, Oklahoma, and into Texas. From San Antonio on, the flight was essentially in a westerly direction, traversing the full length of New Mexico, Arizona and into California. Rodgers may have been the first to apply the term "flying IFR", but since instrument flight was non-existent, it is, as pilots occasionally and

Partially lured by big money and instant fame, these early aviators understood the enormous risks they took and it was this almost death-defiant attitude that earned the pilot's reputation.

jokingly refer to it as, "I Fly Roads, Railways...". In fact, Rodgers' entourage, including his wife and a very busy mechanic, followed him across the U.S. by train. While the train provided Cal with needed parts, fuel and even the comforts of life including warm meals, it also offered a simple means of navigation by following the railroad tracks which traversed the full length of his journey. The simplicity of this method is no more self evident than when entering the "Pass" near Banning, California—one of his stops.

1911 Demonstration of a Wright Flyer at a racetrack.
(Reprinted with permission from the Smithsonian Institution.)

Cal Rodgers first entered the Southwest in the town of Wilcox, Arizona and following a short stay and some quick repairs in a nearby open field, Rodgers went on to Tucson, where he arrived on November 1, 1911. Dazzling the crowds which had assembled at the University Stadium, he finally let down on a open field near east Ninth Street. [7] There, Cal Rodgers was met by Robert Fowler, who had started his cross-country flight from San Francisco, California, on his way to Jacksonville, Florida—a journey that would last 149 days. He suffered from many similar harrowing experiences Rodgers had encountered. [8] As Fowler headed East, Rodgers took to the westbound skies of Maricopa and on to Phoenix. Originally scheduled to land at a large four block square known as "the Circus Grounds", the large crowd forced Rodgers to land in a nearby grass pasture, approximately a half mile from the intended landing site. [9]

Cal Rodgers (r.) and the *Vin Fiz*
(Courtesy: San Diego Aerospace Museum.)

Following the stop in Phoenix, Rodgers, who was beginning to feel the excitement of nearing his goal, anxiously looked forward to finishing the long journey at his intended final destination in the City of Pasadena, California. The flight from Phoenix to Stovall Siding, Arizona was uneventful and upon landing at Stovall, not a sole came out to greet the flyer, prompting Rodgers to dub it "the best place since leaving New York". [10] On Friday, November 3, Cal took to the skies early and with Pasadena less than 300 miles away, decided to forego a scheduled stop in Yuma in order to take advantage of a well running engine. Just as he crossed the Arizona-California border at Imperial Junction however, the motor exploded with a loud bang. Injured by shrapnel from a blown cylinder, Rodgers nevertheless landed the aircraft in a clearing without further incident. Aircraft and engine had been pushed to the edge of limitation but Cal wanted to press on and reach his goal as soon as possible. As repairs were made, Cal located a suitable take-off point at the edge of the Salton Sea. The following day, with the patched up airplane airborne once again, the trip resumed toward the Town of Banning. As Rodgers was setting up for the landing, the magneto, which he had tried to nurse along, broke loose and the engine quit once again. Looking for a landing site, he landed the EX-Flyer without difficulty in a plowed field. [11] The much anticipated arrival in Pasadena would be delayed again.

On Sunday, November 5, Cal took off from Banning only to have to make yet one more emergency landing, this time in Beaumont, not five minutes from Banning. Finally, after one last repair and a quick fuel stop in Pomona, Cal Rodgers and the *Vin Fiz* arrived at Tournament Park, Pasadena, where he came to a full stop on the white marker they had been laid out for him. Carried off as the new hero of the skies, Cal Rodgers was feted everywhere he went. But Cal Rodgers had one more goal. He wanted to reach Long Beach and dip the wheels of the Wright EX-Flyer in the waters of the Pacific Ocean and complete the flight from "sea to shining sea". It would not happen as quickly as Cal Rodgers wanted, for in an attempt to push man and machine one last time, he crashed again and badly injured himself this time. After only a partial recovery and what must have been an interminable wait, Cal Rodgers finally arrived on the beaches of Long Beach on December 10th, his crutches strapped to the airplane. [12] And so ended the first coast-to-coast cross-country flight ever.

Although 54 days past the deadline to collect the Hearst prize, Cal Rodgers nevertheless set a new standard and pushed himself and his plane beyond the known realm. With no airfields or airports to speak of, Cal Rodgers took a rickety airplane and made landing fields where none existed before. From cow pastures to lake shores, and from racetracks to desert flats, Cal Rodgers and the *Vin Fiz* landed when and where needed and in doing so, instantly transformed ordinary fields into fields of flying.

From cow pastures to lake shores, and from racetracks to desert flats, Cal Rodgers and the Vin Fiz landed when and where needed and in doing so, instantly transformed ordinary fields into fields of flying.

Westbound railroad tracks into the pass at Banning, California.
(Photo: Robert Olislagers.)

Robert Fowler arrives in Yuma, Arizona on October 25, 1911
(Courtesy: Yuma International Airport.)

Cal Rodgers dips the wheels of the *Vin Fiz* in the waters of the Pacific Ocean in Long Beach.
(Courtesy: San Diego Aerospace Museum.)

CHAPTER 3

AIRMAIL & THE WAR YEARS 1911-1924

AIRMAIL & THE WAR YEARS 1911-1924

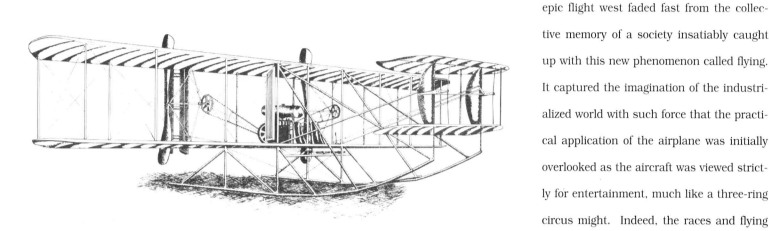

WRIGHT 1909 MILITARY FLYER
Won the bid for first military airplane in
the world July 1909:
(Signal Corps Specification 486)
...stayed in the air 1 hour and 12 min.
...attained an average speed of 42.53 MPH
...carried two people with a combined weight
of 350 lbs.

Stan Mahoney
5/88

1909 Wright Military Flyer (pen & ink drawing).
(collection: Robert Olislagers)

The memory of Cal Rodgers and his epic flight west faded fast from the collective memory of a society insatiably caught up with this new phenomenon called flying. It captured the imagination of the industrialized world with such force that the practical application of the airplane was initially overlooked as the aircraft was viewed strictly for entertainment, much like a three-ring circus might. Indeed, the races and flying demonstrations overshadowed all other early milestones, including the 1909 Wright Military Flyer, the first airplane to meet military specifications. The thought of airfields connecting cities with each other by way of use of aircraft as the "...future mode of transport for both passengers and cargo", was even further removed from the minds of the general public, except for but a few. [1]

1924 Aerial view of Monterey Airport and Monterey Bay.
(Courtesy: San Diego Aerospace Museum)

While much of the world was still preoccupied by flight itself, a few visionaries in a small town in Northern California had dreams of the future. On July 3, 1910, the Board of Freeholders of Modesto, amended the Town's Charter to include language to acquire land for an airport. When the amendment was formally adopted on September 14, 1910, Modesto became the first municipality in the United States to take steps to formally establish a municipal airport. Although the town had its share of nay-sayers and skeptics, the national media nevertheless recognized Modesto for its enterprise, foresight and leadership. [2] Modesto however, was far ahead of its time and as a government agency it stood virtually alone in its efforts to promote air transportation. Although it took another 10 years before funds were made available for an airfield, Modesto continued to promote aviation and intrepid flyers called upon the city in its honor. While Modesto made the first steps to operate a municipal airport, the City of Tucson actually did in 1915, when Fishburn Field was established, making it the first municipally-owned and operated airport in the U.S. By 1925 however, Fishburn Field had already suffered capacity problems and was closed in favor of a new site. Today, the site of the old Fishburn Field is where the Tucson Rodeo Grounds are located.

Other communities too had their initial brush with aeronautical history at the sites where airports exist today. Monterey, California, home of the SWAAAE annual winter conference, was caught up in the spirit of flight when in 1910, a young British pilot by the name of James Radley, demonstrated his aerial skills in his Bleriot at the same site of today's Monterey Peninsula Airport. Like Modesto, it would take time before the airfield would become a permanent reality. By 1913, the site of the present Fullerton Airport had become a regular stop for early aerial demonstrators, as pilots traveled up and down the state to show off their skills with their aircraft of choice. But it was not until after a brief stint as a sewer farm, that the site returned to its former glory as a flying field, and finally in 1927, following the suggestion by two local citizens, the City Council allowed Fullerton Airport to become a reality.

One of the oldest continuing running civilian airfields in the Southwest, is a former barley field, better known as Clover Field and now referred to as Santa Monica Airport. Established in 1919, the airport became home to the Douglas Aircraft Company in 1922 and it was from this field that the venerable DC series aircraft were produced, including the most successfully mass-produced transport airplane ever, the DC-3. Since that time Santa Monica Airport has become one of the busiest single runway airports in the United States. Along with Scottsdale Airport in Arizona, and McClellan-Palomar Airport, Palo Alto Airport and Lindbergh Field in California, these five airports are among the busiest single runway airports in the nation. All are located in the Southwest.

The honor of the oldest continuously operated airfields in the Southwest is shared by two facilities, namely North Island, across the waters from San Diego and the Salt Lake City, Utah airport. Now Naval Air Station North Island, its illustrious history dates back to 1911 when Glen Curtiss established one of the first flight training schools in the United States. He operated the school until 1915 and it was from

The honor
of the oldest
continuously
operated airfields
in the Southwest
is shared by two
facilities, namely
North Island,
across the waters
from San Diego
and the Salt Lake
City, Utah airport.

here that Curtiss flew the first amphibious aircraft, promptly proclaiming hydroaero-planing "the coming sport". The Navy arrived the year after Curtiss set up shop and established Camp Trouble on the northeast landing area. While the Army came and went (1913-1937), the Navy has continued its presence at North Island until the present. Today however, it shares airspace with another airfield named after the first solo aviator to cross the Atlantic, Charles "Lucky Lindy" Lindbergh.

Salt Lake City's early beginnings go back to 1911 as well when the "Great International Aviation Carnival" came to town. A small runway in the middle of a pasture called Basque Flats would remain host to many flyers until 1920, when the city acquired much of the surrounding land to accommodate air mail service. The airfield became known as Woodward Field, after airmail pilot John P. Woodward who was killed on one of his runs for the post office. Renamed Salt Lake City Municipal Airport in the 30s, the airport was renamed one more time in 1968 to Salt Lake City International Airport, to reflect its growth and international standing. One a civilian airfield and one a military facility, together Salt Lake City and North Island have continued their long and great history on the same site for almost as long as flying has been part of the American fabric.

1923 Aerial view of Clover Field.
(Courtesy: San Diego Aerospace Museum)

Indeed, the first commercial customers did fly on January 1, 1914, scarcely a decade after the Wright Brothers' flight at Kitty Hawk.

When Curtiss established his flying school at North Island, aviation was still very much in its infancy. But with the industrial revolution in full swing, it would not be long before the spectacle of flight would transcend its early throws and realize its practical value. After all, Wilbur Wright had shown that one could easily fly with a passenger, the inference being that commercial ferrying of paying passengers would not be far behind. Indeed, the first commercial customer did fly on January 1, 1914, scarcely a decade after the Wright Brothers' flight at Kitty Hawk. The occasion was the inaugural flight of the St. Petersberg-Tampa Airboat Line, a regularly scheduled service between the two Florida cities.[3] The effort was short lived however, as the commercial application was not able to sustain the short haul route financially.

1937 Aerial View of Clover Field.
(Courtesy: Los Angeles County Department of Airports)

1928 Aerial view of Rockwell Field
(Reprinted with permission of the Smithsonian Institution)

Earle Ovington departing for the first airmail flight in the
U.S. in 1911. *(Courtesy: San Diego Aerospace Museum)*

Even the Wright Brothers were not immune from failure. Early on, Wilbur and Orville Wright had attempted to convince the U.S. Army of the virtues of a military application, but it was not until 1909 that the idea was formally, albeit reluctantly, embraced. Its real implication would not be realized however until the campaign against Pancho Villa in 1916, and later during World War I. By that time, the Wright Brothers' role was relegated a back seat due to the legal wranglings between them and Curtiss, as well as others who used the Wright Brothers' "wing warping" concept. But out of the chaos of exhibition flying grew a new form of entrepreneurship in the form of postcards, commemorating this or that flight. The public, eager for a "piece" of history, would covet these mementos much in the same way flags and other mementoes are carried on board today's "first flight" test aircraft and space shuttle flights. Although most of these tokens of early flight were airborne for only a few minutes, it gave impetus to a new idea that would transform itself and aeronautics into a new industry.

Oddly enough, the first airmail flight did not take place in the United States or even France, but in India. On February 8, 1911, a British Captain requested permission to fly an exhibition airmail run from Allahabad, India to nearby Naini. Some 6,000 pieces of airmail were transported on a short five-mile hop by his pilot, a Frenchman by the name of Henri Piquet, making it the first officially sanctioned airmail flight in history. [4] Great Britain, France and Germany soon followed thereafter and in September of 1911, at the International Aviation Meet at Garden City Estates, Long Island, Earle L. Ovington, who would later become Airport Manager at the Santa Barbara Airport, became the first pilot to fly airmail in the United States. [5] Ovington volunteered to fly mail upon hearing that Postmaster General Frank H. Hitchcock had proposed the idea. [6] For the next seven years, mail would be carried by pilots without any compensation by the government, yet each letter was properly canceled and the flights were made with the approval of the Postmaster General. Among the first "batch" of Airplane Mail Courier pilots sworn in at the Long Island meet were Lt. Henry H. "Hap" Arnold and Eugene Ely. Both fliers went on to occupy some of the most distinguished places in aviation history; the former with the Army Air Corps and the U.S. Air Force, and the latter as the first pilot to land and take off from a Navy ship.

Curtiss Again Surpasses All Others
AT THE CHICAGO MEET

Competition Is the Severest Test of an Aeroplane's Worth

THE CURTISS AVIATORS
WITH CURTISS AEROPLANES
HAVING CURTISS POWER PLANTS

By operating in wind that kept all other aviators on the ground and by smashing various records

PROVED

That the Biplane is superior to the Monoplane   That the Curtiss Biplane is the most efficient of all aeroplanes
That the Curtiss Biplane is the safest   That the Curtiss Biplane is the strongest
That the Curtiss Biplane has the best control systems

RECORDS MADE WITH THE CURTISS BIPLANE AT CHICAGO

World's Altitude Record, 11,578 feet, by Beachey
World's Record for Speed with Biplane, by Ely
World's Biplane Record for Quick Climbing, by Ely
World's Biplane Record for Speed with Passenger, by Beachey
World's Record for Gliding with Power, by Beachey
Greatest Distance Made at Chicago Meet, by Ward

The Curtiss Hydroaeroplane proved the greatest sensation of the meet

For prices and particulars address

THE CURTISS AEROPLANE CO.

New York Office, 1737 Broadway   HAMMONDSPORT, N. Y.
JEROME FANCUILLI, *General Manager*   G. H. CURTISS, *General Director*

1911 Advertisement for Curtiss aircraft *(Reprinted with permission from the Hatfield Collection, Museum of Flight)*

Many early "airmail" flights took place at the same time Cal Rodgers made his epic flight, (incidentally he carried a letter from the Mayor of New York, to the Mayor of San Francisco.) [7] In spite of the interest on the part of the post office to support airmail, Congress balked at the idea of funding a full-scale airmail service. A request for a $50,000 appropriation was turned down, but this did not deter the post office in its official support for airmail exhibition flights. In 1916, Congress reluctantly appropriated funds from the "Steamboat or Other Power Boat Service" budget to support airmail service on a trial basis, but it was not until 1918 however, that Congress appropriated $100,000 for an experimental airmail service between Washington, D.C. and New York City. [8]

Meanwhile in 1916, the Pershing Expedition, employing the First Aero Squadron for reconnaissance purposes during the campaign against Pancho Villa, established a "first" of their own by making regular airmail runs between troops spread out over a 150-mile stretch along the U.S.-Mexican border. In the initial campaign, the First Aero Squadron not only conducted airmail runs, they were also engaged in photography and reconnaissance flights and covered 19,500 miles in 346 hours of flight time in 540 missions. All of the sorties were conducted in totally dilapidated Jennies, but once the poor, pitiful Jennies were replaced by new Curtiss R-2's, the squadron performed flawlessly and did not miss a single air mail delivery thereafter. [9] In doing so, the First Aero Squadron made history by not only being the first to demonstrate the aircraft's versatility for aerial photography and reconnaissance, but also to deliver mail on a consistent basis in an official capacity.

The role of the military and the development of airmail service is integrally intertwined with the civilian effort to promote the distribution of

The "upside down" airmail stamp commemorating the first official U.S. Air Mail flight on May 15, 1918.

ARTIE THE ACE   *By Hal Forrest*

1929 Airmail Cartoon. *(Reprinted from Airport Construction and Management magazine)*

mail by air. The U.S. Army was presumed to have the aircraft capable of delivering the mail, as well as having trained pilots to fly the aircraft. When the idea was finally funded by the federal government, it was the military they turned to. Former airmail pilot Lt. "Hap" Arnold and now a Colonel responsible for training new pilots to join the war in Europe, was called upon to set up the experimental service. He would soon realize that this task was not going to be easy. Given less than 10 days to set up the service, Arnold relied on Reuben H. Fleet, his Executive Officer, to make the necessary arrangements. When May 15, 1918 came, six Jennies had been converted to carry the mail. Lt. Boyle, a recent graduate from flight training school, would have the honors of being the first official airmail pilot, thanks in no small measure to his future father-in-law's business dealings with the post office. As President and Mrs. Wilson looked on, Lt. Boyle departed the field and immediately proceeded to turn in the wrong direction, however unbeknownst to the President. The hapless pilot not only had the distinction of being the first official air mail pilot, but also was the first airmail pilot to get lost. To add insult to injury, he crashed the airplane shortly after take off and never did deliver the mail by air. In spite of the inauspicious start, the only noteworthy event of the day was the fact that the post office had printed the commemorative stamp upside down, making it an instant philatelic hit. Not meant to be a commercial success, the airmail experiment was a success nevertheless.

1928 Aerial view of the landing strip at Elko, Nevada.
(Courtesy: San Diego Aerospace Museum)

With "the war to end all wars" slowly grinding to a bitter end, and the airmail experiment by the Army complete, the task of providing airmail service was formally turned over to the post office. New aircraft were ordered and on August 12, 1918, the first airmail runs were completed entirely under the auspices of the post office. In order to compete with rail service, the post office realized that longer distances and faster times needed to be achieved if air mail service was to be the future. The first airway, named the "Woodrow Wilson Airway", was established covering the distance between New York and San Francisco. [10] The "airway" was 80-miles wide and connected the two cities via Cleveland, Chicago and Omaha. The last leg from Omaha westward, included Salt Lake City, Utah, and Elko and Reno, Nevada, before terminating in San Francisco. The southerly connection ran from the City by the Bay, Oakland and Sacramento, on down to Fresno, Bakersfield, Los Angeles and San Diego. These new airways also led to the development of the first airports built to support commercial movement of goods and services by air.

Reuben H. Fleet and Lt. Boyle, May 15, 1918. *(Courtesy: San Diego Aerospace Museum)*

President Woodrow Wilson and Reuben H. Fleet, May 15, 1918. (*Courtesy: San Diego Aerospace Museum.*)

Earl Daugherty in Long Beach
*(Reprinted with permission from
The Hatfield Collection, Museum of Flight)*

The new facilities that were built or existed all along these routes as informal landing areas were no longer sufficient to handle the aircraft that called on the cities connecting the airways. Fresno and Bakersfield both developed their airports during this time as the two small San Joaquin Valley cities became an important link between the Bay Area and the Los Angeles basin. Kern County Airport (No.1) in Bakersfield, is now called Meadows Field after Cecil Meadows, one of the Charter members of the California Association of Airport Executives and predecessor to SWAAAE. It was developed in the early 20s and had some of the best graded and oiled runways in the state. Chandler Field in Fresno boasted all field capability until actual runways were established. Until that time, the airfield, like so many "all field" facilities was lighted from the periphery in. Further south, the City Council of Long Beach established Daugherty Field in 1923, named after local aviation pioneer Earl Daugherty, when it dedicated some 150 acres for airport facilities. Of course, Cal Rodgers had landed in Long Beach long before then and had made the long stretch of sand along the Pacific a favorite landing spot among pilots.

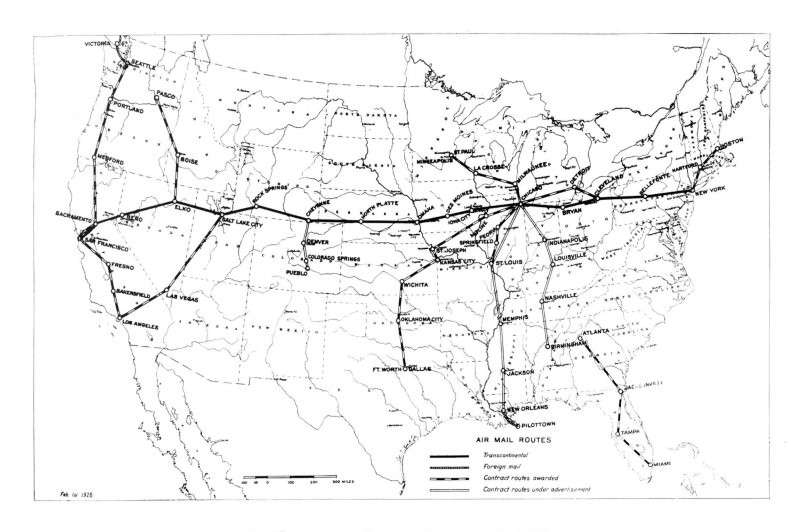

Post Office map. *(Reprinted from Western Flying magazine, March 1926)*

New technologies, such as sophisticated lighted beacons to allow night flying, as well as radio communications technology which provided critical en-route weather data to pilots, would accelerate airport development by connecting critical airways and way points with one another. By 1923, airmail service was becoming routine, and night flying as predicted by its proponents, had a very significant effect on air mail service as demand shot up. With new lighted airways now connecting New York City all the way to Salt Lake City and beyond, the airmail service system had become of age, and the government, which never intended to permanently fund the system, passed the Kelly Act in 1925 to allow the post office to contract with private operators to carry the mail. [11]

Airmail beacon in 1923.
(Reprinted from the Airport Book, M. Greiff)

1931 Aerial view of Fresno Airport. *(Courtesy: San Diego Aerospace Museum)*

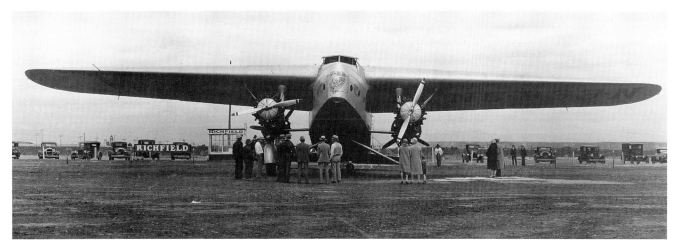

F-32 Fokker at Kern County Airport No.1. *(Courtesy: Kern County Department of Airports)*

CHAPTER 4

THE GOLDEN AGE OF AIRPORTS 1926-1938

FIELDS OF FLYING

THE GOLDEN AGE OF AIRPORTS 1926-1938

With the passage of the Kelly Act, Congress and the Federal government entered a new era in civil aviation. With the Kelly Act, Congress did not merely allow the Post Office to contract directly with private enterprise, it did so in the belief that private investment should play a greater role in developing aviation. However, by trying to privatize, Congress also demonstrated its extreme ambivalence with respect to the role it should play in aviation in the first place. To date, American aviation had been an ambiguous combination of military and civilian interests without a clear purpose, but with a certain future. With ideas abound, but a legacy that was becoming increasingly tragic, aviation was at a crossroads and the Legislature sought to find solutions for this complex mixture of military interests, private investment and regulatory control — at least they would try. From the time Congress appropriated the first few dollars for the experimental service between New York and Washington, D.C. in 1918, until the passage of the Kelly Act in 1925, significant and often contentious debate had taken place in Congress and the topic was among the most important of issues discussed by the 66th, 67th and 68th Congress.[1] Aviation proponents had been instrumental in preventing legislation from being passed that would be detrimental to the "laissez faire" attitude that prevailed from the time Wilbur and Orville Wright had demonstrated powered flight.[2]

However, virtually from the very beginning, aviation had exacted a very heavy toll on those who dared to defy gravity. As the industry matured and more aircraft became available, particularly after World War I when Jennies could be picked up for

U.S. Air Mail logo.
(Reprinted from Aerial Age magazine, February 16, 1920.)

Crash of a "Jenny" belonging to the U.S. Air Mail Service. (Courtesy: San Diego Aerospace Museum)

a few hundred dollars, pilots increasingly had paid the ultimate price. At one point two in every three pilots who took to the skies was killed. The post-war years, an era known as the "Golden Age of Flight" in which the barnstormer, guided by an "anything-goes" attitude, had become the quintessential daredevil, also became the "Golden Age of Airports," but for the exact opposite reason. Congress long perceived this free wheeling industry to be out of control and following the war, debate intensified as issues became even more complicated, with civilian and military aviation clearly headed on divergent paths. Even the National Advisory Committee for Aeronautics (NACA) concluded that "Federal Legislation should be enacted governing the navigation of aircraft in the United States".[3] Now even the industry itself was suggesting that regulation should become a reality.

Two squadrons of Army airplanes at Yuma in 1926. *(Courtesy: Yuma International Airport.)*

Hydroaeroplane ramp in Santa Barbara, 1917. *(Courtesy: Santa Barbara Airport.)*

From a defiant General "Billy" Mitchell, who would later be court martialled for his views and handling of the subject, to the President of the American Flying Club who proclaimed "take American aviation out of the hands of its enemies and place it entirely within the protection of its friends — aviators", it was clear the time had come for some form of regulation. But as General Mitchell wanted control removed from the Army regulars, civilian aviators thought little of elected officials trying to pass legislation for an activity about which they knew nothing and cared for even less. But as with any "hot" topic, just about every legislator jumped into the fray and proposed legislation, whether they had party support or not.

Ultimately it was President Coolidge himself who skillfully brought order to the 69th Congress and with Dwight Morrow as his lead, the Bingham-Merritt-Parker Bill was passed and on May 20, 1926, the President signed the Air Commerce Act into legislation. The new law placed control of civil aviation under the Department of Commerce, headed by Herbert Hoover, who was its Secretary at that time. Aircraft now required registration and certification, and pilots were required to be licensed to fly, as well. Air traffic rules were instituted and penalties to assist enforcement, were also

Airways map of 1926 (Reprinted from Aviation magazine, December 5, 1927.)

LEGEND

Lighted Portions Dec. 31, 1927
Non-lighted Portions Dec. 31, 1927
Non-mail routes, unlighted

enacted.[4] Civil and military aviation would remain distinct as the commerce issue essentially settled the controversy of having one agency oversee both. The new Bureau of Aeronautics was established to handle all civil aviation matters, while the Department of War remained in charge of military aviation.

Allan and Malcolm Loughead (later Lockheed.) *(Courtesy: Santa Barbara Airport.)*

Herbert Hoover
decided to
apply the
"dock" principle,
a precedent
established under
maritime law
and applied
to airports.

Airports were also considered in the bill, but House and Senate versions disagreed over the inclusion of many of the provisions dealing with airport development. The Senate firmly believed that airports would become a burden on the Federal government with runaway federal spending the result. A subcommittee was formed to deal with this issue before the final Bill was passed. Its principal focus, two issues which have remained at the heart of aviation and airport development today; Federal aid to airports and Federal regulation over commerce.[5]

Ultimately, the Air Commerce Act was very specific in that it did not authorize the Federal government to build airports. The huge cost of funding airports was of a major concern and doomed any kind of support from Congress or the President. Skillfully, Herbert Hoover decided to apply the "dock" principle, a precedent established under maritime law and applied to airports. In effect Hoover used the same theory in aviation as was done to

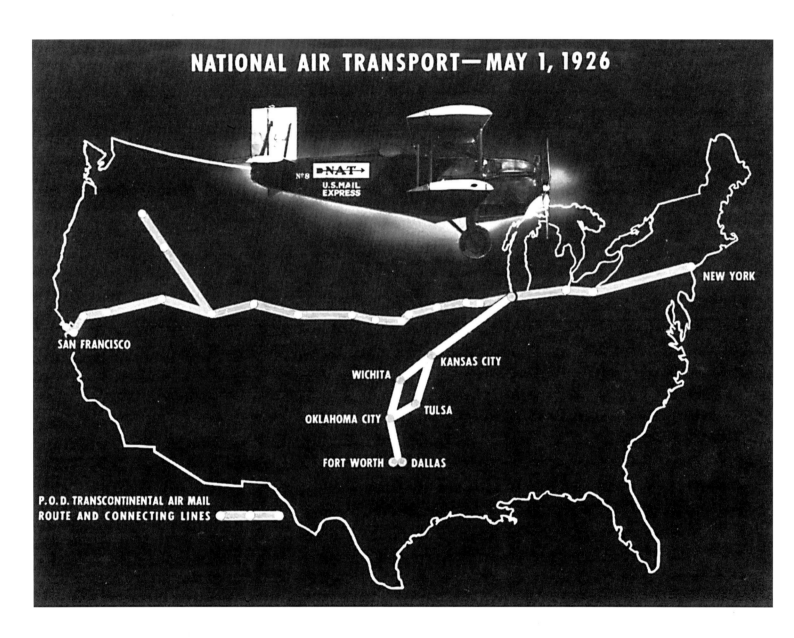

1926 Map of the west coast route of Pacific Air Transport. *(Reprinted from the History of American Air Transportation, 1992.)*

the maritime industry. The premiss was simple. While channels and waterways were built and maintained by the government, docks and harbors were built by local interests. It followed therefore that the Federal government would provide for the development and maintenance of airways, while the development of airports, viewed here as analogues to docks, were a local responsibility. As for commerce, the federal government maintained jurisdictional control over interstate commercial activity, as well as rules pertaining to the airways. It conceded control over non-commercial, intrastate activity, to local government.[6]

With the passage of the Air Commerce Act of 1926, the Federal government took a decisive step and became firmly entrenched in the business of aeronautics. Coupled with the Kelly Act passed the year before, the new regulations applied to aircraft and pilot certification took out a tangible portion of the financial risk that had inhibited commercial aviation to date and it made the odds for successful investment a far better proposition. With government now having made a serious commitment to further developing airways, it was but a matter of time before commercial operators took to the skies in droves. With it came a new demand for aircraft and a burgeoning new manufacturing industry that brought us such venerable names as Vought, Boeing, Douglas, Lockheed, and even Henry Ford, to name a few. It also generated interest in aeronautical research and no effort to advance aviation was greater than that of Daniel Guggenheim who established a $2,500,000 Fund for the Promotion of Aeronautics in 1926. James H. "Jimmy" Doolittle conducted some of the most significant and pioneering flight testing in aeronautics as part of the Guggenheim Fund, and was the first pilot to fly "blind" or on instruments, at is known today.

With the Kelly Act in place, the first airmail contracts were awarded in October of 1925 to five companies selected by the Post Office, including Colonial Air Lines, Robertson Aircraft Corporation, National Air Transport, Western Air Express and Varney Speed Lines. Commercial civil aviation was born and out of these companies would grow some of the giants of today. Colonial became a major part of what is now American Airlines; National and Varney, among others, went on to form United; and Western would become part of what later became TWA.[7] Two weeks after the initial five contracts were awarded, contracts six and seven were awarded to Henry Ford, the automobile manufacturer who, along with William Stout produced one of the most endearing aircraft of the time, the Ford Tri-motor.

But as newly-emerged airlines flew airmail across the U.S., airports were left to develop on their own. The Kelly and Air Commerce Acts had produced everything to jump start the system but the airports themselves. This in no small measure due to the "dock" concept and

With the government now having made a serious commitment to further developing airways, it was but a matter of time before commercial operators took to the skies in droves.

American Airlines, Inc.

Transcontinental & Western Air, Inc.

United Air Lines

Western Air Express Corporation

Pan American Airways, Inc.

1936 Airline logos.
(Reprinted with permission from the Nostalgic Aviator, Inc.)

the fact that airports were enormously expensive to build. Fiorello La Guardia, the New York Congressman after whom La Guardia Airport is named, held much publicized hearings into the cost of building airfields following World War I. Both cost and pork-barrel politics were insurmountable concerns to the Congress of the day, and thus airports were left to fend for themselves.[8]

Only a few airports had developed to any degree by 1926 and most were still nothing more than grass strips, located on city blocks or land sections. With low take-off and approach-to-land speeds, airports were relatively small with short runways if any. Four basic designs existed at the time, including the "all field" rectangular or square airfield, with the windsock located at the center of the field. This layout allowed aircraft to take off in any direction desired, as long as it was into the wind for maximum lift. Landing occurred in the same manner. Where space was a concern, layouts reflected the available land, including triangular, rectangular and L-shaped fields.[9] Other designs included T-shaped configurations or intersecting rectangular fields. Some attention was even paid to such engineering principles as drainage and grading.[10] It was during this time that many cities and towns heeded the call and contemplated entering aeronautics to developed their fields of flying. Those who did not, risked the same fate "as the town that had rejected the railroad", which of course was presumed to be the equivalent of ignorance.[11]

With rules to govern by, and airport development "following the flow of money" as Historian Deborah Douglas has suggested, airports and airlines grew at a tremendous pace during this exciting time. The busiest of today's commercial airports, can trace their origins to this short, four year period, between 1926 and 1930. New facilities were built and existing airfields like Salt Lake City, were expanded during this time. Local Governments put up the money to build these new airports, but equally important was the investment made by the airlines themselves. Among the majors which saw development following the passage of the Air Commerce Act were Los Angeles International Airport, San Francisco International Airport, Phoenix Sky Harbor International Airport, Oakland International Airport, Burbank-Glendale-Pasadena Airport, Reno International Airport, and Lindbergh Field in San Diego.

The busiest
of today's
commercial
airports, can
trace their
origins to
this short,
four year period
between
1926
and 1930.

Of the larger airports, Oakland International Airport ranks as among the oldest continuing running airports in the State of California. Established in 1927, the airport boasted a runway 7,020-feet long, which was the longest constructed runway in the world at that time. Separated into North and South Field, the airport accommodates a large segment of general aviation as well as air carrier aircraft, unique among today's large airports. The South Field, which is host to the air carrier segment of Oakland International Airport sits atop reclaimed land, just like its neighbor to the West and Lindbergh Field in San Diego. Operated by the Port of Oakland, the airport continues to serve its unique market niche in competition with San Francisco International and San Jose International Airports.

Los Angeles International Airport, probably better known by its airport identifier code, LAX, became a reality in 1928, after the city decided to establish a municipal airport. It was known in those days as Mines Field after the realtor who sold the property to the City. The 1928 National Air Races spurred construction of three 7,000-feet runways at Mines Field, but the real goal was to establish an airport following the races. Instead of the airlines flocking to Mines field however, the airport became a mecca for the major aircraft manufacturers at the time and the airport became landlord to such companies as Douglas, Northrup and North American. From those humble beginnings in 1928, LAX has grown into one of the busiest airports in the world and remains the economic heart of the largest of all West coast cities.

Lindbergh Field in San Diego is another international airport which has seen significant growth from the time that intrepid flyer and conqueror of the Atlantic, Charles Lindbergh dedicated the facility in the same year LAX got started. When the doors opened on August 16, 1928, the City of San Diego and the pilot after whom the airport was named, had already established a relationship that began when Lindbergh took off from San Diego to begin his historic flight to Paris, the year before. The *Spirit of St. Louis* was built by the Ryan Aircraft Company in San Diego and coupled with a rich tradition in aviation, beginning with the first flight by John Montgomery, San Diegans have been rightfully proud of their heritage and have dubbed their city "Air Capital of the West".[12] Situated directly across the bay from Coronado Island and NAS North Island, Lindbergh Field is one of the smallest airports among the majors, with 142 of those acres being reclaimed land from what were once tidelands. It lies in the heart of the city, which not only makes it subject to constant noise complaints like so many other airports, but also makes it by far one of the most convenient airports in the

FOUR TYPES OF IDEAL LANDING FIELDS

TYPE A   TYPE B   TYPE C   TYPE D

FIG. 1   FIG. 2   FIG. 3   FIG. 4

Direction Markers for landing to indicate the direction and position of best landing runways in the different shaped fields. These markings should be rectangular in shape and of about the same dimensions as shown in above sketches. Figures 1, 2, 3, 4. The long axes of the marker must parrallel the direction of the runways in the direction affording the least obstructed landing. – See Sketch. The marker can be of any material that can be plainly seen from the air, preferrably white and should be constructed flush with the surface of the ground so as to in no way obstruct the landing of an airplane rolling over it. Cloth or linen can be best used for this purpose. The specifications for landing circles in figures 1, 2, 3, 4 are given in figure 5. The dimension of direction markers are approximate 3 ft. wide and 15 ft. long.

Concrete or cinder runway as shown in Figure 5, for square field, is advocated for Airdromes where heavy rain or snow make field so muddy that the landing and taking off of an airplane is hazardous and liable to result in damage to plane. The runways should parrallel the direction of the prevailing winds provided this arrangement is compatible with the shape of the field and the approach for landing and take off thus indicated is over the least obstructed area. This office does not advise expensive construction of this kind unless the amount of traffic will warrant the outlay. The construction of runways for different shaped fields, will generally follow the same principal of position, although of course of much larger proportions, that is shown for direction markers for landing – in figures 1, 2, 3, 4. These runways should be about 150' long and 50' wide.

Unimproved Landing Facilities — Figures 1, 2, 3, 4, show dimensions for only four types of ideal landing fields and should by no means be accepted as the only type of field that can be used. These are drawn to show the maximum requirements for any present airplane fully loaded and to show requirements for possible use as lighter than air stations. Any field that has a fairly smooth and level surface not obstructed by ditches over six inches deep, clear of obstacles, with a hard surface, with approximately 1500 ft by 600 ft or more can be considered a very usefull landing field provided it is not surrounded by high obstacles which obstruct a clear approach for landing or take off.

International Identification Marker in NW corner of field

Place Circle Marker in center of field and flush with the ground. Concrete runway for landing fields where soil in wet weather makes landing and taking off of Airplanes dangerous on account of mud

Wind Indicator Such as a Standard Aviation Wind Cone placed in one corner of field, preferably on hanger if there is one.

FIG 5

Types of Landing Areas in 1920. _(Reprinted from "Airways and Landing Fields", Air Service Information Circular 5, no. 404. 1923.)_

HARRIS M. HANSHUE
*President
Transcontinental and
Western Air Inc.
Los Angeles, California*

America's Greatest Aircraft Market
Los Angeles County

*Terminal . . . Transcon-
tinental and Western
Air Express adjoining
Alhambra near
Los Angeles*

*Administration Building at 243
acre United Airport, Burbank,
California — near Los Angeles.*

*Grand Central Air Terminal Administration
Building, Glendale, Calif. — near Los Angeles.*

"ANY MANUFACTURER of aircraft or of equipment essential to the aviation industry has but to analyze the records of the various air transport companies of America to discover that his greatest potential (if not present-day) market is in Los Angeles County.

"The five air transport companies whose lines emanate from Los Angeles County operate twelve outgoing and incoming daily schedules serving—either directly or by direct connection — every section of the United States and Canada and important centers of Mexico, Central and South America, Cuba and West Indies.

"Interest in air travel here is particularly strong, flying conditions are good the year 'round, and manufacturing costs are lower than elsewhere.

"These conditions, plus the fact that five major air transport companies have their Western terminals in Los Angeles, obviously, make this the logical location for the profitable operation of the aircraft industry."

Harris M. Hanshue
President Transcontinental and Western Air Inc.

*Complete information including detailed
surveys supplied on request by
Industrial Department
Los Angeles Chamber of Commerce*

LOS ANGELES
Flying All Year
COUNTY

Advertisement of Los Angeles County Airports. *(Western Flying magazine, 1927.)*

Formation fly-by at United Airport on opening day, Memorial Day, 1930. *(Courtesy: Burbank-Glendale-Pasadena Airport.)*

Opening day festivities at United Airport, Memorial Day, 1930. *(Courtesy: Burbank-Glendale-Pasadena Airport.)*

1928 Air Races at Mines Field.
(Courtesy: Los Angeles Department of Airports.)

Country. Having grown from slightly more than 5 million enplaned passengers in 1980, to more than 12 million enplanements in 1995, Lindbergh Field also had the distinction of being the busiest single runway airport in the United States with over 210,000 operations.

Not all airports were the result of local government involvement as a number of airports were developed by the airlines in order to assure themselves of optimum way points on the routes they flew. Phoenix Sky Harbor International Airport also got its start in 1928, but the airport was the result of classic private investment. The airport was privately owned and developed by Scenic Airways, Inc., a regional airline. With the stock market crash the following year, another airline took over, only to sell out to the Acme Investment Company, which in turn sold the airport to the City of Phoenix in 1935 for $100,000. Dubbed "the farm" by local pilots, cattle had to be buzzed regularly to clear the runway for landing. By 1948, the Phoenix Sky Harbor Airport had become the busiest airport in the Nation. By 1980, the airport served more than one million passengers a month and the phenomenal growth has continued to this day, making Phoenix Sky Harbor International Airport one of the busiest in the entire country.

Phoenix was not the only airport to get its start from private investment by airlines. Reno International Airport in Nevada was built in 1929 by Boeing Transport and was known then as Hubbard Field. Sold to United Airlines in 1935, the airport was acquired by the City of Reno in 1953. Following the Airline Deregulation Act of 1978, the airport which had been renamed the Reno-Cannon International Airport, became the fastest growing airport in the nation in 1979, with 2.9 million enplanements. That was nearly triple the number of passengers in 1975. In 1995 the airport was renamed Reno International Airport.

Dubbed "the farm" by local pilots, cattle had to be buzzed regularly to clear the runway for landing.

Burbank too would find its genesis with the airline industry when it was dedicated as United Airport on Memorial Day, 1930. Owned and developed by United Aircraft and Transportation Company, later to become United Airlines, the airport followed the same trend experienced by a number of airports. But Burbank has differed in one respect from other privately developed airports, in that it remained closely tied to private industry and private management longer than any other facility. It became Union Air Terminal in 1934 and was renamed again in 1940 to Lockheed Air Terminal, when the Lockheed Company acquired the airport. Following World War II, most airlines left Burbank for Mines Field, which had become Los Angeles Municipal Airport and would later become LAX. Renamed the Hollywood-Burbank Airport in 1967, the airport would remain in private hands until 1978, when an airport authority was established comprised of representatives of the cities of Burbank, Glendale and Pasadena. To reflect the new ownership, the airport was renamed again, this time as the Burbank-Glendale-Pasadena Airport, by which it is known today. Lockheed however has continued to manage the airport on behalf of the airport authority, making the relationship between public and private enterprise, one of the most unique and enduring in all of airport history.

Not all airports would have such illustrious starts with cities or airlines vying to invest moneys to build runways, taxiways, aprons and terminals. Many airports that date back to the early thirties were carved out of desert flats and remote strips outside of town. Two of these airports are located in the high desert of California, north of what is probably the most unique airfield in the world, Edwards Air Force Base. Inyokern and Mojave Airports both got their start around 1930 and were for a while operated by the County of Kern, which under the leadership of Cecil Meadows, managed at one time some 23 airports around the county, making it the largest county-operated airport system in the country. With the advent of WW II, both airports saw military activity, as Inyokern was converted first into an Army Air Corps training facility for primary flight training in Stearman's and Mojave Airport became a Marine Corps fighter base, operating F4U Corsairs and F-9's. Inyokern converted to a Navy facility and operated as such until 1952, while Mojave remained occupied by the Marines until 1964 when the airport was turned back over to Kern County. Both airports eventually became Airport Districts, Mojave in 1972 and Inyokern in 1985. Through the perseverance and unique styles of management, the airports have become thriving centers of economic activity. Mojave Airport is known as the Civilian Flight Test Center, and mimics in many respects its military neighbor to the South. It even has a test pilot school, the only civilian school of its kind anywhere. Inyokern is

Many airports that date back to the early thirties were carved out of desert flats and remote strips outside of town.

Mines Field in 1929. *(Courtesy: Los Angeles Department of Airports.)*

rapidly becoming a favorite to Hollywood and the advertising industry and a major portion of the airport's revenue is generated by film and commercial shoots requiring the use of runways, taxiways and aprons.

The most significant of all general aviation airports today is Van Nuys Airport. Opened in 1928 as Metropolitan Airport in San Fernando Valley, Van Nuys ranks as the busiest general aviation airport in the world and is the sixth busiest airport in the nation. In 1942, the airport was converted into a military facility and was renamed Van Nuys Army Air Field. Following the war, the airport was acquired by the City of Los Angeles 1949 and renamed the San Fernando Valley Airport. In 1957, the city renamed the airport to its present name and expanded the 6,000-foot runway by an additional 2,000 feet, following completion of the Sherman Way underpass. Situated on 725 acres, approximately 850 aircraft call VNY home. With over 500,000 airport operations a year, Van Nuys remains at the very forefront of general aviation today.

Not all airports are so lucky. Sadly, many airports that saw their beginning during this time are no longer around. One of the most famous of all is without a doubt the Grand Central Air Terminal in Glendale, California. Dedicated on February 22 1929, the guest list that day was a "who's who" in aviation and entertainment. Jack Maddux and Roscoe Turner were on hand, as was Governor C.C. Young. Gary Cooper and Jean Harlow headed the list of Hollywood celebrities.[13] Funded in large part through the private efforts of Maddux, and later by Curtiss who developed the Curtiss Airport Corporation and had bought out Maddux and the Spicer Group in May of 1929, Grand Central Air Terminal would become the quintessential airport for most travel to and from the Los Angeles area. By the time the U.S. entered WW II following the bombing of Pearl Harbor on December 7, 1941, the airport played host to an operational base for P-38 aircraft. Following the war, it reverted back to a civilian airport, but the pressures of industrial and residential development in Glendale, ultimately forced the closure of the grandest of

Grand Central Air Terminal in 1938. *(Courtesy: San Diego Aerospace Museum.)*

TWA DC-1 parked in front of the terminal at Grand Central Air Terminal in 1931 *(Reprinted from Madcaps, Millionaires &"Mose", John Underwood. Heritage Press.)*

Grand Central Air Terminal in 1996; an abandoned office building owned by The Prudential Company. *(Photo by: Robert Olislagers.)*

all airports. Today, the original terminal with its distinctive Spanish arches still visible, stands forlorn and empty among tilt up's and other nondescript industrial buildings and parking lots. Painted over, chipped white paint reveal the original colorful tiles that once decorated the building. High overhead, the corners of the air traffic control tower remain adorned by winged angels holding a propeller. All four seem to pierce into a distant past, as if to guard what once was. In their shadow, eyes closed, you can almost hear the whirl of a Tri-motor, taxing out for one more last flight.

The sudden explosion of civilian aviation cannot be entirely credited to the opportunity provided with the establishment of the Air Commerce Act. While it provided the critical platform for private and public investment, the industry needed a catalyst to convince the public at large of the promise of aviation. On May 20 and 21, 1927, former airmail pilot, Charles H. "Slim" Lindbergh became that catalyst, by crossing the Atlantic in a solo flight that captured the imagination of the world. His great feat earned him yet another nickname, "Lucky Lindy", and nearly 70 years later, his aircraft *The Spirit of St. Louis*, displayed at the Air and Space Museum at the Smithsonian Institution, remains as a testament to his skill, daring and courage and is regarded as the most popular among the exhibits there. Never before, or since, has an aviator been able to stir the emotions of a people to such a degree, or has managed to endure in their minds for so long. From the time he set foot in Paris, France, Lindbergh became the instant ambassador of aeronautics and the growth of civilian aviation and airports is also his legacy. His tour of the U.S. to promote the need for more airports in the Fall of 1927, contributed greatly to the number of cities and towns showing an interest in airport development. The Guggenheim sponsored tour ignited interest like none had before and stands alone in the annals of airport history.

The frenzy that was Lindbergh however, would soon be overshadowed by the Stock Market Crash of 1929 and the Great Depression that followed. It cast a long dark and cold shadow over a people who descended hard from the era known as the "roaring twenties", and into the economic abyss that followed. Although the Air Commerce Act prevented the federal government from funding airports between 1926 and 1938, the great depression would force the hand of the federal government and forge a political polemic which has driven airports ever since. From 1933, the Civil Works Administration (CWA), until it was replaced by the Federal Emergency Relief Administration (FERA) in 1934, spent $11.5 million establishing 585 new airports. FERA also aided another 943 airports, mostly in small communities.[14] In 1935 the Works Progress Administration (WPA) took over the

Today, the original terminal with its distinctive Spanish arches still visible, stands forlorn and empty among tilt up's and other nondescript industrial buildings and parking lots.

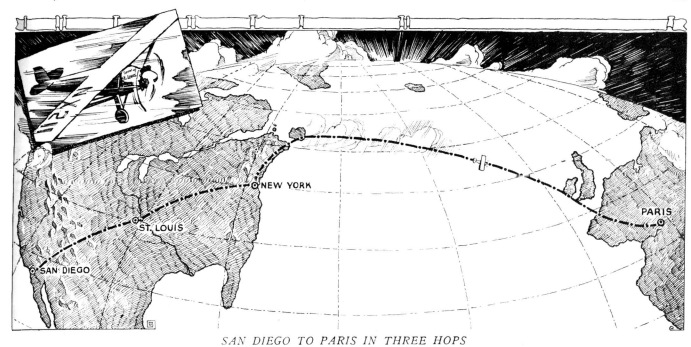

SAN DIEGO TO PARIS IN THREE HOPS

San Diego—New York—Paris in Three Hops Sets Lindbergh at Pinnacle of Aviation

A YANKEE kid did it! Through technical evidence, an eminent Eastern aero engineer a short time ago, demonstrated the impossibility of the New York-Paris flight. It is probable that Captain Charles Lindbergh knew nothing of this demonstration of the impossible. In any event, he failed to take it into his calculations when he hopped off in his Western-made ship "Spirit of St. Louis,' waved a farewell to New York, and some thirty-three hours later reiterated Pershing's memorable words—"Lafayette, we are here.'

This New York-Paris flight for the last decade has been the dream of every leading aviator. It has been tried several times, some have succeeded in the Trans-Atlantic jump—with stop-over allowances. None before Lindbergh ever had accomplished the entire trip in a single flight. Furthermore, prior to this flight none had accomplished the crossing single-handed.

In the great glory that has come to young Lindbergh for his epic flight from New York to Paris, still another record that he established in conjunction with this flight appears to have been overlooked. He made the trip from the Pacific Coast to La Belle France in exactly three hops. Leaving San Diego he jumped to St. Louis; from St. Louis it was merely a step to New York and from Gotham to Paris constituted the third jump. This youth of the air covered more than 7000 miles in these three strides; which probably will be a mark for aviators to shoot at for some years to come.

Leaving New York at 7:52 a.m., on Friday the 20th, Lindbergh arrived in Paris at 5:21 p.m., the following evening, an elapsed time of 33 hours, 10 minutes, in the first successful non-stop Trans-Atlantic flight. Practically unknown, but with a confidence that had inspired certain citizens of St. Louis to back him in his undertaking, overnight Lindbergh became the world's outstanding hero. He took Paris by storm and not since the signing of the Armistice on November 11, 1918, has that city of mirth been quite as jubilant.

In taking off from Roosevelt Field, the Spirit of St. Louis balked, and those watching in the gray dawn were fearful that "Slim" would be unable to make it. The field was muddy and the plane refused repeatedly to leave the ground and when it did, it cleared by a scant ten feet a huge tractor that lay in its path, while only a few feet again cleared him from a threatening of telephone wires. That few feet in either instance would have

Byrd Delays His Flight to Europe

Tmander Richard E. Byrd over the Atlantic with his big Fok-HE proposed flight of Comker tri-motored plane has been deferred until the return of Captain Charles Lindberg to the United States in order that there may be no incident to detract from the attention which Europe is showering upon the hero of the first non-stop trip to Paris.

In the meantime Byrd continues to test his big ship, and in the course of a week or two, after Lindbergh is safely on his way home, he probably will hop off for Europe, taking Bert Acosta as alternate pilot.

Byrd's flight is purely a scientific expedition designed to develop the possibilities of trans-oceanic transportation, and the conditions that must be taken into consideration in establishing any regular service over the Atlantic by air.

spelled disaster, possible death. But Lindbergh "knew his onions," and, the obstacles cleared, he was "off to Paris."

In commenting on the flight, Lindbergh said: "The trip was no picnic." According to his own story of the flight, "we met good weather over New Foundland, but hit sleet and fog for about a thousand miles of the trip. In order to avoid the fog and clouds of ice it was necessary for us to cary our 10,000 feet but I imagine much the greater part of the journey was made at about 100 feet.

"Had we imagined the weather would be as bad as we found it after leaving Newfoundland, it is doubtful if we would have started but as long as we were on the way, there was nothing to do but keep going. The dawn looked mighty good to us but better still was the sight of Ireland which we got at about two o'clock in the afternoon.

"From the maps and what I had read about it, we knew that Ireland was slightly mountainous, that England was hilly, rolling country and France pretty flat. So that when we picked up the high ridges we knew that was Ireland.

"Crossing the English Channel was no particular trick, but we had to take a chance when we hit Cherbourg, but as we had daylight until about twenty minutes out of Paris, that helped considerably. Then we were picked up by the big searchlights on Mount Valerian and at the airdrome. The city lights of Paris were somewhat confusing and without the searchlights we might have had some difficulty in making a landing."

This history-making air voyage was made by dead reckoning; the plane carried no astronomical instruments and Lindbergh does not understand the use of a sextant. This feature of the trip alone has astounded the most experienced pilots of France and Great Britaiin.

Story of the Lindbergh flight from San Diego, to New York, to Paris, France in 1927. *(Reprinted from Western Flying magazine, June 1927.)*

responsibility of airport development, however, the WPA would concentrate on improvements which were of a more permanent nature. Monterey Peninsula Airport and Oxnard Airport benefitted from the WPA program. Even art work, such as the mosaics that grace the original art deco style terminal building at Long Beach airport, were funded by the WPA. Unlike the CWA and FERA programs, the WPA required a local match. By the time the WPA program was dissolved in 1943, employment had rebounded and the federal government was fighting an enemy of a different kind.

By 1938 Congress passed and President Roosevelt signed into legislation the Civil Aeronautics Act, effectively ending the reign of the Commerce Department's direct involvement with aeronautics. Although control would be placed in the hands of the newly-established Civil Aeronautics Authority (CAA), the Commerce Department's influence has had lasting impact on the industry and continues to drive the legislative and legal parameters in which airports operate today.

Advertisement for Mercury Aviation Company, owned by movie mogul Cecil B. DeMille who owned and operated two airports in the Los Angeles area.
(Reprinted with permission from The Hatfield Collection, Museum of Flight)

The Ryan Company at Dutch Flats in San Diego. *(Courtesy: San Diego Aerospace Museum.)*

United Cargoliner DC-3. *(Courtesy of Los Angeles Department of Airports.)*

1941 Aerial view of Lockheed Air Terminal (Burbank) and Grand Central Air Terminal *(Courtesy: Los Angeles County Department of Airports.)*

Amelia Earhart at Lockheed Air Terminal *(Burbank-Glendale-Pasadena Airport.)*

MOJAVE 74
OCT 12-13

SANCTIONED BY THE

PROFESSIONAL
RACE
PILOTS
ASSOCIATION

	ADULT	CHILD 6 TO 12
RESERVED GRANDSTAND	9.00	6.00
GENERAL ADMISSION	6.00	3.00
ADVANCE TICKETS *	5.00	2.50
FRIDAY EVENTS	2.00	1.00
OVERNIGHT CAMPING SPACES	5.00	

* LIBERTY, MUTUAL TICKET AGENCIES

FOR FURTHER INFORMATION CONTACT

AIR RACE MANAGEMENT CORPORATION
16644 ROSCOE BLVD. VAN NUYS, CALIF. 91406

Poster of the 1974 Air Races at Mojave Airport. Races were held from 1969 until 1975. *(Collection: Robert Olislagers)*

Aerial view of Van Nuys Airport in 1933. *(Courtesy of Los Angeles County Department of Airports.)*

State and Federal

*F*UST why there should be such universal acceptance of the idea that the municipality is divinely ordained to shoulder the responsibility for airport establishment, is rather difficult to discern. The onus of providing facilities for other forms of transportation has never been borne by the city, and has invariably been divided between the state and the nation, and it is not easy to see why a distinction should be made in the case of airports.

R APID, reliable and safe transport is one of the greatest of national assets. In peace or war it is equally important to the welfare and prosperity of the whole country. Air transportation is inherently fast, but it can be neither reliable nor safe without adequate airport facilities. It is the responsibility of the federal government to see that the nation is so provided with airports that planes in any number can speed to any locality, no matter how remote, without delay at a time of crisis.

O UR present available airports are with few exceptions built by our large cities. Smaller municipalities cannot afford the vast expense incident to the establishment of a really adequate airport. They have landing fields, of which they are usually very proud, but most of them have no conception of what a real airport involves, and have not the resources with which to finance one if they had.

I F ESTABLISHMENT of airports is left to the individual municipalities it will be many years before this country can derive the full benefit of the fast, all-embracing transport afforded by the airplane. Without the aid of state and nation there will always be localities inaccessible to the plane, localities which under certain conditions it may be very necessary to reach.

T HE responsibility of the state and nation in matters of transportation is an accepted axiom of civil government. It has been exemplified in every mode of transportation in every country since the time of the Romans. In America we have the precedents of vast land subsidies to the railways, great cash subsidies to shipping, hundreds of millions of federal funds expended in river and harbor development, and other hundreds of millions of federal aid for highways. Even in airways the government has recognized its obligation in the establishment on a limited scale of 'intermediate" fields in uninhabited regions, purely for emergency use.

T HE responsibility is not of course 100 per cent federal. It is divided among the federal, the state, and the local governments and each of these subdivisions of government has its definite proportion of

Aid for Airports

the responsibility. At the present time the tendency of the state and federal governments appears to be to push their shares of the burden onto the local governments, which is manifestly unfair and unjust.

THERE is an immediate need for an equitable division of responsibility in airport construction. The division should be made on the basis of proportion and importance of interest. There are some airport projects in which manifestly there is no other interest than the municipal. There is no justification for expenditure of either state or federal funds on such projects. There are other airports which have a definite place in national defense and postal projects, and in the commercial communications system of the state. Such airport projects are in the majority, and at the present time there is no provision for their establishment by other than local resources.

FEDERAL aid for highways was worked out on a basis of a dollar of federal funds for each dollar of state funds, and applied only to roads that fell under certain classifications, and whose specifications complied with federal requirements. The proportion of federal lands within the state had a bearing on the apportionment of aid, and other factors were considered.

FOR lack of a better criterion, the Federal Aid for Highways plan might well be used as a basis from which to work out the proportion of responsibility which state and nation shall assume in airport establishment. The factors peculiar to aviation and the airport will of course modify the final result.

HOWEVER it is done, it is time for action, if the municipality is not to be saddled with the whole responsibility of developing the American airport system. Every city council, every chamber of commerce, every civic organization, and every airport and aeronautical organization should immediately take the problem in hand. A unified body of thought concentrated behind a concerted movement for Federal Aid for Airports, will result in the establishment of an airport system that will consolidate American supremacy in the air—that will immeasurably increase our defensive resources in time of war, and our commercial and industrial resources in time of peace.

UPON this objective will be concentrated every atom of energy and of influence of the Occidental Publications until such time as a complete and comprehensive system of American airports is an accomplished fact. To this cause we dedicate ourselves, and to it we summon the thought and the effort of every friend of American aviation.

CHAPTER 5

THE WAR YEARS 1939-1945

THE
WAR YEARS
1939-1945

The Stock Market Crash of 1929 precipitated one of the most difficult periods in American history and plunged the nation into a deep and prolonged financial crisis. Bereft of capital on both sides of the investment-consumption continuum, not even President Hoover's attempt at jump starting the economy, by infusing $2 billion into the ailing economy, could create sufficient momentum to pull the country out of the crisis. Airlines and airports suffered alike and the growth experienced by the industry during this time, albeit at a slower pace,

Curtiss JN-4 "Jenny" *(Courtesy: McCarran Aviation Heritage Collection/Rockwell Collection, UNLV.)*

must be viewed as extraordinary indeed. The great depression dominated the Hoover Administration and the failure to resurrect the economy, in part, lead to the end of his administration and marked the beginning of Roosevelt's. It also signalled the beginning of a fundamental shift in political economic debate, led by economist John Maynard Keynes. Unlike the Hoover Administration, which followed classic economic doctrine, the Roosevelt Administration was guided by principles set for in Keynes' General (economic) Theory, for which the foundation had been established earlier in 1919 in the "Economic Consequences of the Peace". Keynes postulated that demand, and not supply, would be the driving force in economic behavior, provided government intervention created balance through regulation.[1] This doctrine, particularly as it related to regulation, was designed to allow capital to "flow upward", rather than to "trickle down", as the mercantalist approach of Adam Smith would have it. A modified neo-classical version of this supply side theory re-appeared in the 80s during the Reagan Administration following economic theory postulated by Milton Friedman. In very general terms however, this doctrinal difference in economic theory has characterized modern political debate and it is important to note that the effect on airport

Four More Opinions

On State and Federal Airport Aid

Harry L. Finch
Commissioner of Parks, Salt Lake City

"I WAS very much interested in the editorial in your September issue in relation to State and Federal Aid for the construction of Airports and agree with you that the only way we will ever have a general installation of landing fields which are at all serviceable will be through the assistance of either State or Federal aid or both. This will apply to our sparsely settled states with more force perhaps than in other states where cities of reasonable large population are more numerous than in many of our Western States.

"Then again, the injustice of taking the tax on gasoline which has been used on our airfields and in airplanes and turning it over to the state roads without one cent being returned to the industry in any way, as it is done in our state, cannot be the right system. I would say that our airfield has paid into the state treasury at least one hundred thousand dollars in gasoline taxes without the return of a single dollar in road or other work anywhere leading to or benefitting air transportation in any way. This applies to our own conditions, but I have no doubt other municipal and private airfields are also subjected to the same conditions."

Hon. Tasker L. Oddie
United States Senator from Nevada

"I AM in receipt of the September issue of Airport Construction and Management and note your editorial on 'State and Federal Aid for Airports.'

"I feel that you are doing a fine service in taking the lead in this important enterprise. The airports of the country have not kept pace with the rapid and successful development of aviation. I refer especially to those in the smaller cities and towns which cannot afford to build them as well or on as large a scale as the more populous and wealthier cities. I also feel that our Government should do more than it is doing at present in the development of the airports of the country. More vision and constructive thought and action are needed in certain quarters in order that the necessary airports may be adequately constructed.

"There is an analogy between the aircraft and airport problems, on one side, and the automotive vehicles and highways, on the other, in that the automotive industry has far outgrown our present highway system and is developing much more rapidly and effectively than our highways. The same thing can be said regarding aviation and airports.

"I wish you success in your great work, which the people of the country will appreciate more as time goes on."

Hon. Arthur Capper
United States Senator from Kansas

"I WOULD be in favor of reasonable Federal aid for airports, when an equitable adjustment of Federal, State and local responsibilities is worked out. But I must state also, very frankly, that the extension of Federal aid along new lines is being viewed askance by many.

"I will watch with sympathetic interest your program as it is worked out."

R. W. Hart
City Manager, City of Lynchburg, Virginia

"I WISH to concur with you in the need for State and Federal Aid for Airports, particularly during the present state of this comparatively new method of transportation.

"Aviation needs to be encouraged and I believe should and will receive merited support by the State and Federal Government."

State & Federal Aid to Airports 1929 *(Reprinted from Airport Construction and Management magazine, 1929)*

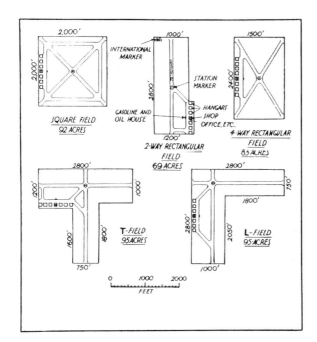

Airport Design Types -1923 *(Reprinted from The Airport Book, M. Greiff)*

Ovington

E ARLE OVINGTON, operates his own private airport at his home at Santa Barbara, Calif., and there is a long standing invitation to every pilot who comes his way to drop in. Incidentally, Ovington's field may soon be extended and built up to become Santa Barbara's major airport.

Ovington attended Bleriot's aviation school in France, returning to this country in 1911 to enter a number of flying races. Among others, he won the 186 mile cross country race sponsored by the Boston Globe, taking a $10,000 prize. On September 23 of the same year he was sworn in as the first air mail pilot, and transported a cargo of mail. During the war he was president and general manager of the Curtiss station at Atlantic City, N. J.

Ovington founded and for the past four years has been commodore of the Santa Barbara Aero Club. He is chairman of the aviation committee of the Santa Barbara chamber of commerce, a member of the Early Birds and the Quiet Birdmen, as well as the Professional Pilots Association, and is listed in Who's Who in America. He was lately commissioned a Lieutenant-Commander in the United States Naval Reserve.

Earle Ovington *(Reprinted from Western Flying magazine, 1927)*

development is deeply rooted within this debate. Although the great depression and World War II would serve as catalysts, funding toward airports has been guided by these policies, starting with the Roosevelt Administration.

It comes as no surprise then, that airports increasingly have come to rely on federal support and only in recent years have the basic policies in airport funding been challenged, as efforts to "defederalize", especially at the larger airports, are viewed as the only remaining alternative to decreasing federal control at the local level. Thus, the debate over contemporary issues such as revenue diversion and rates and charges, is rooted deeply within the economic theories that have guided politics in general. Control remains an important corollary to the larger debate and as local airport sponsors ponder the cost of autonomy, the integrity of what has been viewed as systemic since the Roosevelt era, is challenged by the financial ability to make such choices and by the economic philosophies which lie at the core of political debate.

At the time of the Roosevelt Administration however, the shift in economic policy, known as the New Deal, allowed the country to emerge from the great depression and the construction of more than 500 airports during this time was meant to create opportunity at the bottom first. Many of these airports however, failed to stand the test of time, in part because they were built near small communities not capable of sustaining sufficient economic growth to support air commerce activity over the long run. The significance of so many new airports must be viewed therefore in the context of job creation during difficult economic times.[2] However, the success of the New Deal at the macroeconomic level stands in sharp contrast to the failure of so many airports to sustain themselves in a free market environment and appears to lend support to the basic theory that commercially viable airports are highly dependent on the flow of capital, as suggested by Douglas.[3] It even appears to suggest that the flow of capital and investment over time is not dependent on economic doctrine, but is accelerated or slowed only by the particular form which most favors one over the other. Although other factors must be considered with respect to the success and failure of airports developed during the Great Depression, it does appear to follow in general terms. Even today, the flow of capital continues to have significant impact on airport development, albeit in global, rather than in national terms. One only has to look at the growth and level of investment in airport development along the Pacific Rim to realize the effect commerce, trade and investment has on airport development as a whole.

What remains from the New Deal era can be found principally at airports and in communities willing, and more importantly, able to invest resources and capital at the time. It was in these communities that the importance of having an airport was measured indeed in economic terms and that, to be able to play a role in the national economy, one had to start with transportation infrastructure, including roads, railroads and airports.[4] While capital as a commodity remained scarce, the growth of airports and airlines during this entire period is all the more remarkable and can be measured by both technological, as well as ideological advances in airport development.

As the airmail routes expanded, many new airports, both

Waldo Waterman in 1924 *(Courtesy: Model Colony Room, Ontario Library.)*

large and small, were developed and the airway system, complete with beacons to light up the night sky, greatly enhanced the system of connecting cities and communities. By 1933, over 18,000 airway miles were lit with beacons spaced at 15 miles apart, and auxiliary or emergency fields spaced every 50 miles or less. As the industry matured, so did internal differentiation among airports . First in simple terms, as Earle Ovington, the first pilot to officially fly airmail for the post office and who operated his own airport in Santa Barbara, theorized. Ovington perceived airports to consist of two basic types of fields, one properly referred to as the "airport" and the other, an "airfield".[5] An airport, he reasoned, had to be close to town to handle passengers, mail and other merchandise, while airfields were for teaching and training, and should preferably be located out of town, "beyond the residential section so that those who reside therein may enjoy their homes without fear of a student spinning down through their roof".[6]   Waldo D. Waterman,

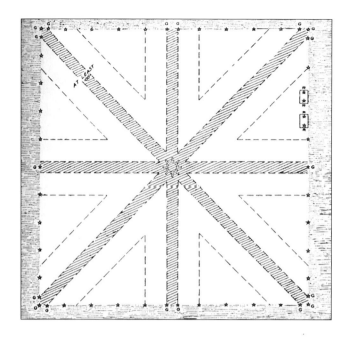

Airport Lighting Diagram -1927
(Airport Construction and Management
magazine, 1929)

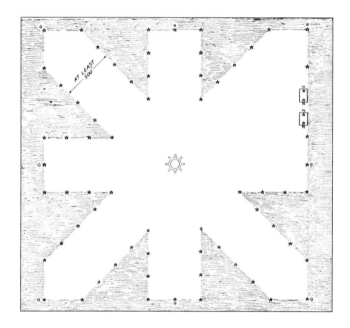

Airport Lighting Diagram-1927
(Airport Construction and Management
magazine, 1929)

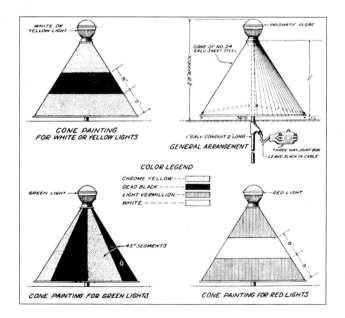

Airport Cones - 1927
(Airport Construction and Management
magazine, 1929.)

General Manager of the Los Angeles Metropolitan Airport in 1929 took differentiation among airports one step further and identified as many as nine different functional classifications. These included, the major all-purpose airfield; the close-in terminal [airfield]; the school field; the dealers' and taxi field; the manufacturing and industrial field; the airline base field; the intermediate field; emergency fields; and individual fields.[7] While most classifications speak for themselves, Waterman argued with parenthetic and somewhat paradoxical logic, that the "close-in terminal" airport needed to be close to a city or town in order to service passengers, but that "the value of such ground would be prohibitive in cost for (flight) schools, manufacturers, and basing (FBO) operations", and only airlines would be able to have (afford) the exclusive use of such facilities.[8] How right he was about cost!

Clover Field in 1937. (*Courtesy: Los Angeles County Department of Airports.*)

Grass fields still characterized most of the airfields in the late twenties and early thirties, but new technologies, first tested and implemented at the major way points for the air mail services and at many of the military air fields, now started to shape the myriad of other airports that dotted the landscape as well. Grass runways and taxiways gave way to oiled runways and taxiways, such as those at Clover Field (Santa Monica Airport) and Maricopa Flats Airport in Arizona. By the late 20s, Kern County Airport too had one runway covered with 60-70 percent asphaltic road oil and when Mines Field was constructed for the 1928 National Air Races, it too featured an oiled runway for take off purposes. Mather Field, near Sacramento and one of the oldest Army Air Corps training facilities in the Southwest, boasted a 3-inch asphaltic concrete apron and taxiway as far back as 1918.

While the reasons for smooth runway and taxiway surfaces may seem obvious to those in the profession today, this was not the case in the twenties when many of the aircraft required little in the way of take off or landing distance. The weight of the early aircraft required only a short roll out before rotation. Similarly, landing speeds were so slow that only a small area was needed to land the airplane. In fact, the early aircraft did not have brakes, as roll out distances on the rough surfaces of pastures and grass strips were sufficiently short to make brakes a luxury rather than a necessity. By the late twenties and early thirties however, the small lightweight aircraft had given way to newer airplanes with greater approach to land speeds and more importantly, load capacity. Loads increased dramatically as the aircraft carried greater numbers of passengers, cargo and fuel. Gone were the days of converted airmail planes and by the late thirties, aircraft like the Boeing 247 and the early DC series aircraft started to dominate the passenger market. By 1933 some 500,000 passengers had taken to the skies and this number would more than double by the time the Civil Aeronautics Act of 1938 was enacted. Thus runways and taxiways needed to evolve with the new aircraft that would use them. The lack of funding made such propositions often a demand based improvement, rather than one based on anticipated demand. Most of the fields of flying built during this era were not fields of dreams as such and found that keeping up with technology was quite a challenge. By 1938, the need for national planning and the need for a national airport system, as a system, started to take shape.

The acceptance of oiling and asphalting runways, taxiways and aprons were not the only innovations in airport development. Site location became an important aspect of planning and engineering, as factors such as weather, physical aspects, accessibility and cost were being considered. In 1929, Richard J. Probert published take-off and landing charts to help establish runway length at various altitudes.[9] A weather station on an airport was also considered a major innovation and an asset to any airport that had its own. In 1929 one could get set up for a little over $1000, with recurring expenses estimated at less than $5,000 per year, which included the salaries of a meteorologist in charge and an assistant meteorologist. The cost was less if the airport did not have scheduled air service.[10] As the airmail system expanded, numerous airports during this time were the beneficiaries of beacons, paid for by the Commerce Department. Many airports added locally funded boundary lights, as all-field, or all-way airports were lighted from the periphery in, rather than by means of runway lights along the length of the landing area. Even planners got in on the act and saw an opportunity to plan properly for this new technology. Recognizing that airports were not isolated from one another, uniformity became of paramount importance, both from a planning, as well as a financing point of view.

Gone were the days of converted airmail planes and by the late thirties, aircraft like the Boeing 247 and the early DC series aircraft started to dominate the passenger market.

ROTOGRAVURE SECTION **Los Angeles Times** SUNDAY FEBRUARY 25, 1940

SOUTHERN CALIFORNIA PUTS WINGS ON THE WORLD

BIRDS OF PEACE AND WAR — Under a peaceful California sun, with the Verdugo Hills in the background, new commercial ships and warplanes are shown on test line at Lockheed's Burbank plant awaiting test flights. The new outlined British bombers are part of the 750 planes ordered from Lockheed by Great Britain. At the left is the 17-place Lodestar, new transport ship.

POWERHOUSE of American aviation is Los Angeles County where an army of 25,000 men, toiling in the area's four major aircraft factories, builds more than 50 per cent of the nation's airplane production. Multi-engined transports for world airlines, swift pursuit ships, combat planes and giant bombers for warring Europe, training planes for American defense — these and craft of a dozen uses come off local assembly lines. Floor space alone totals 3,000,000 square feet. Pressed, these plants together could turn out 8000 aircraft in one year, or 750 a month. Douglas Aircraft Co., Lockheed Aircraft Corp., North American Aviation and Vultee Aircraft, Inc.,—all in Los Angeles County.

BOUND FOR WAR—Grim reminders of Europe's conflict, these British bombing planes made in Los Angeles County are lined up at harbor with wings and propellers removed awaiting shipment to England.

COMBAT SHIP — At the Vultee plant in Downey, recently doubled in size to take care of current production, this new Vultee 51, speedy and agile combat plane, is the pride of military observers.

Special "Photogravure" section of the L.A. Times during WWII, covering a story at Burbank Airport (Courtesy: L.A. Times/Jack Rowe Collection.)

Even the first zoning efforts were being implemented, mostly at the urging of airport managers trying to protect "their" airports from incompatible surrounding land use. The adage that "everything changes and nothing changes", holds true even in airport management.

By 1938, the aircraft manufacturing industry had experienced even greater advances than did the airport industry, which was desperately trying to keep up. The cancellation of the airmail contracts in 1934 and the disastrous effort by the Army Air Corps to carry the mail once again as it had in 1918, forced the industry to take another look at itself. By now the transportation of passengers, rather than mail, had become the primary focus and with it came the realization that the airways, airports and the industry as a whole, were very much part of a system. The Civil Aeronautics Act required the CAA to survey all the airports in the context of a National Airport Plan, as it was to be referred to. With so many innovations in the making, and the recognition that the industry was indeed systemic, Roosevelt acknowledged the need for a reorganization of the airway management and created the Civil Aeronautics Authority, along with the Air Safety Board and an independent administrator, as part of the Civil Aeronautics Act of 1938. It signalled the end of 12 years of formal Commerce Department control. Following some early organizational difficulties, the CAA was once again reorganized in 1940, with the establishment of the Civil Aeronautics Board and the Civil Aeronautics Administration. The CAB became responsible for safety rules, aircraft accident investigation and economic regulation of the airlines, while the CAA was responsible for air traffic control, pilot and aircraft certification, safety enforcement and airway development. Although an independent authority, the CAA Administrator reported directly to the Secretary of the Commerce Department.

Following the German invasion of Poland in 1939, Congress appropriated $40 million for the development of military training fields. Initially 399 airports received aid in the development of landing facilities and this program was later expanded to a total of 986 fields when it became clear that the number of existing facilities was inadequate to address the War Department's needs. Excluding military funding, over $350 million was spent by the CAA in the construction of military facilities and another $9.5 million was spent on civil airports.[11] Many of these military training and operational facilities were constructed to convert to civilian uses following the war and indeed more than 500 airfields were conveyed to cities and counties for civil purposes following the end of World War II. By late 1944, a follow up to the original survey of airports was submitted to Congress, resulting in a sweeping overhaul of the airports and airway development program, including the first formal effort to fund the development of airports. The 1946 Federal Airport Act however, had deep roots dating back to the early Roosevelt days, the New Deal and World War II, which all contributed, in one form or another, to the development of airports in the United States.

Although many of the airfields built under the Development of Landing Areas for National Defense (DLAND) and other programs designed to establish training and operational airfields have disappeared, a remarkable number of them still survive. This is in large part due to the fact that many of these facilities came complete with hangars and other support facilities and were in effect "turn key" operations. A visit today, to any of the airfields constructed during the war years, will reveal a large number of these hangars and barracks still standing. The fact that the offices of the airport managers at Chino Airport and Minter Field for example, are housed in these nearly 60-year-old quarters, is a testament to their durability. Both Minter Field, an Army air field, and Chino Airport, known then as Cal Aero Flight Academy, a civilian and privately-funded operation, were constructed in 1940 for the purpose of training cadets. Stearman and Vultee trainers lined the area in front of the barracks and hangars and literally thousands of pilots were trained at both airfields. Later converted to general aviation airports, Minter Field and Chino Airport continue to share another feature unique among the many civilian airports in the Southwest, which is their concentration of war birds and pilots who fly them in races, such as the Reno National Air Races at Stead Field, Nevada. In addition, both airports have an air museum supported by dedicated volunteers whose goal is to preserve the aeronautical legacy of yesteryear.

The offices of the airport managers at Chino Airport and Minter Field are housed in these nearly 60-year-old quarters, is testament to their durability.

Cadet Lightner on his first solo flight in 1941 at the Cal Aero Academy, Chino .
(Reprinted from LIFE magazine Courtesy: San Bernardino County Department of Airports.)

The Chapel at Minter Field. The chapel was a standard design type CH-1 building.
(Courtesy: Minter Field Airport District.)

Abandoned barracks at Chino Airport in 1960. *(Courtesy: San Bernardino County Department of Airports.)*

Although the City of Fresno had long been a primary stop for United and TAT going back to the days of airmail contracts, all of these flights originated or terminated at Chandler Field, which remains a busy general aviation airport today. North of Chandler Field lies Fresno Air Terminal which is the air carrier facility serving the central portion of the San Joaquin Valley. Fresno Air Terminal too began as a small Army Air Corps training field during World War II and was known as Hammer Army Air Field. Unlike many other airports turned civilian following the war, Fresno Air Terminal still remains actively involved with the military and it is more often than not to see a Boeing 737 waiting for a clearance, holding next to an F-16, operated by the 144th Fighter Wing of the California Air National Guard. The Army and the Marines also have a presence and the joint-use of the airport facilities at Fresno Air Terminal make the airport unique.

Another rather unique airport developed during the war years is Falcon Field Municipal Airport in Mesa, Arizona. Unlike the hundreds of airfields built around the country to train American pilots, Falcon Field, named after the British hunting bird, began as a combat pilot training field for the Royal Air Force after Roosevelt agreed to aid the British with their flight training. Following the war, the airport was turned over to the City of Mesa and Falcon Field now caters to general aviation and industrial interests, just like its neighbor airport to the North, Scottsdale Municipal Airport. Scottsdale came into operation in 1942, as a basic training facility for Army Air Corps pilots. Known as Thunderbird Field II, the airfield was home to over 5,000 cadets during a period of less than two and a half years. Since the City of Scottsdale acquired the airport in 1967, the airport has

Aerial view of Chino Airport in 1985. *(Courtesy: San Bernardino County Department of Airports.)*

grown into one of the busiest single runway airports in the nation. In addition, the airport boasts an industrial park of 2,000 acres, serving many small and mid-sized firms. Completing the triangle of airports in the greater Phoenix metropolitan area is the Phoenix Goodyear airport, which also draws on its roots dating back to World War II. Built as a support facility for the Navy, Phoenix Goodyear now serves as a reliever airport to Phoenix Sky Harbor International Airport and is home to over 135 based aircraft.

Like Scottsdale Airport, Gillespie Field in El Cajon, near San Diego, California has seen tremendous non-aviation industrial growth. It too claims its humble beginnings to the days of the war, but as a Marine parachute training facility. Known as Camp Gillespie, it is one of the few converted airports which has retained part of its original military name. Today, Gillespie Field, owned and operated by the County of San Diego, ranks among the largest airports in the nation in terms of total aircraft with over 800 based planes. It is also home to a speedway, a rifle range and a golf driving range, as well as a soccer field and numerous businesses which all contribute to the airport's revenue base.

A-20s at Los Angeles Airport during WWII. *(Courtesy: Los Angeles Department of Airports.)*

Industrial parks are not isolated to Scottsdale and Gillespie, as economic diversification is becoming increasingly more important at airports to support the core of aeronautical activity at each respective facility. More and more, airports are forced to justify their existence on the basis of direct economic output, rather than the indirect benefits which airports bring as gateways to the local communities which they serve. Like Gillespie, Scottsdale and others, Yuba County Airport has also set aside airport property to bolster the bottom line. It too served as a military facility in World War II, when the Army Air Corps utilized the field as an air support base. It was here that one of the greatest aviators of all time, former airmail pilot, air racer, instrument test pilot and military aviator, General Jimmy Doolittle, practiced with B-25s for his historic raid on Tokyo.

Not all airports who trace their roots to the war years have such an illustrious history, nor are they quite as vocal about the industry they serve today. Known then as Mirage Field, it was built in 1942 in just two short weeks to serve as Auxiliary Field #3 to the Victorville Army Air Field, now Southern California International Airport, but better known in its heyday as George Air Force Base. Since the Army Air Force days, El Mirage Airport built a quiet but solid reputation in the glider industry and later added the Unmanned Aerial Vehicle (UAV) program in 1985. Serving primarily the intelligence industry, the unmanned flights dominate all other activity at El Mirage Airport and restrict flights at the airport during testing. The airport, since it was acquired in 1946, has remained in private hands, making it unique, and sadly among a rapidly disappearing class of airports.

Paint by Numbers? Letters being painted on the runway at Apple Valley Airport. Note the reverse "e" in honor of the 99s, the International Organization of Women Pilots, who have made it their "signature" *(Photo: Robert Olislagers.)*

Another form of airport ownership which has been popular for over 30 years, is the formation of districts, which by virtue of a tax levy assessed on the general population, is able to support the activities for which the levy is assessed. One such airport, developed during the war years, is the Santa Maria Airport District, which like Mojave, Inyokern, Minter Field, Monterey, Apple Valley, Truckee-Tahoe, and other airports, is allowed to collect taxes in support of airport operations and maintenance. Although not all District airports are dependent on taxation to support their operations, most airports have and often to the benefit of the community. The Santa Maria Army Air Field began as a World War II training facility, most notably in 1942 for B-25s, and later for P-38s, including ground crews training. Formed as a District in 1964, it continues to thrive as an airport today. Encompassing 2,600 acres, it serves the commuter air carrier industry, as well as the general aviation industry. Like other airports, the Santa Maria Airport plans to expand into the light manufacturing and industrial base to further support its future activities.

Zamperini Field, once known as Torrance Municipal Airport, also featured P-38s during the war years, when it served as an active fighter base to as many as five

Aerial view of Buchanan Field in 1991. *(Courtesy: Contra Costa County Department of Airports.)*

squadrons. Referred to as the Lomita Flight Strip, the base turned out such aces as General Robin Olds and Colonel Art Jeffrey. Named after Olympian Louis Zamperini, who served as bombardier during the war, the airport had as many as 430,000 operations annually in 1974. Located in a heavily populated residential area, aggressive noise abatement standards have lowered noise complaints, as well as noise violations which were instituted during the last 20 years.

Burbank Airport in camouflage. It was common for airports considered a target during WWII to stage elaborate camouflage schemes. Netting, fabric, feathers, fake buildings and lots of paint made some airports truly blend in with their surroundings. *(Courtesy: Burbank-Glendale-Pasadena Airport.)*

Not all airports developed during this period started out as military facilities. The foresight of local entrepreneurs and elected officials led the Board of Supervisors of Contra Costa County to construct an airport in 1942, but the war years intervened, as the U.S. Army converted the newly built airport into a P-39 training base. After the war, the airport was returned to civilian hands and the county sought to continue the airport as it had once envisioned, naming it Buchanan Field, after one of its own. Like Zamperini Field, Buchanan Field is located near residential development, which has led the Board of Supervisors to restrict aircraft operations to minimize noise effect on a uniform basis. Today, the airport has some of the most restrictive Ordinances in place, yet the airport continues to play an active role within the State's aeronautical activity as one of the top 10 busiest airports. As with all airports, it quietly, but decisively, played a pivotal role during relief efforts to Santa Cruz County following the earthquake of 1989. No measure of direct cost accounting could ever calculate the value of airports like Buchanan Field during such crises, yet countless airports are often asked to justify their very existence in terms of directly attributable value, negating all other intrinsic and indirect contributions.

Sky Haven Airport, now called North Las Vegas Air Terminal was also built during the war years, and like Buchanan Field, it was done so for strictly civilian purposes. It also could not escape the ravages of war. Dedicated on the day Roosevelt said would live in infamy, December 7, 1941, the news of the bombing of Pearl Harbor was carried to the well wishers at Sky Haven Airport by a pilot from Las Vegas Air Base, better known these days as Nellis Air Force Base. Over 150 aircraft had come from afar for the ceremonies and several thousand had assembled to see the show which was canceled upon hearing the devastating news. With the declaration of war, all civilian aircraft were grounded for the period of six months as all pilots were finger printed and re-licensed.

Flight School at El Monte Airport in early 1940s. *(Courtesy Los Angeles County Department of Airports.)*

As the war consumed and simultaneously mobilized a nation, the aircraft and airport industry grew at a rate never before experienced. Although the growth was artificially induced by the war, much like those first tentative steps taken in 1918, it led to new technologies, especially in aircraft development. Jet engines were no longer thoughts on paper and rocketry was already a proven, albeit deadly, commodity. The transition to peace time use of these technologies would benefit the industry like no other in modern industrial society. Airports too benefitted from this legacy, as hundreds of airports were converted to civilian use and with thousands of pilots returning home from the war, a new market was instantly created.

Construction of hangar at El Monte Airport. Early 1940s.
(Courtesy Los Angeles County Department of Airports.)

Aerial view of Brackett Field in 1944.
(Courtesy Los Angeles County Department of Airports.)

Boulder City Airport in 1937.
(Courtesy U.S. Department of Interior, Bureau of Reclamation.)

Art of Deception. Fake house camouflage buildings at Burbank Airport during WWII. *(Courtesy Glendale-Burbank- Pasadena Airports.)*

Mines Field. 1941. *(Courtesy Los Angeles Department of Airports.)*

Aerial view of Edwards Air Force Base. *(USAF Photo.)*

CHAPTER 6

THE CHALLENGE OF THE POST WAR ERA 1946-PRESENT

FIELDS OF FLYING

THE CHALLENGE OF THE POST WAR ERA 1946-PRESENT

A United Airlines DC-3 over Catalina Island.
(Courtesy: Catalina Conservancy.)

The Civil Aeronautics Act of 1938 merely cleaned up a legislative plethora of statutes relating to safety, airmail, pilot certification and other related aeronautical regulation which had accumulated over the course of the 12 preceding years. The most significant component included in the 1938 Act was the recognition that airports were very much part of a system, rather than isolated entities. The first survey conducted in 1939, attests to the importance placed on defining what that system consisted of. Although it did not result in immediate action, the subsequent revised report, submitted in 1944, would become the basis for the 1946 Federal Airport Act.

The reforms however would not have played a major role in Congressional politics if it were not for a number of serious airplane crashes in 1936 and 1937. Safety was not only at the forefront of political debate, but airlines soon realized that safety was also money in the bank. Following the crashes in 1936 and 1937, passenger traffic growth actually shrunk for the first time since records were kept.[1] C.R. Smith of American Airlines, recognizing the correlation, made safety his number one priority and from 1936 until 1941, American Airlines did not suffer a single mishap. Safety would become the hallmark of American Airlines and its share of the market grew to where at one time it carried one third of all passengers in the U.S.[2]

The Air Traffic Control Tower at Ontario International Airport at sunset. *(Courtesy: Ontario International Airport, Public Affairs, Los Angeles Department of Airports.)*

While safety issues focused on airline operations, they spilled over into the realm of airports, specifically as they related to the inadequacies in the distribution of airports as a system of connecting points, local capital investment, and the mere existence of basic amenities. The recommendations of the 1944 revised report of the National Airport Plan called in part for a congressional appropriation of not more than $100 million annually to assist local public agencies with the development of airports to meet present and future demand.[3] Adopted as part of the Airport Development Act of 1946, the need for airport funding was formally recognized and finally became a reality. Of course, airport funding had already been part of the New Deal and during the second world war. With formal approval for airport funding also came restrictions placed on airport "sponsors", as the local agencies operating airports were referred to, including such mandates as conformance to standards, non-exclusivity provisions, and control of rates and charges. The federal government also reserved the right to unrestricted access to facilities receiving federal aid. By 1948, 133 grant offers were made to local sponsors, totaling $13.3 million.[4] The program remained in place until 1958 when the Federal Aviation Act was enacted and the only significant change in the program occurred in 1955 when funding was approved for a four-year period.

As was the case in 1936 and 1937, a mid-air collision in 1956, in which 128 people were killed, spurred a new round of debate on Capitol Hill. This resulted in a report making recommendations for the improvement of the airway system and the 1957 Airways Modernization Act was passed. The report's recommendation to create a more independent Federal Aviation Agency was ignored until three more mid-air collisions occurred in 1958. In record time, Congress passed the Federal Aviation Act of 1958, introducing sweeping new legislation and creating the new agency. At the same time, the statute repealed all prior directives and statutes, including the Air Commerce Act of 1926, the Civil Aeronautics Act of 1938, and the Airways Modernization Act, passed only the previous year. The new Federal Aviation Agency had much broader powers and for the first time, the FAA was charged with the responsibility of coordinating all civil and military air traffic control functions, something the CAA had previously shared with other agencies. The FAA's first administrator, Elwood R. "Pete" Quesada, immediately made airline safety, as well as facility expansion, his top priorities.

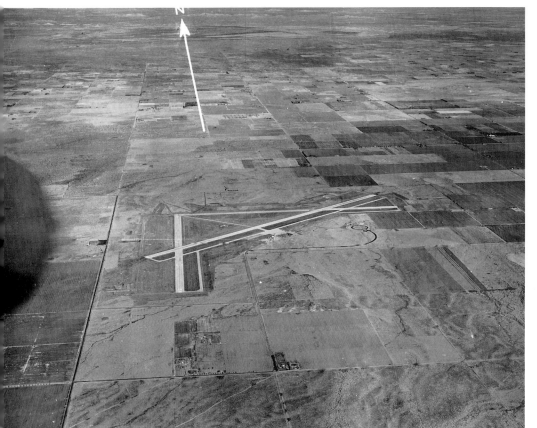

Aerial view of Palmdale Airport in 1952.
(Courtesy: Los Angeles County Department of Airports)

With all facets of transportation experiencing significant growth in the 20 years following the war, President Johnson announced plans in 1966 to create a new cabinet department that would combine all major transportation functions under the auspices of a single department. On April 1, 1967, the new U.S. Department of Transportation became a reality and the Federal Aviation Agency was renamed the Federal Aviation Administration. At the same time, all accident investigation duties were transferred from the CAB to the newly-established National Transportation Safety Board. It also signalled the end of the Federal Aid for Airports Program, which in its 24-year existence following the war, expended some $1.2 billion on airport improvements.

In those 20 years following the war, the nation experienced a remarkable period of growth which would set the tone for the period that would follow and is often referred to as the "Information Age." Spurred by technologies derived from the war and further pushed by the ensuing cold war competition between the U.S. and the former U.S.S.R., the period was also marked by an urgency for people to return to normalcy. In little more than a 15-year period, an entire generation had grown up knowing only the hardship of a depression and the desperation of war. For those who remembered the "Roaring Twenties", lost time had to be made up. For those

The terminal at Santa Barbara Airport in 1947.
(Courtesy: Santa Barbara Airport.)

Open House at Yuma Airport in 1963.
(Courtesy: Yuma International Airport.)

who knew little else, the opportunity for peace and prosperity could not come soon enough and the technological advances of the post-war era brought all the modern conveniences and promise for a better tomorrow. The pace to pick up where peace left off was so intense that it even overshadowed the events in Korea, now often referred to as the "Forgotten War". For most individuals it was a time to recapture what they lost in 1929 and for others it was a time for discovery.

For some who had fought the good fight, however, the flying bug that bit them during the war would stay with them forever. Some stayed in the military, like Chuck Yeager who went on to become a test pilot after the war. On October 14, 1947, Yeager busted the "invisible wall" when he became the first pilot ever to break the "sound barrier" by flying faster than the speed of sound. An ace during the war, Chuck Yeager would eventually retire from the U.S. Air Force as a Brigadier General following a storied career. He continues to test aircraft for the Air Force on a consulting basis, but above all, like Lindbergh, Yeager has remained an inspiration to new generations of pilots, and like Lindbergh, airports have honored him by naming their facilities after him.

Others returned to civilian life, but remained active as pilots. James Nissen was one of them. Nissen, a former naval aviator, became a civilian test pilot following the war and like so many full-time pilots, went looking for an airport to do some more flying after a long day at the office. The city of San Jose, near where Nissen did much of his test flying, did not have an airport but considered building one even before the war. In fact some 483 acres were set aside at one time but with much bureaucratic bickering and nay-sayers opposing the project, the war seemed to all but doom the project forever. Not so for Nissen who, following the war, leased 13 acres on the site originally proposed for the airport and with the aid of friends, carved out a 3,000-foot runway. San Jose had an airport. The airport was formally approved in 1948 and James Nissen became its manager. Today, San Jose International Airport, so named

Aerial view of El Monte Airport in 1960.
(Courtesy: Los Angeles County Department of Airports)

For some who had fought the good fight, however, the flying bug that bit them during the war would stay with them forever.

A B1B Bomber makes an emergency landing at Rogers Dry Lake at Edwards AFB following nose gear problems.
The clay lakebed has saved numerous airplanes over the years and damage to the B1B was minimal. *(USAF Photo/Anne Bryant.)*

Sunset over the dry lakebed at Edwards AFB following Spring rains. This is the only time of year when the lakebeds are not usable. Tiny brine shrimp come to life in the shallow waters after long periods of dormancy, bringing thousands of birds to the base each year.
(March 1993. Photo: Robert Olislagers.)

in 1984, is the fourth busiest airport in California and emplanements topped the nine million mark in 1995.

Cable Airport in 1952. *(Reprinted from Cable Airport: 50 Years of Service to General Aviation.)*

Dewey Cable had the same dream as James Nissen, but followed a decidedly individual path. Rather than seeking the aid of bureaucrats, he built first and then asked for permission! As the war started to wind down, Dewey Cable, who worked on P-38s in a maintenance depot at Ontario Airport, decided to build his own airport after realizing that the lease he had for a flight school at Arlington Airstrip, now Riverside Municipal Airport, was not in his long-term best interest. Having looked all over the Pomona and San Gabriel Valleys, San Bernardino, Pasadena and other places, he finally settled on the only place that was available as well as affordable. The site consisted of a wash in a watershed area between Upland and Claremont; the reason Dewey Cable was not able to get financing to build his airport. Not being able to afford to have the work done either, Dewey and his wife Maude set out to build the airport themselves and not long thereafter, Cable Airport became a reality. To this day, the Cable family continues to own and operate the airport, having turned it into one of the largest privately-owned and operated airports in the country.

Although the flying business was dominated by men in those days, women too were involved in the building of airfields. Pancho Barnes and Eleanor Rudnick crossed paths on a regular basis and each displayed much of the independent spirit for which they were known. Salty-talking Pancho Barnes, a descendant of the wealthy Lowe family and whose life has been portrayed in numerous movies, operated her own airstrip and ranch she built on land that is now the small arms firing range at Edwards Air Force Base. Rancho Oro Verde, better known in those days as the "Happy Bottom Riding Club", a name whose origin is still somewhat shrouded in mystery, became home to many pilots from nearby Muroc Army Air Field. Its heyday

The United States of America
Department of Commerce
Civil Aeronautics Administration

Air Agency Certificate

Number 7 1 4 5

This certificate is issued to

BAKERSFIELD AIRPARK

whose business address is

BARNES AIRPORT
MUROC, CALIFORNIA

upon finding that its organization complies in all respects with the requirements of the Civil Air Regulations relating to the establishment of an Air Agency, and is empowered to operate an approved AIR AGENCY.

with the following ratings:

PRIMARY FLYING SCHOOL
COMMERCIAL FLYING SCHOOL
FLIGHT INSTRUCTOR SCHOOL
BASIC GROUND SCHOOL
ADVANCED GROUND SCHOOL

This certificate, unless canceled, suspended, or revoked, shall continue in effect UNTIL MAY 31, 1952.

Date issued:

May 22, 1950

By direction of the Administrator

A. Harold Bromley
Chief, Airman Standards Branch

This Certificate is not Transferable, AND ANY MAJOR CHANGE IN THE BASIC FACILITIES, OR IN THE LOCATION THEREOF, SHALL BE IMMEDIATELY REPORTED TO THE APPROPRIATE REGIONAL OFFICE OF THE CIVIL AERONAUTICS ADMINISTRATION.

Any alteration of this certificate is punishable by a fine of not exceeding $1,000, or imprisonment not exceeding 3 years, or both

U. S. GOVERNMENT PRINTING OFFICE: 1949—O—818984

Form ACA-390
(12-48)

Operating certificate issued to Pancho Barnes, allowing Pancho to provide commercial service at Bakersfield Airpark.
(Courtesy: E. "Mac" McKendry.)

Colorful RV-3 and RV-4 experimental aircraft line up along the EAA 71 Chapter hangar
at Bakersfield Airpark during a fly-in in 1989.
(Photo: Bob Baker, C&B Flying Service.)

came following the war when pilots like Chuck Yeager would relax there following long days of test flying the latest in aircraft technology. It was Pancho who treated Chuck Yeager to a steak dinner "with all the trimmings" on the day of his record-breaking supersonic flight, knowing he had flown the Bell X-1 with broken ribs from a fall suffered days earlier while riding one of her horses. The steak dinners would become a custom for the "mach busters" as they reached new milestones. Pancho herself was a well-known air race pilot, having raced in the first Powder Puff Derby in 1929 and taking the women's world speed record away from Amelia Earhart the following year. She understood pilots and legend has it she even taught bombing training at Muroc following an episode in which hapless student pilots mistook her ranch house for a practice target. The Happy Bottom Riding Club is no more after the main building burned down and the Air Force obtained the land under imminent domain in 1954. Only ruins and a lone mangled skeleton of what was once a Stearman remain of the site today. Pancho went west in 1975 and it was none other than General "Jimmy" Doolittle who eulogized her commenting; "she's probably up there reminiscing with some pilot or other and saying; I wondered what that little bald bastard was going to say about me".[5]

1968 Aerial view of Catalina Island Airport. *(Courtesy: Catalina Conservancy.)*

Pancho and "Mac" McKendry, her last husband, would often fly to Bakersfield to restock depleted supplies, which meant a visit to Kern Liquor Supply. They would always fly to Bakersfield Airpark, where Pancho even held a certificate to operate a flight school. But it was Eleanor Rudnick who built the strip in 1945 and flew crop-dusters from there and even trained student pilots. While her reputation never attained the legendary status of Pancho's, she displayed all the independence of her counterpart from across the Tehachapi's, making Eleanor a local legend in her own right. She continued to operate the airport until the mid-sixties when a local oil man and inventor took over. One of E.A. Bender's inventions consisted of metal swimming pool covers to prevent children from accidental drowning. When the idea failed to catch on, the ever clever Mr. Bender converted the pool covers to hangar doors which can still be seen on the hexagonal building at Bakersfield Airpark. The City of Bakersfield acquired the airport in 1985, renaming it Bakersfield Municipal Airport.

After completely rebuilding the runway in 1991, deflecting it 30 degrees from its original alignment, the City recently asked the County of Kern, which already owns and operates seven airports, to take the facility over.

Like Eleanor's and Pancho's airfields, many of the airports built after the war were privately owned and operated and remained comparatively small as the airport manager often functioned as fixed base operator (FBO), flight instructor, commercial pilot and mechanic, as well as performing all the maintenance functions that come with the job. It is not that much different

Open House at the Lompoc Airport. circa 1970. *(Courtesy: City of Lompoc.)*

today for some of the 3,000 or so publicly-operated airports in the nation. It is often said that the job of an airport manager requires many hats and this is especially true for the manager of small airports. Even where cities and towns have assumed the responsibility of operating the airport, those tasks are often part of the package. It is not uncommon to visit airports like Oceanside Airport in North San Diego County or Catalina Island, and have your plane refueled by the airport manager. At the same time, the manager may be reviewing schematics for new hangars or negotiating for more obstruction lights with DOT. It is all in a day's work.

The smaller airports which dot the countryside all over the Southwest continue to play an important and often unspoken part in general aviation and in the economy. While many of these airports are struggling to stay afloat financially, they remain the backbone of aviation. It is from these airports that tomorrow's pilots learn to fly. It is from these airports that supplies for relief efforts are flown and it is from these often remote airfields, that the next departing aircraft may be transporting a donor heart. It is from these small fields of flying that a child may be transported to the nearest hospital for life-saving surgery.

AIRPORT MANAGER WANTED

Must have extensive background in aviation—must not be too old or too young—as someone said, "Old enough to know better and young enough to enjoy it."

Must have engineering experience and practical know-how in all phases of building roads, runways, taxiways, hangars, fuel installations, including jet fuel, electrical systems, sewer systems, drainage systems, water systems, gas line systems, and all other utility systems.

Must be familiar with laws pertaining to zoning, taxes, aviation, fire codes, electrical codes, water, plumbing and gas codes, real estate leases, easements, civil service, civil rights, Federal aid to airports, State aid to airports, budgets, bond issues, (general obligation and revenue), traffic, financing in general, and investments.

Must know psychology, insurance, labor mediation, public relations, public speaking, farming, mechanics, politics, horticulture, and pest eradication.

Must be able to understand Township Assessors and Supervisors, Township Road Commissioner, Township Health Commissioner, the Mayor, City Council members, City Manager, City Street Superintendent, City Water Superintendent, City Health Department, City Building inspectors, the Sheriff, Chief of Police, State Police, State Roads and Highways Department, County Highway Department, County and City Zoning Officers, State Aeronautics Commission, Federal District Airport Engineer, FAA Regional Director and his staff, FAA Washington office, including the heads of all the divisions in FAA. He is not required to like these people; just be able to get along with them.

Should be well and favorably known to the Governor, the Congressman, Senators, State Representatives and State Senators, all local newspaper editors, and at least one National Aviation Editor, preferably George Haddaway.

Must be willing to work under a low budget and with little or no job security and be available 24 hours a day, seven days a week—should be able to go without sleep for several days at a time during snow storms, floods, hurricanes, and VIP visits.

Must have FBI clearance and possess visionary and prophetic powers concerning the future of helicopters, VTOL, air traffic, land use, noise abatement, next year's TSOs, FAA's policy decisions next week and next month on flight service stations, weather stations, tall structures, towers, general aviation, and air lines—and be able to predict snow storms accurately.

Must be a first rate housekeeper and landscape man; must know paints, painting and color requirements, tree raising, seeding, fencing, garbage disposal and sanitary landfill techniques and procedures.

Should be able to see his airport and its future from the point of view of the community, the taxpayer, the pilot, the aircraft owner, the passengers and users, and the Airport Commission.

Must be familiar with the prevailing contract and lease terms and prices for landing fees, floor space, parking space, fuel flowage fees, car rentals, restaurant operation, liquor concession, clean towel and window-washing service and the non-discriminatory provisions required in all contracts by FAA.

Must have good basic knowledge of and be able to operate a police department and fire department, and know about wages, salaries, fire and police equipment, including crash procedures off and on the field.

Must be skilled in obtaining surplus equipment for nothing and be able to rebuild and rehabilitate such equipment without cost.

Must have basic knowledge of accounting, particularly cost accounting and its application to airports, and know about insurance plans for employees.

Must be able to conduct a constant program of education, designed to convince everyone of the necessity for and the value of the airport to each man, woman, child and business within the taxing boundaries.

Must be diplomatic in dealing with all local organizations that request use of the runway as drag strips, free land for pistol range, dog and horse shows, dog pound, tennis courts, trap shooting, ball diamonds, sports car rallies, picnics, and free gravel.

Must be patient with representatives of drum and bugle corps, policeman's ball, sheriff's ball, fireman's ball, Boy Scouts, Girl Scouts, Red Cross, Salvation Army, childrens homes, Foundation for Arthritis, cancer, muscular distrophy, heart, mental diseases, polio, home for wayward girls, and church conventions.

Above all he must have a sense of humor and a recommendation from AAAE.

Preference may be given to a Democrat from Texas and we may also consider as trainee, a Socialist from Minnesota.

Write Box 13 and do not contact present manager—he doesn't know he's leaving.

("Airport Manager Wanted" was included in the talk given by Foster Smith, Chairman, Rockford Airport Authority at the AAAE Annual Conference in Fort Worth, April 27, 1965)

Airports like Dinsmore, Garberville, Kneeland, Murray Field and Rohnerville in Humboldt County serve many of these functions; some even providing service as fire attack bases. The Humboldt County Aviation Department is one of only a handful of departments still involved in maintaining and operating county-wide airport systems as part of an overall policy to provide public service. In addition to Humboldt County, San Diego County, San Bernardino County, Riverside County, Los Angeles County and Kern County, all still operate airport systems of at least four airports or more. The cities of Los Angeles, Phoenix, Sacramento, Fresno, Las Vegas and Reno, are also committed to running multiple airports departments in an effort to maintain regional systems vital to the growth and strength of

The terminal at Kern County Airport No. 1 in Bakersfield in 1952.
(Courtesy: Kern County Department of Airports)

the respective local economies. The notion that the best thing for an airport is another airport still rings true. Contra Costa County is the latest county in the Southwest to continue its commitment toward a regional airport system, with the dedication of Byron Airport in 1994, which replaced the old airport. The sad reality, however, is that few new airports in fact are being built. Although some 17,000 airfields, airports, heliports and air strips exist across the country, the majority are privately owned and restricted air strips located near remote homes and ranches not available to the public. The Aircraft Owners and Pilots Association has reported the closure of an airport in the U.S. at an average rate of one a week. Byron Airport and even McClellan-Palomar Airport, built as a replacement for the old Del Mar Airport when Interstate 5 was built in the fifties, are exceptions and not the rule.

While many general aviation airports are looking to redefine their basic position within a market that has experienced zero growth in the last 15 years, (except in the business aircraft segment of the economy) it is the large metropolitan airports which have dominated the industry for the most part. Not surprisingly, they are very much a reflection of the design and manufacturing component of the aircraft industry, in particular as it relates to load capacity. Whereas general aviation has remained largely static in its basic design of aircraft, the air carrier industry has seen radical new design changes over the years which have had a corresponding affect on airports. Starting with Boeing 247's and the DC-series aircraft in the early 30s, to the introduction of jet aircraft, first with the Boeing 707 in 1958 and the DC-8 in 1959, but especially the Boeing 747 10 years later, airports and the airway system as a whole have made several major transitions in its short history in order to accommodate these new class of aircraft. From longer, wider runways, to docking aircraft in every possible configuration imaginable, including the use of jetways, airports have had to adjust to the pure physical component of aircraft design. Increased aircraft speed also factored in the overall management of airports as airlines developed hub and spoke systems in order to accommodate the concentration of resources at specific locations. Unexpected pull-outs, however, by some airlines at these hub airports have had a devastating effect as the airports sought to regroup virtually overnight. Affordability too has had an impact on the industry and the popularity of PeopleExpress before it collapsed, and Southwest Airlines, celebrating its 25th anniversary in 1996, are indicative of price elasticity at its best. They made air travel available to a whole new segment of the population heretofore unable to afford it.

Aerial view of the ramp and the terminal at Sacramento Metropolitan Airport in 1971. *(Courtesy: Sacramento County Department of Airports.)*

The growth in commercial air travel since the late sixties and early seventies, and the gradual decline in general aviation starting less than a decade later, are powerful reminders of where the industry as a whole may be headed in the near future. This growth has also challenged airports everywhere as demand for air service continues to increase, while the capacity to meet that demand is severely constrained. Increased security threats over the years have placed an additional burden on the system as airports and airlines seek to find alternative ways at handling passenger safety without compromising convenience.

FAA Maintenance facilities
at a sleepy desert airport.
(1996. Photo by Robert Olislagers.)

Tucson International Airport-1994.
(Courtesy: Tucson International Airport.)

The Air Traffic Control
Tower at Tucson
International Airport-1994.
(Courtesy: Tucson International Airport.)

The B-2 "Stealth" Bomber is being refueled over Barstow–Daggett Airport (behind refueling boom.)
(USAF Photo/Ron Hamm Aviation.)

As far back as 1938, complaints were heard that the DC-3, introduced only two years earlier, and other "large" aircraft, had brought about "a failure to balance aviation's technical progress with suitable landing fields". This complaint has been heard ever since, as airport development is typically behind aircraft technological development and passenger demand. While demand may shoot up overnight with the introduction of a single low-cost carrier into a new market, the development of infrastructure and support facilities to handle that new demand may take years. It has been estimated that it takes an average of 10 years to build a new runway. Airport master planning therefore seeks to anticipate growth by establishing a blueprint for future development if, and more often, when such development is needed. Airports are stationary objects and are far less liquid than the customers it serves. Some airlines, who are far more liquid than airports and who often participate in the cost of financing facilities at airports, do not always share the same philosophy as the short term needs to the bottom line and dividends are often contradictory to the long-term needs in providing infrastructure and adequate service to the very customers they serve. The days of airlines-owned and operated airports have long since gone and the particular struggle for airports does not end there. The constant challenges of noise impacts, environmental concerns, safety, security, and convenience to name a few, are part and parcel of the daily routine of an airport, if one can call it a routine.

1961 Aerial view of Brackett Field.
(Courtesy: Los Angeles County Department of Airports.)

The federal government has continued to be a major player in providing the balance between funding and regulating the industry. Funding of airports has continued unabated since 1946 and became a user fee based system in 1970 when President Nixon signed the Airport and Airway Development Act (Title I), and the Airport and Airway Revenue Act (Title II), allowing an 8-percent ticket tax to be collected to fund the system. The Airway Trust Fund, as it is known, has amassed billions of dollars over the years to provide funds to air-

Ontario International Airport at dusk.
(Courtesy: Ontario International Airport, Public Affairs, Los Angeles Department of Airports.)

ports on a discretionary as well as an entitlement basis. The basic Airport Development Aid Program (ADAP) has remained intact to this day, although the airport funding provision was changed to the Airport Improvement Program (AIP) in 1982 when the Airport and Airway Improvement Act of 1982 was signed into law by President Reagan. Over the years, many funding provisions and entitlements were added, as were mandates to perform under the grant offer provisions.

The most profound effect on airports however came in 1978 with the passage of the Airline Deregulation Act. The deregulation of many provisions on the books for over 40 years profoundly transformed the airline industry as air carriers were quick to drop routes that were not profitable. Virtually overnight, airports were left without air carrier service and empty terminals could be found everywhere, except where subsidies to airlines allowed them to continue to operate in poorly performing markets under the Essential Air Services provision of the deregulation act. Scheduled to sunset in 1998, the essential service provision has repeatedly been attacked by some legislators as pork and praised by others as critical to prevent isolation in rural and remote areas which would otherwise be without service. The deregulation act spawned new regional airlines and commuter services in many of the communities which were abandoned by the majors. The restructuring of airlines, mergers, and bankruptcies among airlines, including many prominent flagship carriers, also changed the relationship between airlines and airports as stability no longer existed and airports were forced to look in other directions for joint funding of terminals and support facilities traditionally shared with the airlines.

Having it all! Hangar and home on the flight line at Rosamond Skypark, California. *(1996 Photo by Robert Olislagers.)*

Considerable debate over funding has continued to dominate the legislative agenda in the 90s and in particular the focus on air traffic control and safety, as well as airport capacity, have been at the forefront of that debate. The ticket taxing authority which has been in place since 1970 was allowed to lapse for the first time in late 1995 as Congress struggled to approve the 1996 Federal Budget. But the shift in control on Capitol Hill in 1995, from Democrats to Republicans, is the first major shift in political power in 40 years and poses the same questions which were raised in the days of Hoover and Roosevelt. The fundamental principles which govern both have not changed significantly and the push for block grants in the 90s for example must be viewed in the same context as Hoover's dock concept in the late 20s and early 30s. Although it keeps the government involved, it further separates the Federal government from State and local government, with the ultimate goal being local self sufficiency. Although it may take many more years, it appears that the shift in debate will keep the fundamental question of airport systems, and airports as systems of airports, at the core of debate. Diminishing resources will no doubt serve as a catalyst as the demand for entitlement funds from the general fund in the federal budget becomes greater with time.

James and Jane Montgomery 1950.
(Courtesy San Diego Aerospace Museum.)

Rust hole reveals a Cessna 140 at Flabob
Airport in Rubidoux, California.
(1996 Photo by Robert Olislagers.)

As aviation approaches its first centennial celebration in the year 2003, the legacy of the Wright Brothers is as complex as the efforts were to make flight a reality.

But in no other country in the world, have its citizens the ability, the freedom, flexibility and convenience to board an aircraft as they do in the United States. And in no other place on earth has the legacy of flight developed to the extent it has in the United States. And nowhere else may one find as many fields of flying to make the dream of flight a reality.

Fly safe...

World War II vintage nose-docks at Barstow-Daggett airport still in use today.
(1996 Photo by Robert Olislagers.)

Arizona's Airport TUCSON

PHOTOS ART & EARLY PROMOS

Santa Rosa Airport 1929.
(Courtesy, San Diego Aerospace Museum.)

San Rafael Landing Field, 1927.
(Courtesy, San Diego Aerospace Museum.)

Dedication of Lindbergh Field. San Diego, 1928.
(Courtesy, San Diego Aerospace Museum.)

Lindbergh Field Air Terminal. 1933.
(Courtesy, San Diego Aerospace Museum.)

Montgomery Field. Spider's Aircraft Service, 1955.
(Courtesy, San Diego Aerospace Museum.)

Midway Airport. San Diego. 1928. Only person identified is Robert F. Bryon on far right. From Union Tribune Photo Dept.
(Courtesy, San Diego Aerospace Museum.)

Travel Air 2000 over Oakland Airport, 1933.
(Courtesy, San Diego Aerospace Museum.)

National City Airport looking west. National City, California. Circa 1959.
(Courtesy, San Diego Aerospace Museum.)

La Mesa Airport circa 1954. San Diego.
(Courtesy, San Diego Aerospace Museum.)

Boulder City Airport. Nevada, 1933.
(Courtesy, San Diego Aerospace Museum.)

Del Mar Airport. Del Mar, California. Circa 1958.
(Courtesy, San Diego Aerospace Museum.)

Kelly's Airport north of Los Angeles, Circa 1920's.
(Courtesy, San Diego Aerospace Museum.)

Long Beach Airport, circa 1933.
(Courtesy, San Diego Aerospace Museum.)

Santa Maria Airport, 1931.
(Courtesy, San Diego Aerospace Museum.)

Aerial view of Nut Tree Airport, California, 1961.
(Courtesy, San Diego Aerospace Museum.)

Curtiss JN-4 "Jenny" in front of hangar at Reno Airport. Circa 1920s.
(Reprinted from Great Airports Worldwide.)

Western Air Express hangar at Salt Lake City Airport. Circa 1930.
(Reprinted from Great Airports Worldwide.)

The Classic Ford Tri-motor built by the automaker. 1928.
(Reprinted from Airport Construction and Management — 1929.)

Opening day at United (Burbank) Airport. Memorial Day 1930.
(Reprinted from Great Airports Worldwide.)

Aluminum palm trees inside the terminal at McCarran International.
(Reprinted from Great Airports Worldwide.)

Interior of the terminal at Reno International Airport. 1988.
(Reprinted from Great Airports Worldwide.)

Terminal at John Wayne Airport. 1994. *(Courtesy Orange County Department of Airports.)*

The Tanforan Race Track near San Francisco. 1911.
(Reprinted from Great Airports Worldwide.)

Interior of the terminal at San Francisco's International Airport. 1930.
(Reprinted from Great Airports Worldwide.)

Aerial view of San Francisco International Airport and the Concorde Supersonic Transport Jet.
(Reprinted from Great Airports Worldwide.)

ATCT at San Jose International Airport. 1984.
(Reprinted from Great Airports Worldwide.)

Ramp at Tucson International Airport. 1957. *(Reprinted from Great Airports Worldwide.)*

Publicity photo of the new Tucson Airport logo, circa 1960s.
(Reprinted from Great Airports Worldwide.)

Poster promoting Brown Field, San Diego, CA. 1988. *(Reprinted from Great Airports Worldwide.)*

"We Made
Flying Possible.
Sacramento Metro
Made Flying Easy."

— Orville and Wilbur Wright
for Sacramento Metro Airport

fly
Sacramento
METRO AIRPORT

**When You Fly To Boston
From Sacramento Metro,
You're Really Using The Old Bean.**

It's smart to fly to Beantown from Sacramento Metro. The alternative? A 2-hour, 100-mile drive to San Francisco Airport. That wastes valuable time, and time is money. Sacramento Metro is a quick drive from downtown. And Sacramento Metro has nearly 100 flights a day bound for top destinations. Like Chicago. Washington, D.C. And Boston. And don't forget: It can cost $50 or more in gas, tolls and parking to drive to San Francisco Airport. So get your next trip off to a flying start instead of a driving one. Book a Sacramento Metro flight.

fly
Sacramento
METRO AIRPORT

Advertisements used by Sacramento Metro Airport in the 80s to promote air service.
(Reprinted from Great Airports Worldwide.)

Pancho Barnes. 1930.
(Reprinted from Great Airports Worldwide.)

Big Bear Airport and east end of Big Bear Lake. 1934.
(Courtesy, San Diego Aerospace Museum.)

Early "ARFF" vehicle at Oakland Airport. 1928.
(Courtesy, San Diego Aerospace Museum.)

Hangar no. 1 at Oakland Municipal Airport.
(Reprinted from Great Airports Worldwide.)

Art Deco artwork from Western Flying Magazine. 1929.
(Reprinted from Western Flying Magazine.)

Art Deco art. Cover of Western Flying. 1929.
(Reprinted from Western Flying Magazine. 1929.)

Art Deco artwork from Western Flying Magazine. 1929.
(Reprinted from Western Flying Magazine.)

Art Deco artwork from Western Flying Magazine. 1929.
(Reprinted from Western Flying Magazine.)

DOUGLAS

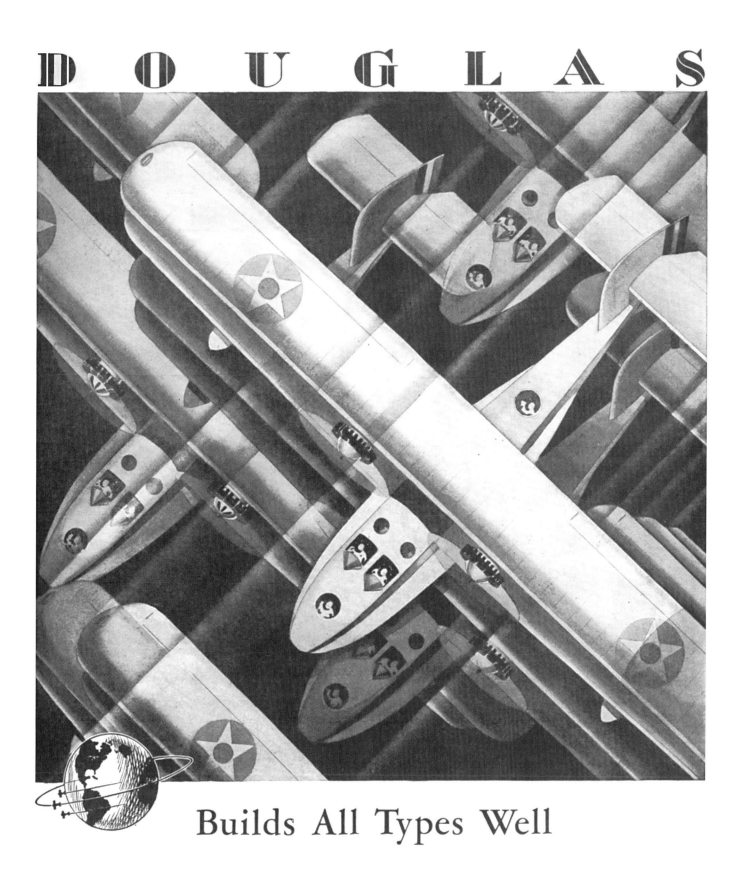

Builds All Types Well

Art Deco artwork from Western Flying Magazine. 1929.
(Reprinted from Western Flying Magazine.)

ATCT and Theme Building at Los Angeles Airport. 1995.
(Courtesy, Chad Slattery with permission from Landrum & Brown.)

Theme Building at Los Angeles Airport. 1995.
(Courtesy, Chad Slattery with permission from Landrum & Brown.)

ATCT and Theme Building at Los Angeles Airport. 1995.
(Courtesy, Chad Slattery with permission from Landrum & Brown.)

CONTENTS

CONTENTS

CONTENTS

CONTENTS

PATRON
ERECT-A-TUBE,INC.

EL MIRAGE AIRPORT

El Mirage Airport, situated in the picturesque El Mirage Valley of the western Mojave Desert, lies 45 air miles northeast of downtown Los Angeles in the northwestern portion of San Bernardino County. Now listed on the Los Angeles Sectional as "L69 RESTRICTED/CLOSED", El Mirage Airport, located at 117° 36' W, 34° 37' N, is 10 miles west of Victorville/Adelanto and 23 miles east of Palmdale/Lancaster. The El Mirage community is small, rural and focused upon alfalfa and onion farming, growing orchard fruits, a modest dairy industry, a few other prosperous small and varied industries, and a wide variety of individual and family recreational activities.

El Mirage Airport borders to the north upon the 7-mile-long, 3-mile-wide El Mirage Dry Lake and the encompassing, newly created 24,000-acre (federal) El Mirage Desert Recreational Park and Preserve. Park recreational activities include: camping; model airplane flying; offroad vehicle use (quads, dune buggies, dirt motor biking, dirt bicycling, etc.); the flying of light recreational aircraft (ultra lights, autogyros, gyrocopters, light gliders, etc.); mud running (when the authorized area is wet and muddy); sand-sailor/land yachting; television, movie and video site producing; and more. To the south, the nearby 10,000+ foot San Gabriel and San Bernardino Mountains support several ski resorts during the winter and excellent boating, fishing and hiking in the summer.

Climate and topography provide the El Mirage Valley with some of the best conditions in the world for year-round flying. Skies at El Mirage are virtually permanent VMC for VFR flying with IMC/IFR being a rare condition. Glider/sailplane pilots, in particular, enjoy the El Mirage Valley due to the strong updraft thermals, smooth, steady mountains waves and uplifting shearlines. Due to the unusual surrounding topography, strong desert surface windstorms, common in other upper and lower desert regions are uncommon near El Mirage.

The "High (Mojave) Desert" has supported a uniquely dense and rich concentration of aviation activities over the past 50 years. Palmdale Airport, 23 miles west, supports major aircraft production facilities for McDonnell Douglas, Lockheed, Northrup and Rockwell and is home to both B-1 and B-2 productions. Edwards AFB, the world's premier governmental flight test facility and a NASA Space Shuttle recovery base, is 21 miles to the northwest of El Mirage. Mojave Airport and its Civilian Flight Test Center, 37 miles northwest, host many unique civil aviation developmental enterprises, such as Rutan's record, round-the-world "Voyager" flight. George AFB, 11 miles east, had a long and distinguished military past in the High Desert and is now being operated for the public sector as Southern California International Airport. Four of Southern California's eight total residential airparks are situated in the High Desert area. Neighboring Ken Brock Field is the world's foremost center for the manufacturing, testing, training in and sale of autogyros and gyrocopters. At El Mirage Airport, many glider records have been set. Today, El Mirage is home to General Atomics Aeronautical Systems, Inc., a world leader in the design, developement, manufacture, the flight testing and the marketing of Unmanned Aerial Vehicles (UAVs). The "Mojave High Desert" has in the past and continues today, to be a hotbed of aviation accomplishments.

The scenic El Mirage Valley facing southwest.

El Mirage Airport "Triangle"
with dry lake bed to the north (left).

El Mirage Airport first entered service in 1942 as "Mirage Field" or "Auxiliary Field #3" to the "Victorville Army Air Field" (Victorville AAF later became George AFB and is now Southern California International Airport). "Mirage Field" was built in two weeks for the US Army Air Forces by the Corps of Engineers as part of the Federal Mobilization "Victory Program". Mirage Field was utilized as a flight training field for World War II pilots and as a dispersal field in case of coastal attack. In the WWII haste to construct a hundred airfields and train pilots for combat, there was not time for local wind studies to be conducted. Construction was done in the then US Government standard 3,700-foot triangle pattern with Mirage Field having a fourth runway added through the center of the triangle. With this design, one runway would always have suitable wind conditions for the crosswind-sensitive aircraft of the WWII time. Most of the WWII "Mobilization Airfields" across America later served as the beginnings of many of the present major civil airports and military air bases. George AFB, Palmdale and Mojave Airports are local desert examples. At the close of WWII, the US Government put many surplus airfields up for public sale. Mirage Field was one such air field offered for sale to the general public through an auction.

Gus Briegleb, later a nationally-famous glider (designer, builder, and instructor pilot) enthusiast, first spotted Mirage Field in May 1945 from the cockpit of his 'Taylorcraft' airplane. The thermals over the field were perfect for soaring and the adjacent dry lake bed provided additional landing space. When it became available for sale in 1946, Gus, aided by the War Assets Administration with a couple of war defense bonds, won the bid to purchase Mirage Field for $12,000. The Briegleb Soaring School moved into the new "El Mirage Field" where gliders and sailplanes, rather than pilots training for combat, now soared through the desert skies overhead.

When purchased in 1946, El Mirage Field had four paved runways and two wood buildings. A 10-mile desert dirt path was the only road leading into the nearest towns of Adelanto and Victorville. There were no people and no water at El Mirage Field. To operate the Briegleb Soaring School, Gus dug a well by hand. The two wooden buildings were converted into a bunkhouse and a lunchroom. During the Korean War, Gus "leased" El Mirage Field to the Air National Guard for training in trade for a couple of new buildings. At its peak early in the 1960s, El Mirage had a dozen buildings, 22 gliders and a thriving glider school. Gus Briegleb was designing, building, and maintaining gliders, flying as test and chief instructor pilot.

Gus Briegleb circling El Mirage Field
in his BG-12 Sailplane in 1968.

Briegleb founded the Southern California Soaring Association. The US Army Glider Corps flew his two place BG8 and his single place BG6 and BG-12 gliders. Gus Briegleb's credentials, his enthusiasm and his expertise in the glider world, put El Mirage Field "on the world soaring map". From the 1950s through the 1970s, Briegleb and El Mirage Field served as host to many regional soaring competitions. Several sailplane records were established in the skies over El Mirage including two world records by Briegleb. The 1962 National Soaring Championships were held at El Mirage Field. At several El Mirage regional competitions, well over a hundred aircraft participated from El Mirage Field.

In the early 1960s, Briegleb accepted a NASA contract to build the first full-size prototype of a wingless glider. Briegleb's prototype later became a base point of design for the space shuttle. NASA's Paul Bickle at Edwards AFB gave Gus a contract to build his wingless glider "for an amount less than $10,000!"

Pancho Barnes' hangar

Gus "came in at $9,998!" Briegleb still has the blueprints of his forerunner of today's space shuttle. Briegleb was later inducted into the National Soaring Society of America Hall of Fame.

Gus Briegleb brought many other activities to El Mirage as well. With underground water plentiful, Gus built up an agricultural base around the runways. This eventually included 420-acres of alfalfa farming and some orchard fruit production. As a young man prior to WWII, Briegleb had worked in Hollywood, assisting movie producers on the sets. Using these prior Hollywood connections, Briegleb brought motion pictures, TV and advertisement productions to El Mirage Field and to the nearby dry lake bed, as well. He planned a weekend desert recreational oasis for El Mirage Field, but limited funds prevented him from completing this venture.

A colorful neighbor and friend to Briegleb and a frequent fly-in visitor to El Mirage Field was world famous aviatrix, Pancho Barnes. Her Happy Bottom Riding Club was situated just south of Muroc Army Air Field (now Edwards Air Force Base). Barnes was a top American female pilot in the 1920s and 30s. She wrested the world's speed record and many race championships away from Amelia Earhart and Louise Thaden in the 1930s. Barnes performed as a barnstormer and movie stunt pilot; organized the Hollywood stunt pilots against movie mogul Howard Hughes; and trained WWII Air Corps cadets in her Civilian Pilot Training program. She owned and operated her Happy Bottom Riding Club and Ranch, a second home to the military men of Muroc Air Field. A flamboyant and sometimes controversial figure, Pancho Barnes was a close friend and colleague of many well-known military and civilian pilots and leaders of her era, including General (later President) Eisenhower, Air Force General Hap Arnold, Tokyo raider Jimmy Doolittle, mach breaker Chuck Yeager and glider expert Gus Briegleb.

In 1953, after an unfortunate fire and a forced acquisition of Barnes Ranch property by the expanding Edwards AFB, all that remained of Pancho Barnes' legendary ranch were her airplanes and two airplane hangars. Briegleb purchased the larger hangar from the government in 1954 and moved it to El Mirage Field, piece by piece, reassembling the hangar where Pancho Barnes Hangar #1 stands today.

Ownership of El Mirage Field changed hands in 1980, when the airport was purchased by Mark Thompson. The farming, flying and filming operations continued much the same. Thompson also brought in his Aviation Warehouse (an aviation salvage business supplying

1994 Rollout of General Atomics Predator UAV at El Mirage Airport

motion picture mock-ups, scenes, "props" and sets to the studios) and his Library (supplying technical aviation manuals) businesses. In 1982, Gus Briegleb reacquired the airport from Thompson. Thompson's Aviation Warehouse businesses remain prosperous to this day at the southwest corner of El Mirage Field.

In 1985, Leading Systems Inc. (LSI), owned by Abraham Karem, leased the airport on an exclusive use agreement with an option to buy. LSI designed, developed, flight tested, manufactured and marketed Unmanned Aerial Vehicles (UAVs) for surveillance and reconnaissance at the now "El Mirage Airport". LSI added two new hangar buildings at mid-property, including a single and 60 by 80 foot hangars, resurfaced the center runway and added runway lights. Following four years of good business and promise, LSI purchased the airport from Briegleb in September of 1989, ending 41 years of his ownership. LSI business soon thereafter declined during the difficult times of the 1990s recession. After two failed sale attempts, one with Hughes Aerospace, LSI fell into bankruptcy. Both LSI and El Mirage Airport were available for sale.

Carter Clark
monitoring
progress
of construction
on Airport

General Atomics of San Diego purchased the UAV business portion of LSI as an expansion and diversification to their other corporate businesses. While not interested in purchasing the airport itself, General Atomics desired to remain at El Mirage with their newly-acquired UAV division. General Atomics has earned and experienced significant business success and growth since their acquisition of LSI. Now, as "General Atomics Aeronautical Systems, Inc." (GA-ASI) with Thomas J. Cassidy, Jr. as President, they have secured a longer term lease and have added improvements at El Mirage Airport, including a recently-completed main hangar. They continue to design, develop, manufacture, flight test and market a variety of UAVs, (their latest being the "Predator") for use by the US and other governments for civil and military surveillance and intelligence purposes. General Atomics will most likely remain at El Mirage Airport well into the 21st Century. El Mirage Airport is closed at present due to frequent UAV flight test activities. For your safety, please remain well clear of El Mirage Airport at all times! Do not fly into the flight vicinity.

Carter Clark first spotted El Mirage Airport from the cockpit of his F4E Phantom, while stationed at George Air Force Base in 1979. He later visited the airport during the filming of the pilot movie for the *Hart to Hart* TV series. Clark had considered developing a residential airpark in the West as a post-military retirement pursuit. While driving back from Victorville to their Edwards Air Force Base home in 1991, Clark drove through El Mirage to show his wife, Diane, an airfield he'd seen many times from the air. "It's a great airport ... an ideal site for an airpark." Gus Briegleb was closing the gate as the

Clarks pulled up. After introductions, Briegleb and the Clarks discussed El Mirage Airport. Knowing that LSI was considering selling the airport, Briegleb took the Clarks' phone number, and called a few weeks later with news that El Mirage Airport was for sale. The Clarks closed a purchase of El Mirage Airport in June 1992.

With uncongested and clear VFR skies, ample acreage, excellent runways, beautiful and peaceful surroundings, plentiful water and power, friendly communities not too close but nearby enough, the proximity to the entire Los Angeles metropolitan basin, a host of recreational activities immediately at hand and an adjacent dry lake bed ideal for recreation ... and emergency landings, El Mirage Airport is ideally suited for many possible aviation uses. Future options for El Mirage Airport include its continued use as a premier flight test facility for General Atomics Aeronautical Systems, Inc.; Clark's plan for a full-

"Newly completed GA-ASI main hangar"

scale residential airpark; a warehouse/supply trans-shipment aeroport for Southern California businesses; a public use, private, general aviation airport; a recreational aviation center including glider, ultralight and skydiving activities; its continued use for motion picture, TV and advertisement productions; general property use for agriculture; and any compatible combination of these activities.

PHOENIX SKY HARBOR

INTERNATIONAL AIRPORT

Pick a decade and the image of Phoenix Sky Harbor International Airport mirrors the state of the City of Phoenix at the time. Try 1928 when the city was a small rugged town surrounded by mountains and desert. Early aviation enthusiasts, including a young Sen. Barry M. Goldwater, flew out regularly on Sky Harbor's dusty runways, and Scenic Airways, the region's first commercial airline, had begun flying passengers up to the Grand Canyon.

Nicknamed "The Farm," Sky Harbor consisted of 285 acres of land and a few buildings the City purchased in 1935 from the Acme Investment Company. Pilots had to buzz the field before landing to clear it of grazing cows, but for $35,300 cash and a $64,700 mortgage, Phoenix launched itself into the world of aviation. Before long, American, TWA and Bonanza airlines began operating regular service out of the old pueblo terminal building that served Sky Harbor during the early years.

By the 1950s, however, GIs were returning to Arizona in droves, anxious to leave the snow and sleet behind and make new lives for themselves and their families. The demands of this influx of newcomers prompted the City to construct a new, modern terminal. That compact facility, with an open air baggage claim area, opened October 13, 1952. It was touted that it would meet the needs of Phoenix into the 1970s.

Befitting the new age of air travel, the star of Terminal 1 was a Civil Aeronautics Administration control tower with state-of-the-art radar and navigational equipment. Both the tower and the terminal were air conditioned -- a great rarity in the desert during the 1950s.

When it opened, Terminal 1 was used by nearly 300,000 passengers. But, by 1961, more than 900,000 passengers were passing through its gates. Like Phoenix, Sky Harbor was outgrowing itself fast. A second, larger terminal was planned. Terminal 2 opened in 1962, the year the airport broke the 1 million passenger mark.

Like the style of the City, Terminal 2 was low slung and contemporary. Larger and more sophisticated in design than Terminal 1, Terminal 2 was an airport built to serve a city rather than a town. Designed for service, flexibility and beauty, its panel mosaic mural by artist Paul Coze became a community landmark.

Yet once again the experts were fooled by their figures. Terminal 2 was supposed to replace Terminal 1 and provide airline service for Phoenix until the year 2000, but by 1971, it was clear another facility was needed. A larger, more contemporary terminal was approved as part of the Master Plan.

Just as Phoenix was booming, so was air travel. In less than 10 years, passenger usage had tripled. By the 1970s, Phoenix was sporting a new highrise skyline and Sky Harbor welcomed a new, multi-storied facility -- Terminal 3.

Terminal 1 was once again scheduled for closure, but deregulation of the airline industry changed that scenario, and all three terminals remained in use. By 1984, Terminal 3 was expanded by 10 gates and an additional 100,000 square feet was added to the complex. But even this could not contain the growth of the Valley and

In 1935, the City of Phoenix purchased the 285-acre airfield for $35,300 cash and a $64,700 mortgage. Before long, TWA, American and Bonanza airlines began operating regular service out of a small pueblo building optimistically referred to as the terminal building.

Opened in 1990, Terminal 4 features a dual level roadway to separate arrivals and departures, a moving sidewalk, escalators and a state-of-the-art international concourse designed to accommodate Sky Harbor's growing international passenger traffic.

By the 1970s, Phoenix was sporting a new highrise skyline and Sky Harbor welcomed a new, multi-storied facility – Terminal 3.

the demand for air service.

Three years later, in 1987, ground was broken for an even larger, multi-storied structure -- Terminal 4. Terminal 1 had been built at a cost of $835,000. Thirty-five years later, Terminal 4 carried a $284 million price tag -- the largest capital improvement project in the City's history.

Opened in 1990, Terminal 4 features a dual level roadway to separate arrivals and departures, a moving sidewalk, escalators and a state-of-the-art international concourse designed to accommodate Sky Harbor's growing international passenger traffic.

In 1991, its first full year of operation, Terminal 4 handled 15.4 million passengers -- 70 percent of Sky Harbor's total traffic. With the Goldwater terminal in service, Terminal 1 was finally closed.

Scenic Airways, the region's first commercial airline, began flying passengers up to the Grand Canyon out of Sky Harbor Airport in the late 1920s.

Just as Terminal 4 was being brought on line, the Federal Aviation Administration completed a capacity study that recommended an additional runway at Sky Harbor. As expected, by 1995 Sky Harbor's aircraft traffic climbed from 490,015 in 1994 to 514,079 annually. Passenger traffic increased by 8.7 percent in 1995 to more than 27.8 million passengers and is expected to continue to rise for the next several years.

To prepare for the anticipated growth, in 1993 the City began land acquisition and design development to relocate the Arizona National Guard and numerous other projects necessary to make way for a third runway. Runway construction should commence in 1998 and be completed in 1999.

Today, Phoenix Sky Harbor International Airport looks again to the future. What is certain is growth -- both in the Valley of the Sun and the airport. A new Master Plan process is underway to identify issues and opportunities so that Sky Harbor can continue to serve a burgeoning and increasingly sophisticated business and leisure traveler.

As Phoenix Aviation Director N.A. Bertholf observes, "We are planning the airport our children and grandchildren will use well into the 21st Century."

If the past is an indication, the future of aviation in Phoenix will continue to soar.

PHOENIX DEER VALLEY

A I R P O R T

The City of Phoenix became the proud owner of Deer Valley Airport in August 1971. Since then, a series of extensive improvements have enabled Deer Valley to emerge among the leading general aviation airports in the nation.

In 1972, the City of Phoenix Aviation Department bought and operated the airport's first air traffic control tower. The Federal Aviation Administration opened the present tower in 1975, the same year the airport's main terminal was completed.

Deer Valley is traditionally one of the busiest airports in Arizona, averaging 220,000 takeoffs and landings per year. Located in northwestern Maricopa County, Deer Valley is classified as a general aviation reliever airport for Phoenix Sky Harbor International Airport, and is home to more than 900 based aircraft.

To help maintain Deer Valley's place among the nation's finest general aviation airports, the City has continued to make improvements to the facility. In 1987, a project to lengthen the main runway (7R/25L) was completed. The airport's second runway, (7L/25R) was lengthened from 3,800 to 4,500 feet in the spring of 1993.

The master plan for Deer Valley charts the airport's future into the next century. Improvements and upgrades designed to enable the airport to accommodate a large percentage of the nation's general aviation fleet mix is among the City's highest priorities for Deer Valley.

In addition to airfield improvements, the airport's master plan has also called for upgrades to tenant facilities. In 1991, 117 T-hangars were added on the northeast side of the airport, and in 1995, 118 additional T-hangars were constructed to accommodate growing demand.

Plans in place to manage the anticipated growth include expanding the airport's parking and aircraft storage inventory to include additional tie-downs, covered tie-downs, T-hangars and executive hangars.

Purchased by the City of Phoenix in 1971, Deer Valley Airport is traditionally one of the busiest airports in Arizona, averaging 220,000 takeoffs and landings per year.

A series of extensive improvements have enabled Deer Valley to emerge among the leading general aviation airports in the nation – serving as home to more than 900 based aircraft.

PHOENIX GOODYEAR
A I R P O R T

Once operated by the United States Navy, Phoenix Goodyear Airport's roots reach back to World War II. The airport was built in 1943 to serve as a field support facility to the adjoining Aircraft Division of the Goodyear Tire and Rubber Company.

The Navy expanded the airport in 1951 for military aircraft storage. This was the airfield's mission until 1965, when the General Services Administration took over operations intending to eventually phase out the facility. However, the airport's future was secured in July 1968 when the City of Phoenix bought and began operating Litchfield Airport.

Since acquiring ownership of the airport, the City of Phoenix Aviation Department has transformed the airport now known as Phoenix Goodyear into a general aviation airport serving western Maricopa County. Phoenix Goodyear is home to more than 135 based aircraft and is included in the Federal Aviation Administration's National Airport System Integrated Plan. The airport is classified as a reliever airport to Phoenix Sky Harbor International Airport.

The City has made numerous improvements at Phoenix Goodyear, including new T-hangars, ramp space, tie-downs and an upgraded airfield.

The major tenant at Phoenix Goodyear is the Airline Training Center Arizona, Inc., (ATCA). A subsidiary of Lufthansa Airlines, ATCA provides basic flight training for pilots destined for careers with Lufthansa and other air carriers.

In 1991, Lufthansa completed a $10 million, two-year expansion project at Phoenix Goodyear. The expansion included building additional dormitories, increasing student amenities, erecting new maintenance hangars and adding more aircraft to the fleet.

Located in one of the fastest growing areas in Maricopa County, the master plan for Phoenix Goodyear charts the airport's future growth into the next century. A second parallel runway of 4,200 feet is one of several airfield improvements planned for the airport in the coming years.

Since acquiring ownership of the airport in 1968, the City of Phoenix has transformed Phoenix Goodyear Airport into a general aviation airport serving western Maricopa County.

More than 135 aircraft are based at Phoenix Goodyear. The airport's major tenant is the Airline Training Center Arizona, Inc., a subsidiary of Lufthansa Airlines.

SAN FRANCISCO INTERNATIONAL AIRPORT

A   D E S T I N A T I O N   M A G N E T

Adventuresome and talented pioneers initiated aircraft flight in the San Francisco Bay Area dating back twenty years prior to Orville and Wilbur Wright's first mechanically powered air machine. Their famous aircraft experiment flew 105 feet in three and one half seconds above the sands of Kitty Hawk, North Carolina on December 17, 1903. Professor John Joseph Montgomery with the University of Santa Clara in California, successfully made the first glider flight in the United States in 1883.

These brave pioneers whose experiments were considered interesting but impractical, loved San Francisco. Since an airport did not exist, they landed in fields, on golf courses and in sand dune valleys. In January, 1911, they conducted a flying meet on the bay shore side of the San Francisco Peninsula, near the site of the former Tanforan race track, now developed into the Tanforan Shopping Center.

Flying enthusiasts and local citizens recognized the need for a proper airfield. The decision was made after a few years of successful landings at a San Francisco Marina District airfield to start an airport project at a site to be selected outside the city's 44.82 square miles. The Marina District airfield was located adjacent to the San Francisco Bay Waterfront, where the U.S. Army Presidio now stands. This location required, as you can imagine, expert landing skills over the waterfront's dramatic and precarious geographical setting. On November 2, 1926, San Francisco voters approved a Charter Amendment that would permit the city to purchase land for development of an airport outside the city limits of San Francisco. The vote was: "Yes," 81,552; "No," 16,592. The nearly five-to-one "Yes" vote was one of the largest majorities given a municipal proposition in the history of modern San Francisco. The San Francisco Municipal Airport was first constructed on Mills Estate, owned by a wealthy San Mateo County family, located 14 miles south of San Francisco. The space was 150 acres, leased at $100 an acre, or $15,000 a year. The San Francisco Board of Supervisors approved

Ground loading at San Francisco's old executive terminal.

Pan American Airways Boeing Stratcruiser. Existing international terminal background.

two $25,000 appropriations, one for development of the land, the other for hangar construction. "This placed San Francisco on the airlanes of the world," stated Supervisor Milo Kent, Chairman of the Special Airport Committee.

New international terminal building.

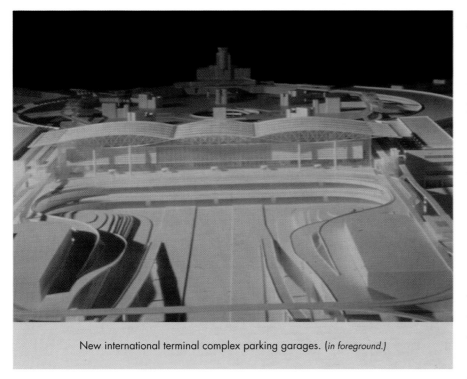

New international terminal complex parking garages. (*in foreground.*)

Plans to expand this first class airport became an active reality in 1995, in response to the enormous growth occurring in the San Francisco Bay Area and the Pacific Rim, the fastest growing market for air travel in the world. By the year 2000, forty percent of the world's passenger traffic will be in the Pacific Rim, compared to 18 percent in 1989. SFIA's total passenger traffic will increase from 35.5 million in 1995 to 51 million in 2006.

The continuation of high standards set forth by the San Francisco Airports Commission for processing passengers and offering excellence in traveller services, today commands an expansion of the International Terminal in this already extremely efficient Airport. Demands on the airspace system have resulted in peak hour delays as passengers are cleared through U.S. Customs and Immigration, aircraft wait for available gates, and increasing automobile volume challenges all access roadways. Growth and progress dictate the construction and reconfiguration of Airport facilities to maintain the already high levels of service for passenger convenience and safety.

Twenty-six new International gates will accommodate the largest, most quiet (Stage III) aircraft, the 747-400, versus ten gates today. Plans are being contemplated to accommodate the "stretch jumbo," the 747-500x and 747-600x aircraft. Upon completion of the expansion, baggage claim capacity will handle arrival of twelve simultaneous international flights, versus four today. Customs and Immigration facilities will be able to process 5,000 passengers per hour, versus 1,200 today. Twelve hundred feet of ticket counters will expedite check-in versus 500 today. One hundred forty thousand square feet of retail concessions versus 61,000 square feet today will offer increased convenience for travellers and provide added revenue generation for the Airport and the City of San Francisco. The new facilities will almost double the square footage of the current combined three terminals.

Today, seventy years later, San Francisco International Airport is the fifth busiest airport in the country, the second busiest in origin and destination passengers, and the seventh busiest in the world in terms of passenger volume.

New international terminal departure level lobby.

New international terminal at night.

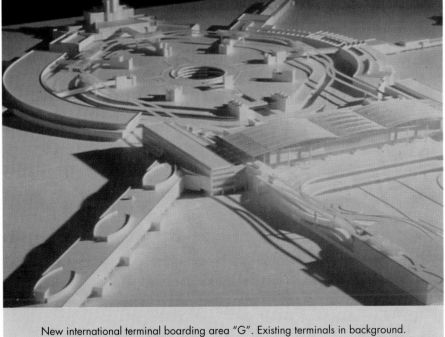

New international terminal boarding area "G". Existing terminals in background.

In addition to the above services, passengers will be able to enjoy a FREE Airport Light Rail System which will connect terminals, rental car facilities, ground transportation, remote parking, aircraft maintenance and cargo areas. Elevated circulation roadways, a Ground Transportation Center, increased space for rental vehicles, additional parking structures and, eventually, BART (Bay Area Rapid Transit) including a BART train station at the ticket counter level of the New International Terminal, will set San Francisco International Airport apart as a leader in the industry. Future travellers will be offered state-of-the-art passenger services.

This progressive project will be financed from Airport revenues. The San Francisco General Fund and local tax revenues will not be used to finance the Master Plan. Currently, San Francisco International Airport generates $6.8 billion a year in personal income and 229,400 airport related jobs. The Airport provides more entry-level and blue-collar jobs for San Franciscans than any other industry in the Bay Area. Including all of the jobs in San Francisco, 88,000 are generated by visitors who arrive at SFIA. After construction is completed, 11,600 new jobs will be created, including 4,000 during the construction. The Master Plan Program will generate $43 million in Bay Area tax revenue, including $10 million in San Francisco tax revenue.

San Francisco International Airport continues to be a leader among world airports in safety, security, customer service and business operations. Recognizing the need for new facilities to carry the Airport into the 21st Century, the Airports Commission and staff developed, and are in the process of implementing, the $2.4 billion Master Plan. The Master Plan will ensure that San Francisco International Airport continues to be a premier international gateway, a valuable economic asset to San Francisco and a major contributor to the economy of the Bay Area.

The implementation of the expansion and resulting excitement generated by this large-scale project is expected to become a serious economic stimulant for the vitality of the San Francisco Bay Area.

AT&T was incorporated in 1885 for the provision of long distance communications. In 1889, the first public phone brought this service to the masses and the rest is history. Part of that history is the significant contribution that AT&T Bell Laboratories made (and still makes) in the field of aeronautics and aviation.

1917: AIR/GROUND COMMUNICATIONS

At the Army's request, AT&T developed the first air/ground communications system for aircraft in 1917. The system, designated SCR-68, also provided communication between two occupants of an airplane, who had previously been limited to hand signals.

Development of the SCR-68 was begun in May 1917 and was completed in December of that year. The system's transceiver used circuits and vacuum tubes developed by Western Electric. (In those days and until 1925, Bell Labs was the Engineering department of Western Electric.) The antenna consisted of a wire trailing from the tail of the aircraft. Transmission was in the 600-to-1,500 kHz range, and power in the aircraft was obtained from a wind-driven generator, fixed to the aircraft within the propeller slipstream.

1936: RADIO ALTIMETER

AT&T Bell Labs developed and demonstrated the first practical radio altimeter in 1936. Altimeters using essentially the same features were still being used in military and commercial models in the late 1970s. Earlier types of altimeters had been based on barometric pressure and were considerably less accurate.

The radio altimeter, based on the frequency modulation principle, was invented by L. Espenschied. This system used a broadband receiver to pick up FM radio signals that were reflected from the earth's surface. Other inventors had used a narrowband receiver whose tuning had to track continuously varying signal frequency. All subsequent altimeters used the Espenschied principles.

1938: RADAR

Radar was a major contributor to victory in World War II. Approximately half the total AT&T Bell Labs defense effort during those war years was devoted to developing a variety of major radar systems. More than 50 such systems (at least half the national total) were produced in large numbers by Western Electric and used in

combat. Included were all the fire-control radar used on Navy ships; several submarine radars; mobile radars for the Marine Corps; various types of navigation and bombing radars for the Army Air Force; and Army radars, including an integrated search radar and, for the first time, fully automatic tracking radar.

After the war, the AT&T Bell Labs R&D effort continued, but with a new emphasis on large scale national defense systems involving radar. A major radar advance of the early 1950s was the invention of the Chirp or pulse compression radar technique. The Chirp concept led to many other scientific advances, not only at Bell Labs but around the nation and the world.

1940s: MULTICAVITY MAGNETRONS

AT&T Bell Labs contributions to the development of the multicavity magnetron, an alternating-current power source, helped make the critically important microwave radar available to the Allies during World War II. Later, multicavity magnetrons also had non-

E.B Craft, Ralph Bown, Nathan Levinson and N.H. Slaughter using early Western Electronic apparatus to carry on two-way conversations with an airplane. (*August 1917 - Morris Rosenfeld*)

Terrain and clearance altimeter for use inside airplane. (*June 1943*)

military applications in airport and weather radar and in microwave ovens for home and industrial uses.

1956: AIR TRAFFIC CONTROL COMMUNICATIONS SYSTEM

Beginning in 1956, Bell Labs, in cooperation with AT&T and the Civil Aeronautics Administration, designed what was then the largest non-military, private-line, air traffic control communications system in the world. This system connected air route traffic control centers with airports and airline dispatching facilities, weather bureaus, military aircraft control stations, and other control centers.

For the Air Traffic Control Communications System, Bell Labs designed the 300 Switching System. This system was extremely adaptable and able to handle a large volume of calls. It consisted of racks of wire-spring relays and crossbar switches, and also included equipment inside a central control room where as many as 212 consoles and access to as many as 30 lines. Each console featured special keys, lamps, loudspeakers, and telephone sets. When the first installations were completed in 1962, the 300 System included signaling, switching, and voice-communication facilities capable of handling as many as 40,000 calls a day among 23 locations. For many years it remained state of the art.

1963: MICROWAVE ULTRASONICS

The Bell Labs development of microwave ultrasonic devices that operate at room temperature within magnetic insulating oxides made possible the use of these units in sophisticated radars, in self-calibrating altimeters in high-speed aircraft, and in information storage and retrieval.

1985: KARMARKAR ALGORITHM

It's an old, familiar, universal problem: how does a traveling salesman determine the most efficient route to follow in covering his territory or a phone company maximize the flow of traffic through a telecommunications network or an airline determine the most effective way to schedule crews and fuel loads?

At age 28, Dr. Narendra Karmarkar, a Bell Labs mathematician, created a new "linear programming" algorithm a step-by-step procedure that permits computers to solve such resource allocation problems at previously impossible speeds. Although linear programming had been used as a decision-making tool in business

Telephone receiving helmet for airplane radio.

and industry for some time, the procedures commonly applied were becoming relatively slow for increasingly complex problems. Dr. Karmarkar's new interior point approach could quickly solve problems 10 to 100 times larger.

Out of this breakthrough has grown systems purchased by the U.S. Air Force Military Airlift Command and Delta Airlines and others. It has also brought together mathematicians, computer scientists and engineers, working as teams to further expand the frontiers of knowledge by using concepts underlying the interior point method.

AT&T

AT&T continues to develop and deploy innovative technology years ahead of actual use. As aviation expands to bring the world together, so does AT&T as it reaches for the stars. Aviation brings the stars to us as AT&T satellites knit a tighter communications web around the world.

BURBANK-GLENDALE-PASADENA AIRPORT

Burbank-Glendale-Pasadena Airport opened in 1930 as the first multimillion dollar airport in the United States and has been at the center of much of this nation's aviation history ever since.

United Airport, as it was known on opening day, was home to many of the early legends of U.S. aviation — Lindbergh, Earhart, Post, Hughes — due largely to their association with various Lockheed aircraft. Indeed, Lockheed bought the airport outright in 1940 and re-named the facility Lockheed Air Terminal as it entered its heyday as the primary passenger airport for Los Angeles, a status which lasted until 1947.

With the advent of World War II, the airport was simultaneously the center of passenger traffic and a cornerstone of military aircraft manufacturing throughout the war. This dual role was to continue for decades, with Lockheed's manufacture of military aircraft such as the U-2, SR-71 Blackbird, P-3 Orion and F-117 Stealth Fighter and commercial transports like the Constellation, Electra and L-1011.

Today Lockheed has moved its aircraft manufacturing to other parts of the country, but Burbank Airport's popularity with the traveling public is at an all-time high. It was purchased from Lockheed by the Burbank-Glendale-Pasadena Airport Authority in 1978 and now plays an increasingly vital role in the transportation system of the greater Los Angeles area.

Burbank-Glendale-Pasadena Airport is located just 13.3 miles north of downtown Los Angeles and has enjoyed a remarkable resurgence in the past six years. The annual passenger count has jumped 81% since 1989 to 4.9 million, and a remarkable 1386% over the past 30 years when the total was just over 300,000 in 1965.

Why this popularity? Burbank's location and convenience have always been attractive to the traveler, and Burbank's natural access to major western cities has raised Burbank's profile with the airlines, too, as they have competed more vigorously for regional market share.

Burbank offers an alternative to air travelers who are tired of the freeway traffic and bigness of LAX. And Burbank offers the airlines access to more than 2.5 million people within a 15-mile radius of the airport. The result has been more flights offered and more tickets sold.

Six major airlines — Alaska, American, America West, SkyWest, Southwest and United — now serve Burbank with a wide array of nonstop flights throughout the West, and those flights account for

Opening Day on Memorial Weekend

Burbank Airport

nearly 80% of the seats sold. But increasing numbers of travelers are taking advantage of the one-stop connections at hub cities to all major U.S. destination markets as well as prominent markets of the Pacific Rim and Europe. In addition, cargo operators such as FedEx and United Parcel are drawn to Burbank when heavy auto traffic makes it difficult to carry last-minute shipments to their other bases.

Burbank may seem like a neighborhood airport to some, but it's also a gateway to the world.

Burbank Airport is close to L.A.'s business areas — from downtown Los Angeles to the Glendale financial district and the film

Terminal Today

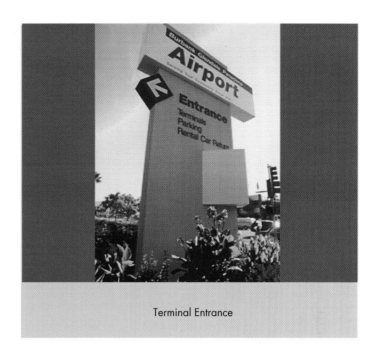
Terminal Entrance

industry and service industries of the greater San Fernando Valley. Burbank is also closer to so many of the prominent tourist attractions of the Southland — Hollywood, Universal Studios, the Rose Bowl and Norton Simon Museum in Pasadena, Dodger Stadium, Magic Mountain, the L.A. Zoo and Gene Autry Western Heritage Museum in Griffith Park.

Burbank Airport is also ideally situated to the major freeways feeding north/south travel in the county (Los Angeles/Magic Mountain) or the ever increasing east/west flow (Ventura/San Gabriel Valley). It is located next to two major converging rail lines, and in 1995 it became the first airport west of the Mississippi to have a rail stop directly at the airport boundary, within easy walking distance of the main terminal. Both Amtrak and Metrolink commuter trains stop at the airport today.

The airport itself has steadily increased the amenities it offers its patrons. A new concourse was built in 1987 enclosing all gate areas in air conditioned comfort. Parking availability is always a nice surprise. Burbank's "remote" lots would be considered next to the terminal at many airports, and they are served by frequent shuttles to the front door.

In 1990, the airport began offering valet parking directly in front of the terminal at prices only slightly higher than self-parking in the daily lot. This service has grown constantly and is especially favored by the many travelers who use Burbank for short-duration trips up and down the coast.

Valet parking takes the hassle out of getting to the flight, but it's also handy for the returning travelers, who will have their cars waiting for them by the time they collect their baggage.

Offering a close-in location and convenience to the traveler, Burbank-Glendale-Pasadena Airport is proud of its first-rate, economical nonstop service to the West and one-stop service to the world.

The importance of Burbank-Glendale-Pasadena Airport is certain to carry well into the future, assured by the existing population base and the airport's strategic location near multiple modes of ground transportation, business centers and major recreational attractions. Additionally, the ability of modern aircraft to use modest runways and likely improvements in efficient air space management will mean continued reliance on Burbank in the years to come.

The airport's highest priority in the near term is to replace its current passenger terminal, which is located closer to the runways than modern design standards allow. In all likelihood, the new terminal will open its doors just after the year 2000, a fitting way to start the 21st century.

GILLESPIE FIELD AIRPORT

The Gillespie Field Airport is owned and operated by the County of San Diego, Department of Public Works. It is located in the city of El Cajon, 15 miles east of downtown San Diego. El Cajon lies in a valley surrounded by foothills with higher mountains to the east and southeast.

As dramatic as its setting, the history of the airport is equally as colorful. Gillespie Field Airport was originally commissioned in mid-1942 as a training facility for Marine Corps parachutists, Camp Gillespie (later named Gillespie Field), served in that capacity until 1944 when Marine parachutists were phased out. After WWII, the training field became a civil air facility serving the city of El Cajon. In 1953, Camp Gillespie was officially deeded to the County of San Diego. Over the years, the county acquired surrounding properties to assure that surrounding development would be compatible with the airport's activities. In 1980, the County of San Diego created the Airport Enterprise Fund (AEF) to fund airport operations and the development of the surrounding and buffer properties held by Gillespie Field.

Today, Gillespie Field is not only a full-service executive airport that can accommodate small aircraft and jets, but it's also home to a thriving business/industrial park.

Each year more than 200,000 flights arrive or depart from Gillespie Field. The airport has a FAA air traffic control tower, it encompasses 775 acres and has more than 800 aircraft based on site — with FBOs occupying 323 acres at the facility. Gillespie Field is a center for vital and life-saving services, including County of San Diego Sheriff's ASTREA, Civil Air Patrol's Search and Rescue operations and Life Flight services.

In addition to airport businesses and activities, the facility is home to the El Cajon Speedway, a tree farm, an Aerospace Museum, a golf driving range, a soccer field, a rifle range and numerous business enterprises. The corporate headquarters of Chemtronics, Taylor Guitars and Vowels Poultry are just a few of the businesses who have located in the adjacent Gillespie Field business/industrial park — a center for commerce in East San Diego County.

Gillespie Field in El Cajon is a thriving airport and business park that is within easy reach of downtown San Diego. Primary transportation is by automobile via Interstate-8, but with the opening of the San Diego Trolley East-County line that goes through Gillespie Field, the airport has never been more easily accessible. Freight

Business Park

Aerial View of Gillespie

TAYLOR GUITARS

Business Park

services are available via air and rail and there are common carriers that provide El Cajon with overnight air and motor freight to Los Angeles, San Francisco and Phoenix.

Whether you're in San Diego for business or pleasure, Gillespie Field is a facility that can meet your needs.

MᶜCLELLAN-PALOMAR AIRPORT

McClellan-Palomar Airport (CRQ) is owned and operated by the County of San Diego. Located 35 miles north of the City of San Diego three miles from the coast line in the City of Carlsbad, the Airport has it all; location, commuter services, on-demand charter services and three full service FBO's. With so much to offer, it's no wonder it's one of the busiest general aviation airports in the United States. McClellan-Palomar logged 204,191 operations in 1995.

From its beginnings, the McClellan-Palomar Airport has been a general aviation airport that attracted the attention of the commuter market. In fact, in the airport's inaugural year, Bonanza Air Lines initiated commercial service with instrument approach at Palomar Airport. It was opened in 1959 as a replacement to the general aviation airport in Del Mar that was closed due to the construction of Interstate-5, the major north-south link between San Diego and Los Angeles.

McClellan-Palomar Airport is a short driving distance from the cities of Del Mar, Encinitas, Oceanside, Vista, and San Marcos. Over the last five years, the airport has become the commuter airport of choice for both North County residents and visitors to San Diego County's exclusive resort communities. Today, McClellan-Palomar is home to more than 500 general aviation and corporate and commercial aircraft. Two commercial airlines, American Eagle, and the United

Express, operate from McClellan-Palomar, and provide commuter service to Los Angeles International Airport seven days a week.

The airport is a key component in north San Diego County's economic development. Industries want the easy access to corporate jets that McClellan-Palomar Airport provides and have located to the area spurring industrial development, creating thousands of jobs. In addition to the recent location of Lego-Land U.S.A., and the presence of numerous golfing industry corporate headquarters in the area immediately surrounding the airport, a recent economic benefit study determined the airport generated $59 million in revenue annually for the City of Carlsbad.

The next few years will be key years for McClellan-Palomar Airport as it moves to update, modernize and expand the existing general aviation services to meet the ever increasing demand for general, corporate and commercial facilities. Planned improvements include increased hangar space, increased fuel storage capacity, more parking facilities, and a new commercial terminal.

LONG BEACH AIRPORT

During the early 1920s, the only "airport" in Long Beach was the city's huge, crescent-shaped beach. Landings and takeoffs were best made at low tides, and it was common to see fabric-covered biplanes lifting off the sand amidst ocean spray.

In 1923, the Long Beach City Council set aside 150 acres near the intersection of Spring and Cherry Streets for use as an airfield. Named Daugherty Field (after Earl S. Daugherty, one of the area's pioneer aviators), the new airport enabled Long Beach to gain access to the nation's infant air transportation system.

The first airport operator's lease was issued on April 7, 1925. Significant development began when the city built hangars and administrative facilities for the Army and Navy in 1928-30. During the mid-1930s, two runways were constructed and in 1936, the Civil Aeronautics Authority (now the Federal Aviation Administration) formally activated a control tower.

"The art deco style terminal building has been a fixture in Long Beach aviation history since its dedication in 1941."
(photo by John W. Cleveland)

By 1941, Daugherty Field had increased to 500 acres. That same year the Airport's art deco style terminal building was completed. Architects W. Horace Austin and Kenneth S. Wing, Sr. designed the building. Three federally-funded mosaic masterworks created by Grace Clements under the Works Progress Administration/Federal Art Project (WPA/FAP) served as the finishing touches on the building.

As smaller capacity aircraft such as the DC-3 and Constellation were phased out of service in favor of large jets such as the Boeing 737 and Douglas DC-9, the Long Beach terminal needed to grow. In

"Long Beach Airport covers 1,166 acres with five runways and is home to over 200 businesses. (photo by Harry Merrick)

1984, a new concourse area and pre-boarding lounge were constructed immediately south of the existing terminal building. This improvement project, while retaining the 1940s character of the terminal, provided better accessibility for patrons with disabilities, improved mobility in the passenger screening process, and improved ticketing and check-in processing of airport users. Since the distinguishing architectural characteristics of the terminal were not altered, the building was named a City of Long Beach Cultural Heritage Landmark in 1990.

In celebration of the 50th Anniversary of the Terminal Building in 1991, the Long Beach Airport Historical Aviation Exhibit was dedicated, displaying relics and photos from the early aviation years. Exhibits such as Daugherty's trophies and awards are featured on the second floor of the terminal. Photos of members of the Long Beach Squadron of the Women's Air Corps Service Pilots (WASP) are also displayed.

Over the years, the Long Beach Airport (LGB), a facility steeped in aviation history has played a major role in the development of the City. It was the airport, along with an abundant amount of vacant adjacent land, that first attracted the attention of Donald Wills Douglas in 1940. Today McDonnell Douglas Corporation provides jobs for more than 20,000 workers, making it the city's largest employer. The Long Beach plant

"A 1927 air race starting at Daugherty Field and visited by Charles Lindbergh's *Spirit of St Louis*, displayed in front of the Earl S. Daugherty hangar." *(photo courtesy of Long Beach Airport)*

serves as the final production and assembly center for the MD-80 and 90 series commercial twin-jet, the wide-body MD-11 tri-jet, and the U.S. Air Force's C-17 short take off and landing (STOL) cargo transport.

The airport is well-situated halfway between the major business and tourism areas of both Orange and Los Angeles Counties. Currently, there are over 200 businesses located on airport property, including nearly 100 acres of mid-rise business park and hotel uses, several top-rate fixed base operators and specialty aviation service companies, as well as Cessna Citation and Gulfstream Aerospace aircraft service centers.

Presently, Long Beach Airport covers 1,166 acres and has five runways, the longest being 10,000 feet. It is a hub of corporate aircraft activity, as well as being one of the world's busiest airports in terms of general aviation activity. Scheduled airlines also provide passenger and cargo service.

Owned and operated by the City of Long Beach, the Airport is an important part of the Long Beach community. The Airport contributes time and resources to two Long Beach area elementary schools. Also, it donates all Airport waste recycling proceeds to those schools. The Airport's volunteer tour program offers an invaluable learning experience. Each year, these tours give over 3,000 children and 500 adults the opportunity to explore a major aviation transportation, manufacturing and business center which contributes significantly to the local economy.

As we head into the next century, LGB will continue to power the region's economy and provide safe and efficient aircraft facilities and services. Still a testament to the visions and dreams of a not-too-distant yesteryear, the Long Beach Airport continues to constantly change in a never-ending effort to meet the growing demands of the future.

M^CCARRAN INTERNATIONAL AIRPORT

1995 marked the 75th anniversary of flight into Las Vegas, and the 75th anniversary of passenger travel. On May 7, 1920, Randall Henderson settled his Curtiss JN-4 Jenny on a makeshift runway, and let Jake Beckley climb out and visit his home town. This milestone flight from Blythe, California, marked the beginning of what has become one of the major sources of travelers to Southern Nevada.

Las Vegas and Clark County joined the commercial air travel routes in 1925, when "Pop" Hanshue negotiated landing rights with Leon and Earl Rockwell. Rockwell Field became the landing field for the new Western Air Express. The first flights on April 26, 1926, heralded a form of travel which today accounts for more than 25 million travelers in and out of Clark County.

In 1930, Western Air Express, working with P.A. "Pop" Simon, founded a new field, known as the Western Air Express Field. This airport attracted the U..S. Army Air Corps and became a Gunnery training school during World War II. In 1941, the field was renamed McCarran Field, honoring Pat McCarran, United States Senator from Nevada. During the war, the name was changed to the Las Vegas Army Air Field.

After the war, the Air Force closed its local base, and commercial air traffic continued to use the field. In 1947, the Air Force decided to reopen the local base because of the proximity of target ranges and testing areas, and offered to do so if commercial air traffic could be moved to another airport.

The County reviewed possible sites throughout the valley and settled on a private airfield located on Las Vegas Blvd. The field was called Alamo Field and had been founded in 1941 by George Crockett. A Missouri native, Crockett, came to Southern Nevada as a representative for Stinson Aircraft, and saw a need for a general aviation field near Las Vegas.

Crockett purchased the property of a Civilian Pilot Training Program, which had gone out of business in Iowa, and started building his Alamo Airport. By 1942, he was open for business, giving lessons and servicing the needs of private pilots. During World War II, some commercial aircraft had also used the field when

access was not available at the Las Vegas Army Air Base.

Crockett and his wife, the former Peg Nickerson, agreed to sell the private airport to Clark County, and in 1948, the second McCarran Airport was dedicated at the old Alamo Airport site. Using the new terminal building were four commercial carriers, Bonanza, Western, United and TWA, offering 12 flights daily.

During that first year, 35,106 passengers used the new airport (today 35,206 travelers pass through in 11 hours). The old McCarran reopened as the Las Vegas Air Force Base, and was renamed Nellis Air Force Base on May 20, 1950, in honor of a local hero, Lt. William H. Nellis, who was killed during the Battle of the Bulge over Bastogne in 1944.

Promotions by local casino/resorts increased the number of visitors to Las Vegas. Airplane travel expanded, and the public came to depend on commercial aviation. By the mid-1950's, expansion at the airport was needed, and a complete redesign of the field was undertaken. After extensive study, the County decided to expand the runway's length from 6500 feet to 10,000 to handle the new jet aircraft. Another expansion need was a new terminal. When a bond issue for $2,000,000 was presented to the voters, it passed overwhelmingly.

During the redesign process, Las Vegas and Clark County became better known in aviation circles through the successful

Randall Henderson and Jake Beckley made aviation history when they made the first airplane flight to Las Vegas in 1920. Henderson stayed a week, selling sightseeing rides over the city in his Curtiss JN-4 "Jenny" for $10.00.

McCarran International Airport's entrance, circa 1974.

The Concorde departing McCarran International Airport. Nearly every kind of current commercial aircraft is seen at McCarran. Photo by J. J. Balk.

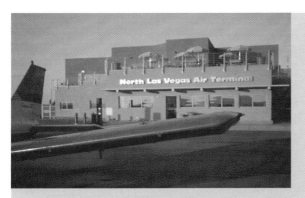

Founded in 1941, North Las Vegas Airport is also part of the Department of Aviation for Clark County. It is widely used by general aviation and charter airlines. Photo by J.J. Balk.

McCarran International Airport, showing the new C gates. Part of the famous Las Vegas Strip can be seen in the background. Photo by J.J. Balk.

completion of the World Endurance Flight and the World Congress of Flight, both in 1959. In the World Endurance Flight, Bob Timm and John Cook flew a Cessna 172 for 64 days, 22 hours, and 19 minutes without landing. Inflight refueling was accomplished from a truck speeding on a closed desert highway, and Timm and Cook set a record which still stands.

The newly lengthened runways at McCarran were well used during the World Congress of Flight in 1959. This international event was held both at the new County Convention Center, Nellis Air Force Base, and McCarran Airport. Missiles, aircraft, systems and products were introduced at the show, and McCarran saw its first DC-8 and Convair 880 land at the field. The next year TWA began the first scheduled jet service into McCarran flying Convair 880s.

With all this promotion, passenger traffic at the field kept increasing. By 1959, daily flights had risen to 73, and the annual passenger total to 686,268. New airlines, including National, brought in even more travelers. The existing airport facilities became inadequate to handle the increases, and a new terminal was planned.

The new terminal was designed for the opposite end of the field from the existing 1948 structure. It was opened March 15, 1963, and airport operations moved to the new building. An average of

128 daily flights and a total of 1,444,700 passengers used the airport that year. The former terminal building became the headquarters for Alamo Airways, a model general aviation facility which continued to be operated by George and Peg Crockett.

In July 1966, McCarran Airport was officially removed from the tax rolls and became totally self-supporting. Since that time, the airport has paid for itself through generated revenues.

In 1967, the Crocketts' involvement with McCarran Airport ended when Howard Hughes bought their general aviation facility. Hughes had known the Crocketts for many years, and the new Hughes Aviation Services continued to service the general aviation market.

McCarran continued to grow, with another $30,000,000 expansion project, started in 1970 and completed in 1973. In 1971, the airport became a "Port-of-Entry", which led to further growth.

During the late 1970's, expansion of the runway system, Hughes Aviation Services, new commercial carriers, and passenger use of the terminal led to the creation of an ambitious plan, "McCarran 2000." McCarran 2000 projected 20,000,000 to 30,000,000 users of the airport by the year 2,000. The terminal was projected to cost one billion dollars, and would be able to handle this level of traffic.

To fund this expansion, in 1982 the largest single sale of airport revenue bonds ever issued at that time, $315 million, were sold. The first major part of this expansion was completed in 1985, with the addition of a new parking structure, a new satellite gate, and an automated transport system linking the new satellite and the main terminal.

During the last decade, with the completion of the first three phases of McCarran 2000, it became obvious that the next phase was going to be needed sooner than expected. The 25,000,000 annual passenger mark was passed in 1994, a year which also saw the completion of the longest commercial runway in the United States at Las Vegas. Phase IV of McCarran 2000 has now begun to provide facilities for commercial air travel and freight growth into the next century.

Will this be the end of expansion for McCarran? It seems unlikely. Since the first Jenny carried the first passenger to Las Vegas in 1920, air travel has grown to become be a vital part of Southern Nevada tourism. Today, every kind of aircraft, including the supersonic Concorde, flies in to McCarran. In addition there are five other airports in the Clark County Aviation System. McCarran will continue to anticipate the growth in Clark County and expand to meet the needs of its customers.

MONTGOMERY FIELD

On August 28, 1883, 25-year-old John J. Montgomery and his brother James sneaked away from their parents' ranch house on Otay Mesa. They carried rifles and a long, bulky package of sticks and cloths. The package was the real purpose for their early morning jaunt. The rifles were props: If anyone asked, they were going rabbit hunting. The neighbors knew something about the strange package, and they thought John was a bit balmy.

When they got to their destination, they assembled the sticks and cloth into a glider. John got into the craft, and James took hold of a 40-foot-long rope. In 1950, James recalled that long-ago morning: "I towed John into the air in his little glider. He flew over my head and landed beautifully about 600 feet down the hill. It was a beautiful, graceful flight."

So went the world's first controlled-wing, heavier-than-air flight, predating the Wright brothers' feat at Kitty Hawk by more than 20 years.

Although this 492-acre field that boasts 260,000 operations annually today carries Montgomery's name in honor of that first flight, it started out with the name of another aviation pioneer in San Diego history: Bill Gibbs.

In the early 1930s, Gibbs was a pilot teaching flying students at National City Airport. At the same time, he was working at nights and going to school during the day. The National City Airport was not the best airport in those days. It was in the Sweetwater River valley, and it would often get muddy. In 1936, it flooded, endangering a hangar Gibbs had built there. So Gibbs looked around for a better site. He found it on the mesa where Montgomery Field is now situated. Not only did it not get muddy, the morning fog, for some reason, always cleared away from that spot first.

In 1936, Gibbs bought 25 acres for $250 (Terms: $50 down, $25 every three months). The next year, he bought an additional 30 acres for $450 cash. Of this purchase, 10 acres were at the present airport site and the other 20 acres were on the other side of the freeway. Over the next few years he continued to acquire contiguous land. In 1937, the first aircraft operation started from a single 1200-foot runway and Gibbs Flying Service was born.

In 1939, he improved the airport, putting in three runways. In early 1940, he leased the airport to Ryan School of Aeronautics for the instruction of Army Air Corps cadets and went to work for Ryan instructing the corps.

The city of San Diego condemned the airport and the surrounding land for a total of 1,800 acres in all, in 1948. For 209 acres of it, Gibbs received $60,000 for the land. He was paid an additional $48,000 for the improvements he had made. At the time, the city was planning on making it the major international airport to replace Lindbergh Field. But the U.S. Navy balked: You're too close to our own air field, they said. So the city sold off the surrounding land for industrial uses and the airfield remained a general aviation airport.

The name was changed from Gibbs Field to Montgomery Field on May 20, 1950.

Today, Montgomery Field is home to 600 aircraft and is the 11th-busiest noncertificated airport in the country (the busiest in San Diego County). A runway extension completed in November 1995 increased the runway's length from 3,400 feet to 4600 feet. Now Montgomery can handle 95 percent of the general aviation fleet — airplanes weighing 12,500 pounds or less.

Montgomery Field is one of the few general aviation airports in the country that is totally self-sufficient. It uses no tax money for its operations. Moreover, the field in 1988 (the latest year for which figures are available) contributed more than $114 million to the economy of San Diego and makes more than 2,000 jobs possible.

San Diego Aviation
Since 1883
Montgomery Glider

In 1938, Montgomery Field (then Gibbs Field) was just one year old, isolated on a mesa.

The dedication of Gibbs Field as Montgomery Field, honoring John J. Montgomery, who made the first controlled, winged flight in the world, was on May 20, 1950.

BROWN FIELD

Situated very close to the California-Mexico border (just three miles northeast of Tijuana), Brown Field is a port-of-entry into the United States and is used by the majority of general aviation air traffic coming from Mexico into California.

The field began as an aerial gunnery and aerobatics school in 1918. At the time, it was called East Field after a Major East who had been killed in 1918 in New York. From 1938 to 1939, it was used for U.S. Navy drone experiments. In 1943, the field's name was changed to NAAS Otay Mesa. Later that year, the name was changed again, to NAAS Brown Field in memory of a Lt. Commander Brown who had been killed elsewhere in 1936. After World War II, in 1947, the field turned civilian. The armed forces took it over again for the Korean Conflict from 1951 to 1953, and held onto it until 1962, when it became a civilian field again.

Currently, Brown Field is serving the general aviation needs of the South Bay area, and accommodates 160,000 operations per year. Military use averages over 500 landings per month, as Brown Field is ideally situated for supporting parachuting exercises and other military activities. Brown Field is also heavily used by federal, state, and local law-enforcement agencies and is home base for the U.S. Border Patrol. And, of course, it is the airport of choice for travelers who wish to shop in nearby Tijuana.

One of Brown Field's unique features is its 8,000-foot-long, 200-foot-wide runway, which accommodates any aircraft, including the world's largest, the Russian-built Antonov-124.

Although close enough to San Diego proper to make it a thriving hub, Brown Field's 900 acres are in an isolated area with no residential areas nearby. Because of this, the problem of noise is of little concern. In addition, the field is totally flat, being on a mesa, and there are no obstructions to the west.

Given all this, together with the North American Free Trade Agreement (NAFTA) and other economic bonds being made between the United States and Mexico, Brown Field has much potential for the future.

Oakland International Airport is one of the fastest growing airports in the United States. From its historic beginnings in 1927, today Oakland International enjoys the popularity of being the Bay Area's most convenient airport with the best fares and most frequent flights. The airport is located just 10 miles from downtown Oakland and only 22 miles from downtown San Francisco.

Oakland is a business-friendly airport. It is open 24 hours a day to accommodate the demands of the airlines, including the air cargo carriers. The airport is also the most centrally located airport in the Bay Area, placing it in the middle of the fourth largest metropolitan population area in the United States.

Oakland International Airport is owned and operated by the Port of Oakland, which also operates the fourth largest seaport in the nation and manages extensive commercial real estate interests. The airport employs more than 7,200 people, with approximately 2,600 in positions related to air cargo.

The airport pumps roughly $4 billion annually into the local economy, and is responsible for generating 2,200 indirect jobs such as those that provide services for airport employees like gas station attendants, bank tellers and grocery store clerks, and up to 44,000 visitor/tourism jobs, such as hotel staff, taxi and charter bus drivers and tour guides.

The 2,600 acre airport is comprised of two airfields, South Field and North Field. The primary commercial runway (11/29) located at South Field, is 10,000 feet long and has clear overwater approaches at both ends. There are plans to extend it to 11,600 feet to meet the demands of Pacific-bound air carriers. South Field is home to a number of air carriers, including Southwest Airlines, Federal Express and United Parcel Service.

North Field, the original site of Oakland Airport, has three runways -- a pair of parallel east-west runways of 5,020 and 6,200 feet and a cross-wind runway of 3,300 feet -- and is used primarily by general aviation aircraft.

The 6,200 foot runway is also an FAA-certified air carrier runway, but is only used as an alternate for runway 11/29 when it is out of service for maintenance or emergencies. Between the two airfields, Oakland handles more than half a million operations annually.

North Field is also the home for cargo operators Airborne, Emery Worldwide and Ameriflight. The U.S. Postal Service also operates a 40,000 square foot Airport Mail Facility at North Field for sorting mail that has been transported by scheduled passenger airlines for the Bay Area region.

HISTORY IN THE MAKING

Oakland International Airport is the San Francisco Bay Area's oldest airport. Built in 1927, the airport has played a pivotal role in San Francisco Bay Area aviation history. The airport began with just one 7,020 foot runway which at the time it was constructed was the longest in the world and built in a mere 23 days.

In the early years, Oakland was host to many historical flights. In June 1927, Lieutenants Lester Maitland and Albert Hegenberger were the first to fly from Oakland to Oahu and made the trip in 25 hours and 49 minutes.

In August 1927, the airport was the starting point of the widely publicized Dole Races from Oakland to Hawaii, sponsored by pineapple magnate James Dole. Thousands of spectators lined the runway to watch nine airplanes start the race. Only two would finish.

In December 1927, Boeing Air Transport, the forerunner of United Airlines, inaugurated transcontinental passenger and airmail service between New York and Oakland. The carrier then inaugurated West Coast passenger/airmail service between Oakland and Southern

Oakland International Airport's Terminal Two at dusk

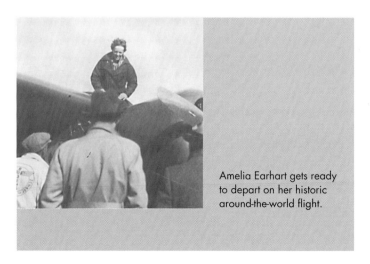

Amelia Earhart gets ready to depart on her historic around-the-world flight.

California in February 1928. Even today, United continues to serve Oakland and several Southern California points with its Shuttle by United service.

Amelia Earhart made several trips to Oakland, her first in June 1931 in an "autogiro," a hybrid airplane/helicopter. In May 1937, Ms. Earhart and her navigator Fred Noonan left Oakland for the last time as they took off on their ill-fated around-the-world flight.

Oakland Airport played an important role as a military marshalling point for all planes bound for the U.S. forces in the Pacific beginning May 1943. All of Oakland's commercial flights were diverted to Mills Field, the predecessor of San Francisco International Airport.

After the war ended, commercial flights returned to Oakland but many of the airlines kept their primary operations in San Francisco. Port of Oakland officials were determined to bring carriers back and to also attract new carriers, so plans were drawn up to expand the airport to accommodate jet aircraft, which was approved by Oakland voters in April 1953.

The new airport, also known as South Field, was built on reclaimed land from San Francisco Bay. A 4.5 mile dike was built and more than 50 million cubic yards of sand was deposited behind it to make way for the new 600-acre complex.

Metropolitan Oakland International Airport was opened in September 1962, with two days of air shows and ceremonies attended by 500,000 people. The new $20 million complex included a new 13 gate passenger terminal topped by an 11-story control tower, a cantilevered jet hangar and a separate air cargo building.

In May 1985, the airport expanded again with a new $16.3 million terminal, adding seven new gates to the airport's existing 13 gates.

A NEW ERA

In 1983, three million passengers transited Oakland International Airport. By 1995, that figure had more than tripled to 9.8 million. The arrival of Southwest Airlines to the airport in May 1989 brought low fare, high frequency flights to Oakland and the Bay Area and spurred the airport's unprecedented growth. The carrier offers more than 100 flights daily and accounts for approximately 60 percent of Oakland's annual passenger traffic.

Southwest continues to expand its presence at Oakland International Airport. In November 1994, Southwest Airlines opened a crew base at Oakland, bringing as many as 495 flight attendant jobs to the area. In March 1995, Southwest also opened a pilot base at the airport that is home to 300 pilots. The addition of the two bases brings Southwest's total employee population at Oakland to 1,150, making the airport the fifth largest city in Southwest's system in terms of staffing.

FedEX's regional hub (with the skyline of the City of Oakland in the background) processes more than 250,000 domestic and international documents and parcels a day.

Air cargo has grown at a dizzying double-digit pace annually since the mid-1980s. In 1983, the airport handled 7.5 million pounds and by 1995, more than 1.2 billion pounds of air cargo moved through Oakland. Much of this growth is attributed to the establishment of the Federal Express hub in 1988.

The hub is a 23-acre regional sort facility just west of the passenger terminals at South Field where some 250,000 parcels and documents are processed daily.

In September 1995 Federal Express opened its Customs Clearance Center to process parcels and documents from the Pacific Rim. Between the two facilities, Federal Express employs 1,100 people.

As demand grows for expanded passenger and cargo services, Oakland International Airport plans to implement a group of 20 improvement and expansion projects called the Airport Development Program (ADP). The projects are identified under such categories as landside improvements, airfield improvements, air cargo expansion and airline and airport support services.

The airport has teamed up with the Federal Aviation Administration (FAA) to develop the ADP as a joint document. Currently it is going through an extensive environmental process that will culminate in the release of an environmental impact report and statement in 1996. Once approved, the ADP is expected to take five to seven years to complete and when fully implemented, will create 4,000 new jobs at the airport, with 80 percent of those positions in cargo.

As Oakland International Airport looks to the new century, it will continue to build upon the things that make it successful -- convenience, customer service, central location, low fares, frequent flights and a pro-business philosophy -- all of the things that make it a Bay Area original.

SAN DIEGO INTERNATIONAL

A R I C H   H I S T O R Y   A N D   A   G O L D E N   F U T U R E .

It's hard to imagine that more than perhaps a few of the 30,000 travelers who pass each day through San Diego International Airport, Lindbergh Field, might take this gateway to 'America's Finest City' for granted.

After all, in what other major airport could you at once be located conveniently near downtown, surrounded by stunning scenery, and be certain of clear blue skies and a pleasant temperature just about any day of the year?

However, Lindbergh Field — situated at the north end of San Diego Bay on tidelands administered by the Port of San Diego — is more than an especially appealing major commercial airport serving a key region of the Southwest. It is testimony to the rich history of aviation itself. San Diego's near-perfect climate turned this area into a favorite testing ground for pioneering aviators in the early 1900s, and history has been made here ever since.

The world's first successful seaplane and first controlled-wing flight took off from San Diego airfields. And this is where the world's first airmail service, and the first naval aviation school, got off the ground.

San Diego Municipal Airport Terminal on Pacific Highway.
(May 1952)

San Diego was also the first city to issue a complete set of air ordinances, and the first to set up a municipal board of air control. Of note, too, are T. Claude Ryan and B. Franklin Mahoney, the founders of San Diego's first aircraft manufacturing plant. After their company, Ryan Airlines, introduced another first — a year-round daily passenger service between San Diego and Los Angeles — Ryan opted to sell his holdings and launch a soon-to-be-famous venture of his own. It was to Ryan's new manufacturing company, Ryan Aircraft, that Charles A. Lindbergh turned for the design and construction of the "Spirit of St. Louis." On May 10, 1927, Lindbergh left San Diego for New York. From there he made the first transatlantic flight to Paris.

San Diegans marked Lindbergh's takeoff from their city to be the first leg of that epic journey and welcomed him back

immediately afterwards in fine style. On August 16, 1928, San Diego dedicated its brand new airport, Lindbergh Field, in his honor.

HUMBLE BEGINNINGS

Once no more than part of a vast, tide-washed mud flat, Lindbergh Field was created through a harbor project funded by the 1927 sale of a $650,000 bond issue.

Engineers deepened the Bay north of the B Street Pier and established deep water berthing along the Embarcadero. The dredged material was then used to reclaim 142 acres of tidelands. In 1929, after the airport area had been graded and surfaced with decomposed granite, the airport's first building — a 50 ft by 100 ft hangar — was erected by Air Tech Flying Service, Ltd.

On October 16, 1934, Lindbergh Field earned an A-1 rating from the U.S. Department of Commerce and was elevated to the status of permanent international airport of entry by the U.S. Treasury Department.

More dredging projects (conducted by the City Harbor

Former President (then governor of California) Ronald Reagan speaks at Lindbergh Field opening ceremonies. (February 1965)

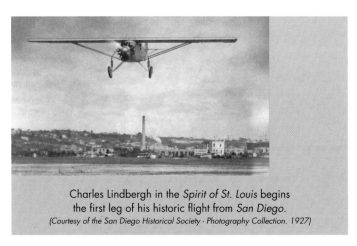

Charles Lindbergh in the Spirit of St. Louis begins the first leg of his historic flight from San Diego.
(Courtesy of the San Diego Historical Society - Photography Collection. 1927)

192   F I E L D S   O F   F L Y I N G

AIRPORT, LINDBERGH FIELD

Development, the U.S. Navy, the U.S. Army Corps of Engineers, and the Works Progress Administration) yielded more construction material. By the outbreak of World War II, Lindbergh Field had grown to 450 acres.

In 1942, the U.S. Army Air Corps took control of the field, adding facilities and relocating and extending runways to suit

New pedestrian and transportation plaza.

New terminal 2 consolidated baggage claim area.

larger aircraft, such as heavy bombers. Only one of these runways is still in use: the main east-west runway, which was extended to its current size of 9,400 ft by 200 ft in 1972.

A dramatic increase in passenger air travel during the 1960s prompted a $6 million reconstruction project to be started in November 1965. On March 5, 1967, at the opening of the updated airport terminal on its current Harbor Drive site, President Ronald Reagan (then governor of California) delivered a speech that underscored just how far Lindbergh Field had come.

By 1977, however, this airport was moving further ahead. In readiness for a new generation of wide-bodied commercial aircraft, an additional terminal was constructed — the West Terminal — which opened to the public in 1979.

SETTING NEW STANDARDS

These days, the Board of Port Commissioners can take pride in the fact that it is helping to set new standards among major California airports. Lindbergh Field was among the first to adopt a comprehensive, state-approved noise monitoring system. Now, over 90 percent of commercial jets landing here are the quieter Stage III-type aircraft, while a nighttime flight restriction balances the need for limited noise with the necessity for convenient air transportation services.

A $165 million airport upgrade and renovation project was launched in 1992. There's now a convenient automated parking system, and fast and secure baggage conveyors. Comfortable new seating is complemented by brighter surroundings and easier-to-read signage. There's plenty of retail space, too, and an up-to-the-minute business center with greeting kiosks for conventions and meeting groups. By the time this airport's ongoing multi-million-dollar upgrade is completed at the end of 1997, even more

New Terminal 2 addition facade.

improvements will be evident.

Thanks to an initiative taken by the Port in November, 1995, eight new passenger gates and 280,000 square feet of additional space are currently under construction around the existing West Terminal. Major improvements to the roadway system are also under way. Dedicated access routes and pedestrian overpasses will ensure a smooth traffic-flow in and out of the airport.

Certainly, Lindbergh Field has enjoyed a rich history. And now its focus is firmly set on a golden future — one from which every visitor flying into San Diego stands to benefit.

This gateway to America's Finest City has never offered a warmer welcome!

SAN JOSE INTERNATIONAL AIRPORT

In 1939, two independent events occurred in California's Santa Clara County which would be the genesis of a world-changing transformation.

Hewlett-Packard Company began manufacturing electronic devices in David Packard's Palo Alto garage. Twenty miles south, through countless fruit orchards and vegetable fields, a young businessman and aviation enthusiast, Ernest Renzel, Jr., coordinated the purchase of 483 acres for the future site of San Jose Municipal Airport.

In the next fifty-six years, the tapestry of orchards and fields blanketing Santa Clara Valley would surrender to the headquarters of the world's leading high technology companies. The "Valley of the Heart's Delight" would become "Silicon Valley," yielding such world-changing wonders as the microprocessor, the personal computer, the video game and the birth control pill. And the land optioned by Ernie Renzel would become the site of San Jose International Airport, the "Gateway to Silicon Valley."

San Jose Municipal Airport administration building in 1948. Test pilot James Nissen (seated far right) helped build SJC's first runway and became its first Airport Manager.

Progress, however, does not often come without a fight. For every visionary with an eye toward the future, there seems to be at least one vocal detractor rooted in the past. Those opposed to the airport disdained, "Why get a great big piece of property like this for an airport? It's like building a four-story garage for one automobile."

For the next two years, local opposition and bureaucratic roadblocks frustrated the airport's progress. On December 7, 1941, the attack on Pearl Harbor brought it to a grinding halt, as construction of all civilian airports was suspended. Still, behind the scenes, Renzel and his allies continued to lobby the Civil Aeronautics Authority (CAA) to approve the original site for San Jose Municipal Airport.

Slick Airway's C-46 was under contract in 1947 to transport California cherries. Initially, fresh produce was SJC's primary cargo. Today the region manufactures 75% of the world's electronics.

Following the war, James Nissen, former Naval aviator and research test pilot for NACA (now NASA) Ames Research at nearby Moffet Field heard, "San Jose was working on getting an airport together." Nissen and a few friends, "Came down to see what we could do."

On November 13, 1945, Nissen and his partners secured a one-year lease for sixteen of the original 483 acres. Deploying every tractor and disc he could borrow, Nissen battled fierce rains, hard-pack adobe and the stench of rotting cauliflower to finally complete a dirt runway, less than 3,000 feet long. Humble as it may have been, San Jose had an airport. And although it was a private venture, the fact that it was located on the proposed Municipal Airport site bolstered the hopes of Renzel and those who shared his vision.

On June 21, 1948, nine years after the original parcel was purchased, San Jose Municipal Airport received CAA approval and its federal airport grant. Later, it was learned, the CAA chief engineer was fired for approving the San Jose site. Nonetheless, a permanent runway was built and James Nissen was hired as Airport Manager. Despite opposition warnings that the airport would become a "municipal white elephant," it was soon running in the black. Never mind that the primary source of income was a pear orchard. This was no doubt a harbinger of the entrepreneurial spirit that would become the hallmark of San Jose and the Silicon Valley.

In the next three decades, Santa Clara County was the fastest growing county in the state. As the region's economic focus turned from agriculture to aeronautics and electronics, San Jose Municipal Airport continued to expand, accommodating and encouraging the boom.

By 1964 a new terminal was built, but was already straining to satisfy its tenants' demands for gates. Still, the airport had its detractors who claimed, "nothing will ever fly out of here except puddle jumpers." The first transcontinental flight rose from the San Jose runway in 1969, and in 1984, the airport was renamed, San Jose International Airport, to reflect its status as a center of global trade. That same year, a $100 million future expansion plan was approved.

In 1996, San Jose International Airport is the fourth busiest airport in California, serving the travel and cargo needs of one of the nation's most dynamic regional economies. Fifteen hundred of the world's 2,500 largest electronics firms are located within thirty miles. Fourteen commercial airlines depart and arrive over 400 times a day from two terminals. Passenger counts now top 9 million per year and cargo revenues exceed $273 million.

Always an innovative and responsive business partner, San Jose International is renowned for its entrepreneurial philosophy toward its tenants, as well as its Silicon Valley business community. In fact, one recent event drew the attention of the entire industry, as airport officials managed to turn a potentially disastrous situation into a boon for three airlines, local travelers and the airport itself.

A major airline was downsizing its hub operation at San Jose International, but still needed to connect travelers to its profitable long-haul flights out of Los Angeles. In an experimental, yet elegant symbiosis, two regional carriers were swiftly moved in to provide connecting service. The airline's problem was solved, two additional carriers entered the

market, and local travelers are enjoying new, low-fare service throughout the west. Furthermore, air traffic is no longer dominated by one carrier and airport consumer-generated revenues are up.

Many airports have lost hub operations, but few have experienced an astonishing 19 percent increase in passengers the following year. This has truly been a win-win-win situation for the airlines, the flying public and San Jose International Airport.

Recently, San Jose International extended its runway to 10,200 feet for flights to the far east, and gained official status as a Port of Entry in 1995. What's more, the FAA has built a state-of-the-art control tower on-site. The next phase of expansion includes a third terminal to accommodate the 14 million passengers expected by the year 2000.

San Jose International is a completely self-supporting public enterprise requiring no taxpayer assistance. Each year it generates 71,249 jobs in the San Jose area, nearly $4 billion in business revenue, $928 million in personal income, and $475 million in local and state taxes. These contributions are direct, and will continue nonstop, as San Jose International Airport meets the on-going travel and cargo needs of Silicon Valley.

San Jose International Airport is a far cry from the "municipal white elephant" the doomsayers had predicted not so long ago. Today it is the hub of a global economic force; The Gateway to Silicon Valley; the accelerator of change, challenge and creativity; a leader in commercial aviation.

SCOTTSDALE AIRPORT

Scottsdale Airport began in 1942 as Thunderbird Field II, a basic training facility for World War II Army Air Corps pilots. Two years, three months and 24 days later it was deactivated.

While in operation, Thunderbird II underwent a transformation that took it from a small piece of isolated desert to a primary training school. This transformation is largely attributed to visionary Air Force officers such as General H.H. Arnold and Lieutenant General B.K. Yount, and the civilian contract school operated by Hayward and Connelly and supervised by Army Air Force personnel, who played a key role in creating a program that would help build the world's most powerful aerial striking force.

Since its inception in June 22, 1942, Thunderbird II graduated more than 5,500 students, a total of three times greater than the entire total contemplated by the Air Forces' original expansion program. In addition, Thunderbird II flew nearly 26.5 million miles— more than 3,000 times around the world at the equator.

One of three Southwest Airways' training schools in the Valley, Thunderbird II's first class of cadets, arriving before the field was pronounced ready for occupancy, had to be trained at Thunderbird I in Glendale. Not until July 22, could all personnel, consisting of little more than 28 flight instructors, move to the Thunderbird II location in Scottsdale.

Thunderbird II, 1942 Scottsdale Airport, Scottsdale Arizona.

Throughout WWII, Thunderbird II devoted its every facility to the training of more and more cadets. As war clouds thickened over Europe, the quota of men to be trained increased with virtually every class. In November 1943, the peak was reached: 615 cadets who flew an average of two hours a day, making 1,845 separate take-offs and landings. In a period of ten weeks, students received a total of 65 hours of flight training and 109 hours of ground school. In spite of the intensified training, the field gained a widespread reputation for thoroughness of instruction and high calibre graduates.

An increase in the number of students brought about a similar gain in the number of persons employed, until in January, 1944, Thunderbird II's payroll boasted 508 employees, with a total monthly salary expenditure of $115,246.87.

Gradually the tempo slowed. World War II came to a close. The civilian contractors did so well in completing their initial assignment, that by August 4, 1944, only 40 of the original 64 primary schools were still in operation. At the closing of Thunderbird II, only 15 remained open to complete the task of primary training. Thunderbird II's mission was accomplished—a great Air Force was built in far less time than anyone ever dreamed possible.

After the war, Arizona State Teachers College (now Arizona State University in Tempe, Arizona) acquired the airport in order to implement its own aviation program. Distance from the college campus and the cost of operating an aviation program soon convinced the college to abandon its plans.

The Arizona Conference of Seventh Day Adventists purchased the Airport in 1953 and established Thunderbird Academy. Former barracks became dormitories. Hangars were adapted to house a wood products industry and a vocational education center offered training in mechanics, woodworking and welding. The airfield itself became a training field for missionary pilots.

In 1963, in order to finance renovation of its physical facilities, the Academy commissioned the first combined-use design of a clean industrial park surrounding an airport.

The City of Scottsdale acquired the airfield portion of the Academy's property in 1967 and has continued to own and operate it since that time. The first fixed base operator was selected in April 1967 and the first business jets landed at Scottsdale Airport in

August 1967. The first Airpark tenant, Casa Precision, broke ground for its first building unit in August 1968. By December 1969, 127 aircraft and 20 helicopters were based at Scottsdale Airport (SDL).

Today, there are over 400 aircraft based at Scottsdale Airport, from single engine recreational planes to large business jets. Approximately 200,000 takeoffs and landings occur each year, making Scottsdale one of the top five busiest single-runway airports in the country, and the busiest corporate jet facility in the State.

Scottsdale Airpark, the 2,000-acre industrial area which surrounds the airport, has become a national model for airport-based business parks. This model has been achieved through the efforts of numerous City of Scottsdale civic and community leaders. Several important factors have contributed to the success of the Scottsdale Airport/Airpark—it is the headquarters for over 25 national/regional corporations; home to more than 1,200 small to medium-sized businesses; workplace of more that 13,400 employees, and has easy airport access and seven miles of taxiway access. The workforce within its boundaries has tripled on the past decade, making it the second largest employment center in a community of 165,430.

One of the most significant aspects of Scottsdale Airport is the major economic stimulus that it provides to the City of Scottsdale and the north Valley region. A recent study indicates that the airport generates more than $91 million annually in revenue to the region's economy and the combined annual impact of the airport/airpark is approximately $1 billion.

The City of Scottsdale is known throughout the country as a community where quality of life and economic progress are synonymous. As Scottsdale Airport develops into one of the major markets of the Southwest, Scottsdale Airport plays a key role in linking the Scottsdale economy to the Southeast and the nation.

The outstanding facilities of the airport and the amenities of the Scottsdale area have attracted a large number of businesses that desire to locate on or near the airport. These same facilities and amenities draw general aviation and corporate business travelers from all over the country to visit Scottsdale for business and recreational purposes.

Scottsdale Airport

ZAMPERINI FIELD

A steady westerly sea breeze coupled with protection from coastal fog and swirling air currents led to the placement of the Lomita Flight Strip in an ideal location to train P-38 fighter pilots during World War II. Today the field is a dynamic part of the All-American City of Torrance, a balanced community of industrial, commercial and residential components. Renamed Zamperini Field, the Torrance Municipal Airport in the heart of the bustling Los Angeles South Bay, is poised to support the 21st–century growth of business, industry and commerce throughout Southern California.

Zamperini Field evolved from a rich heritage of aeronautical and agricultural tradition. From June 1942 through April 1944, five squadrons of P-38 Lockheed Lightning fighters were based there, each with 40 officers, 200 enlisted men and 25 aircraft as they fine tuned their combat skills prior to deployment to bases in England.

By mid-1944 with its training mission completed, Lomita Flight Strip was turned over to the Sixth Ferry Command at Long Beach. Field activity quickly grew to 2,500-3,500 movements per month as ferry pilots checked out in every type of warbird prior to delivery throughout the world.

Film actor Wallace Beery based his Waco YKS-7 cabin biplane there during the war. Brigadier General Robin Olds, famed ace of WW II, Korea and Vietnam and later Air Force Academy Commandant of Cadets began his career here as a fledgling P-38 pilot. Colonel Hubert Zemke, leader of the "Wolfpack" 56th Fighter Group, also led the 479th Fighter Group that trained at the Lomita Flight Strip. Colonel Art Jeffrey, a leading ace of the 8th Air Force with 14 aerial kills, led "C" flight of the 434th Fighter Squadron from Lomita. Record-setting Olympian Captain Louis Zamperini, a bombardier and Torrance native, returned from the dead after WW II to have the field named in his honor. TWA Captain Bob Herendeen

housed his Pitts Special here while he was the World and National Aerobatic Champion from 1965 through 1971.

Ironically, in late 1945, 1,000 Japanese-Americans returning from internment camps found temporary lodging at the Lomita Flight Strip–600 billeted in empty barracks and 400 in special trailers as they began rebuilding their lives and families.

By late 1946, upon recommendation of the CAA, the field was

GENERAL AVIATION CENTER

ROBINSON HELICOPTERS

DECEMBER 1945

DECEMBER 1995

deeded to the City of Torrance despite heavy private demand for its 490 prime acres. A Master Plan released in 1948 envisioned a second parallel runway and a bevy of commercial shops and aeronautical services to support the burgeoning prosperity of postwar Torrance. A new control tower sprang up in 1961, the second runway, taxiways, lights and other improvements were completed by 1963, and annual aircraft movements reached 430,000 by 1974.

Today the airport is home for several contemporary shopping centers, dozens of retail and manufacturing businesses, eight FBO's, a modern General Aviation facility next to the 5-story FAA control tower and accommodations for 530 aircraft in modern T-hangars and flightline tie-downs. Airport resources are producing a healthy $2 million annually for the City of Torrance.

As airport prosperity grew with the surrounding community, the City kept pace by establishing firm yet fair regulations, attracting national attention as it grappled with pioneering noise standards. In effect for almost 20 years, noise violations now comprise less than one half of one percent of today's 190,000 annual movements.

A 10,000-square-foot General Aviation facility completed in 1992 houses a pilots' lounge, flight planning facilities, meeting rooms, the noise abatement center and administrative offices. Annual Air Fairs, popular from 1958 through 1972, were resumed in 1992 and recently attracted 12,000 visitors to this popular October event. A new Air

Park is currently in design that will add an aviation museum, restaurant, outdoor picnic areas and additional maintenance and FBO shops to the flightline.

In 1994 Robinson Helicopters, the nation's leading manufacturer of civil helicopters, chose to locate its 260,000-square-foot manufacturing facility on Zamperini Field. To date, over 2,600 two-place R22s have been delivered in 40 countries in basic, law enforcement, marine and IFR trainer configurations. The R22 holds every world record in its weight class including speed, altitude and distance. Moreover, 250 new four-place R44s have been delivered in 20 countries and will soon surpass the R22 in popularity with 400 employees currently producing four aircraft per week.

As the 21st century approaches, the future of Zamperini Field never looked brighter. A phalanx of FBO's, many on the field for over 30 years, stand ready to meet every need of the aviation community with pilot training and supplies at all license levels, air taxi and charter services in both fixed and rotary-wing aircraft, banner towing and aerial photography services and an abundance of sales, fuel, maintenance and warbird restoration shops. Close by are top quality hotels, restaurants and office space, and the field has the positive support and encouragement of the City.

CAMARILLO AIRPORT

The genesis of Camarillo Airport can be traced to 1942 when the California State Highway Department constructed an auxiliary landing field with a 5,000 ft. runway. In the 1951 response to the emerging cold war, and the potential need for bolstered coastal air defense, the Army Corps of Engineers extended the runway to 8,000 ft. Additional construction on the then-named Oxnard Air Force Base neared completion in 1957 and the base was equipped with the Northrop F-89 "Scorpion" aircraft, as part of the Los Angeles area Air Defense Command. By 1958 the new Air Force base boasted four alert hangars, concrete ramps and a 9,000 ft. Runway, complete with an ILS, VOR and safety overruns. It was an entire community with administration buildings, enlisted housing, recreational facilities, a theater and even a gas station. In 1960, the supersonic Mc - Donnell F-101 B "Voodoo" interceptor aircraft, equipped with "Genie" tactical nuclear missiles, arrived on the Oxnard plain, serving there for almost a decade.

For nearly eighteen years dedicated Air Force personnel provided air defense protection for the Southern California area. In December 1969 the Department of Defense deactivated Oxnard Air Force base and transferred its aircraft and personnel to other facilities. The land became surplus property.

The County of Ventura pursued acquisition of the airfield portion of the facility for air carrier service and general aviation while other governmental and educational organizations were attracted to the 60 buildings. For seven years the battle for the surplus property continued, with opposition the heaviest from the neighboring city of Camarillo. City representatives strongly objected to any kind of airport replacing the now abandoned Air Force base. Finally, an agreement was reached which provided for an airport limited to general aviation and a 6,000-ft. runway.

In October 1976 the General Services Agency approved the county's application for 650 acres of land, including some buildings. Other agencies expressed an interest in the remaining

Camarillo airport tie downs and hangars
(view east from control tower).

100 acres. The property was conveyed to the county by quitclaim deed which outlined specific use restrictions. With the ownership defined, the County of Ventura assigned management of the airport to the county Property Administration Agency. In 1985 airport management was successful in separating the two county-owned airports from the Property Administration, thus creating the County of Ventura Department of Airports.

Camarillo Airport has progressed from a sleepy, tower-less facility to a bustling reliever airport with an FAA air traffic control tower and annual operations numbering 190,000. Today the airport boasts a diverse collection of over 560 production, home built and WWII aircraft, with active chapters of the Experimental Aircraft Association and the Confederate Air Force. With increasing congestion in the Los Angeles basin, pilots and aircraft owners find Camarillo's location, size and weather to be significant factors in using the airport.

The draw of recreational and corporate aircraft paints an encouraging picture for the future of Camarillo Airport. At this writing, the Department of Airports is conducting a master plan study to determine upcoming operational and/or design requirements. As the region grows, Camarillo Airport will be ready to play its role in serving the needs of general aviation in Ventura County.

EAST KERN AIRPORT DISTRICT

MOJAVE AIRPORT - CIVILIAN FLIGHT TEST CENTER

Located in the high desert of the Antelope Valley of California, just 20 miles northwest of Edwards AFB, the premier flight test center in the world, lies a small town that caters to travelers from far and wide. At the cross roads of state routes 58 and 14, Mojave is a bustling little town, dotted by gas stations, fast food restaurants and inexpensive but clean motels, ready to provide the weary traveler with a square meal and some much needed rest. But before any motorist can even begin to make out the distant outline of this desert community, something unusual appears on the horizon no matter from which direction one travels. By day, tall tail sections of Boeing 747's first peak above the horizon as if to greet the unsuspecting wayfarer with one more mirage. By night fall, the sweeping white and blue-green alternating light from the airport beacon emanates from a seeming infinite distance that only the wide open expanses of the desert can produce. Its steady on-again, off-again colors seem surreal against the light of the moon.

But Mojave Airport or East Kern Airport District, as the airport is official known, is no mirage or the product of too many miles and tired eyes. Instead, the airport, also referred to as the Civilian Flight Test Center, is a close facsimile to its military neighbor to the southeast. From classified research in aeronautical science, to flight testing prototype aircraft, Mojave Airport did not acquire the name Civilian Flight Test Center by accident. It is also home to the National Test Pilot School, the only civilian program of its kind in the world. In fact many of the instructors at NTPS are former instructors from the test pilot school at Edwards AFB. The two facilities share the skies above as much as possible and flight testing is rarely interrupted due to poor weather conditions.

The arid climate also provides another benefit and one which sets it apart from Edwards AFB; aircraft storage. Mojave airport specializes in long term storage of new and older aircraft. The aircraft are "pickled" or preserved, using special solutions which prevent corrosion and still allow the engines to be cycled regularly in order to maintain "mission readiness". It is not uncommon to see brand new aircraft already delivered to airlines patiently waiting to be put into service. Other aircraft pickled for future use still sport familiar logos of airlines long gone by.

A desert air strip developed in the 1930s, it was converted to a Marine Corps Air Station during WWII and remained a military facility until 1964. The County of Kern operated the airport from 1964 until 1972 when farmer turned airport manager Dan Sabovich, converted the facility into an airport district with the aid of former Congressman Barry M. Goldwater, Jr., whom he had befriended. Through the ingenuity of Dan Sabovich, and low ground rates coupled to a proviso which required the purchase of fuel at the going rate, Mojave Airport slowly grew into the facility it is today. Passed retirement age, Dan Sabovich continues to run the airport and with the aid of friends, recently established a new bank in town, the Mojave Bank, in order to assist the 2,000 some employees at the airport with their purchases of homes and cars when the local name brand bank would not. Dan Sabovich and Mojave Airport are a lesson in perseverance.

THE FRESNO AIR TERMINAL

The FRESNO AIR TERMINAL (FAT) is owned and operated by the City of Fresno. The Airport is located approximately 7.5 miles northeast of downtown Fresno. Commercial airline service began at FAT in 1946 after service was moved from Chandler Downtown Municipal Airport (FCH). During the 1950's and early 60's, FAT continued many military and corporate functions. In 1953, North American had a major F-86 assembly plant at FAT that employed more than 3,500 people and had a payroll of $12 million annually.

The original terminal on the north side of the Airport was built as part of Hammer Army Airfield in the 1940's. Construction of the current terminal building on the south side of the Airport was completed in 1962. In 1993 a $6.5 million major renovation project was completed. Future terminal plans include a $35 million expansion which will add jetways, additional gate space, and international facilities by the year 2000.

The Airport has two primary runways; 11L-29R is 9,222 feet in length and 150 feet in width equipped with a CAT I ILS and center line lighting system, 11R-29L is 7,206 feet in length and 100 feet in width, for use by smaller, lower-performance aircraft and commuter aircraft. The Airport has a 24-hour Federal Aviation Administration air traffic control tower with approach and surveillance radar.

FAT is currently the largest commercial service airport serving the Central San Joaquin Valley. This six county region has a population of 1.5 million people and Fresno County is the world's most productive agricultural County with more than $3 billion in products each year. More than a million passengers, O&D, use the Fresno Air Terminal every year. Through the 70's and into the deregulated decade of the 80's, FAT, like most airports, experienced tremendous growth in airline jet services. In the 1990's, as the second generation of deregulation occurred and the airline industry adjusted, Fresno like many second tier communities experienced dramatic turnover in their air service providers. From 1982 through 1995, FAT had more than 28 airlines come in and out of the airport. In 1996, twelve airlines offer fares from FAT and the potential for international travel remains a high prospect and goal for the Airport.

The Airport is also home to a large number of general aviation and government aviation installations. At present, there are over 250 corporate and privately owned aircraft based at the airport. There are three Fixed Base Operators and numerous subtenants, who offer a wide range of services. Both the U.S. Forest Service and the California Department of Forestry operate an Air Attack tanker base at the Airport for fighting forest fires. The California Highway patrol has a flight facility for helicopter and fixed wing operations.

The Airport is home to three military aviation activities. The largest of these is the California Air National Guard which maintains Headquarters for the 144th Fighter Wing and five subsidiary air defense command units which operate F-16 aircraft. The California Army National Guard maintains an Aviation Classification Repair Activity Depot (AVCRAD) at the Airport. The AVCRAD's mission is to perform high level repair and overhaul of Army aircraft. The U.S. Marine Corps Reserve maintains an air defense activity on the field.

1946-1962

1962- PRESENT

HNTB CORPORATION

AN EXPANSIVE PAST, AN EXCITING FUTURE

The story of HNTB Corporation is the story of a once-small bridge design firm determined to keep pace with the growth and development of the United States throughout the 20th century -- and into the 21st.

Now, more than 80 years after its founding, HNTB ranks among the top design firms in the nation and offers clients a multidisciplinary range of services in the practice areas of architecture, engineering and planning.

Aviation experience gained in runway and related airfield design work during World War II led HNTB into the field of commercial aviation engineering. Nearly a decade later, HNTB began a general consulting relationship with Miami International Airport that would span more than four decades. From that original foundation, the firm's aviation practice has grown through significant expansion and diversification of services.

Serving airports, airlines and related aviation clients for the past 50 years, HNTB calls upon its nationwide network of more than 35 local design offices to deliver innovative solutions that are tailored to each client's unique needs.

The firm's aviation professionals are active in the southwestern United States and throughout the western half of the nation. HNTB aviation practices in Los Angeles, Irvine, Oakland, San Bernardino, Calif., Las Vegas and Phoenix offices are joined by a strong corps of aviation architects and engineers in the firm's Seattle-area office. HNTB's aviation professionals have led major planning and design assignments at international airports in Phoenix, Los Angeles, Sacramento, San Jose and Oakland, Calif., Salt Lake City, Portland, Ore., and Seattle-Tacoma, as well as at regional, reliever and general aviation airports through the Southwest and West.

In the mid-1980s, HNTB provided fast-track design and construction administration services for reconstruction of Runway 24L at Los Angeles International, as well as for multiple connecting taxiways and related facilities. Since that time, HNTB has handled numerous airfield engineering assignments at LAX. At Phoenix Sky Harbor, HNTB updated the airport's master plan in the late 1980s. And at Salt Lake City International, the new 12,000-foot runway that opened in late 1995 was led by HNTB's program management, design and construction management professionals.

In its 50-plus year of airport planning and design, HNTB has handled more than 2,500 airport projects. In the United States alone, it's estimated that four of every five domestic airline passengers board an airplane at an airport for which HNTB has provided professional services.

The staff of 200-plus aviation specialists includes airport architects, engineers, planners and construction inspectors, as well as airport traffic control specialists, aviation economists, aircraft noise analysts and air carrier service analysts. HNTB's list of comprehensive services encompasses airfield engineering, aviation architecture, planning, construction management, access system and parking facility design and a range of high-technology specialty services.

As the nation's Southwest continues to enjoy -- and be challenged by -- steady growth in population, industry and tourism, its commercial airports will be challenged to keep pace with increasing air traffic demand. HNTB, with a proven record of quality service and on-time, on-budget delivery, will continue to partner with airport operators to develop the next generation of airside, landside and passenger terminal facilities.

Viewing each airport passenger terminal as a gateway to the community it serves, HNTB designs terminals for operating efficiency and user convenience.

HNTB designs runways, taxiways and other airfield facilities that enhance capacity, while minimizing impacts on ongoing airport operations.

KENNEDY/JENKS CONSULTANTS
SERVING AIRPORTS AND THE AVIATION INDUSTRY FOR OVER 45 YEARS

Kennedy/Jenks Consultants has provided engineering and consulting services to airports and the aviation industry for over 45 years. The firm's airport work has ranged from small general aviation facilities to military air bases and large commercial airfields in the western United States and in the Pacific Basin.

Kennedy/Jenks' airport projects have included the renovation or expansion of existing airport facilities and systems and construction of new facilities. The firm has provided both design and construction management services for runways and taxiways, water supply and wastewater treatment facilities, site utilities, aviation safety studies, hazardous waste treatment and management, and remedial investigations.

A PIONEERING ENVIRONMENTAL FIRM

One of the oldest, continuously operating consulting firms on the west coast, Kennedy/Jenks was founded in 1919 by Clyde C. Kennedy in San Francisco. Kennedy went on to design many of California's and Nevada's first water and sewerage systems. Early clients included Eureka, Santa Rosa, Sunnyvale, Richmond, and San Francisco in California; Reno and Sparks, Nevada; and Phoenix, Arizona.

4th Air Carrier Runway-McCarran International Airport, Las Vegas, Nevada

Co-founder Harry N. Jenks worked with Kennedy in the mid-1920s, left to become a professor of sanitary engineering, then returned to open his own engineering office in 1933. In his lifetime, Harry Jenks invented and patented several new processes in water

and wastewater engineering. Jenks designed the first wastewater treatment facilities for many California cities such as San Mateo, San Leandro, and Palo Alto.

Both offices became established independently before merging in 1980 to become Kennedy/Jenks Engineers (later Kennedy/Jenks Consultants). Today, the firm is employee-owned, but the Kennedy/Jenks presence is still strong. The firm is headed by a third-generation Kennedy, David D. Kennedy, Grandson of Clyde. Harry Jenks' son, John Jenks, served as Senior Vice President until 1992 and remains involved with the company.

EXTENSIVE AVIATION EXPERIENCE

From World War II to the end of the "Cold War" in the late 1980s, the firm was active in providing engineering services to the U.S. Military, both within the continental United States and in the Pacific Basin. Kennedy/Jenks has completed many aviation projects at military facilities in the western states, including the Alameda Naval Air Station (NAS) Beale Air Force Base (AFB), McClellan AFB, Moffett Field NAS, San Diego NAS, Travis AFB, and Vandenberg AFB in California, and Fallon NAS in Nevada. Projects in the Pacific Basin included Anderson AFB in Guam, Clark Air Base in the Philippines, Kadena Air Base in Okinawa, Japan, Wake Island Air Station, and Barbers Point NAS, Hickam AFB, Marine Corps Air Station, and Wheeler AFB in Hawaii.

Today, the major share of the firm's aviation projects involve the development of commercial airport and aviation facilities throughout the west. Recent designs and construction management projects have included runways, taxiways, and apron projects at Reno Tahoe Airport, John Wayne Airport and the Chino Airport. A major new runway facility was also designed for the Las Vegas McCarran Airport. This airport is one of the worlds top 15 busiest airports and the new runway and taxiway system designed by Kennedy/Jenks will accommodate current and anticipated air traffic into the next century. Other recent projects have included deicing fluid treatments, flood control, surface drainage, access roads, utilities, hangars, and maintenance facilities. Kennedy/Jenks is currently relocating the utilities at San Francisco International Airport in anticipation of the new international terminal building.

LANDRUM & BROWN

As the Southwest Chapter of the American Association of Airport Executives celebrates its Golden Anniversary, Landrum & Brown is preparing to celebrate its 50th, as well. Formed in 1949 by Charles O. (Charlie) Landrum and John Brown, our firm was one of a select group which helped to define the commercial aviation industry for years to follow.

Landrum & Brown was created as a consequence of a landmark decision in the late 1940s. Immediately after World War II, the major airlines were faced with a critical question, "Who would own/operate the nation's large air carrier airports?" The answer, as we all know now, was that local governments would typically provide airport facilities and private industry would provide airline service. Charlie Landrum and John Brown not only helped to shape that answer, but went on to define a service that is a cornerstone of today's airport industry—airport management consulting.

Nearly a half century later, Landrum & Brown has grown to a firm having more than 100 full- and part-time employees. In recent years, we have provided development and management consulting services to 42 of the top 50 U.S. Air carrier airports, to several major foreign airports, and to many smaller air carrier and general aviation reliever airports. In the process, we have assisted airport clients during the transition from propeller to jet aircraft, from narrow-body to wide-body aircraft, from a regulated to a deregulated airline industry, and into the age of environmental protection.

Landrum & Brown has been committed to the development of sophisticated, state-of-the-art analytical capabilities and to the creation of staff expertise necessary to address airport development issues that are complex, controversial, and time critical. The firm offers four broad areas of advisory services to our clients:

- Master Planning
- Terminal Planning
- Environmental Planning
- Financial Management

The core of Landrum & Brown's traditional business is master planning—the planning and implementation of airport facility development programs and the identification of operational improvements to expand capacity. The ongoing master planning program for Los Angeles International Airport epitomizes this type of service. At LAX, Landrum & Brown is functioning as the Technical Integrator of a multi-discipline team charged with undertaking a complete rethinking of how LAX will function in the future, from its runway system to its ground access system. A similar program conducted by Landrum & Brown in the 1980s resulted in the redevelopment of the world's busiest air carrier airport, Chicago's O'Hare International. Other airport whose present-day forms were molded by Landrum & Brown's facilities planners include Pittsburgh, Detroit, Miami, Cincinnati, Phoenix, Nashville, St. Louis and new Denver.

Landrum & Brown knows that the issues which airports will face over the next 50 years are no more predictable now than they were at our firm's beginning. Whatever the challenges—privatization, alternative funding, changes in airline route structures, or totally new issues—Landrum & Brown is dedicated to providing excellence of service to the aviation industry.

Serving the Southwestern United States and the Pacific Rim from its Los Angeles office, Landrum & Brown also maintains full-service offices in Chicago and Cincinnati.

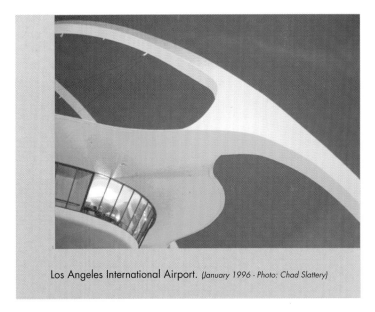

Los Angeles International Airport. *(January 1996 - Photo: Chad Slattery)*

Los Angeles International Airport. *(January 1996 - Photo: Chad Slattery)*

MINTER FIELD

Minter Field has enjoyed a colorful and busy past. Since the Army Air Corps commissioned the field in 1940, Minter Field has been the home to aviators and aviation enthusiasts such as Bill "Tiger" Destefani, Eddie Van Fossen, Robert Converse, all of air racing fame. Over the years Minter Field has served as a back drop for TV commercials, a test site for acoustics trials in the FAA certification process for several different aircraft, participated in the design and testing of a Space Shuttle crew escape device, and even the fog played an important role in testing a radar that could pick out the runway in zero visibility. The Gossamer Condor that set an endurance record for man-powered flight completed an extensive testing program at Minter. It is also the home of the Minter Field Air Museum.

The field was completed in August of 1941, and named Lerdo at first. But on February 7, 1942, the Army Air Corps commissioned the field as Minter Field, in honor of a flying officer, Lt. Hugh C. Minter, a local man that was killed in a mid-air crash on July 8, 1932. Minter Field as a Primary Flight Training Facility, graduated more than 11,200 cadets in four years. Minter Field served as the Jet Propulsion training headquarters for the P-59 Comet, and on April 13, 1945, the last Primary class graduated and the new bombing school opened. In June 1945, Minter Field was used as a flight training facility by the Chinese Air Cadets. Minter Field was deactivated in December 1946.

The County of Kern gained possession of Minter in 1947. It became officially known as Kern County Airport No. 14. During 1950 and 51, 110 Indonesian pilots received flight training at Minter Field. Most of Indonesia's highest ranking officers were trained at Minter Field. In 1984, a group of tenants and interested citizens joined together and petitioned the County to allow the formation of a Special District to govern the airport. In November 1984 the Minter Field Airport District was born.

Through almost six decades beginning in 1941, Minter Field has survived and served as a continual leader in the community, contributing to the economic growth and welfare of the local area as well as Kern County. Minter Field will celebrate its 55th birthday this spring and continues to provide a quality airport for the general aviation flying public. Most of the old buildings are gone, the runways have been realigned and repaved, new lighting systems and fancy electronic gates installed, but the feeling is still there. You can almost hear the growl of the old BT-13 Vibrator's as another flight of cadets take to the air over the town of Shafter.

MONTEREY

Monterey's aviation history began in 1910, when British flyer James Radley staged exhibition flights over the site of today's airfield in his Bleriot plane.

The 1920's saw the inauguration of commercial flights by Maddux Airlines. Local interest in aviation was whetted by performances of the Gates Flying Circus, which made a promotional stop in Monterey.

In 1932, in order to promote business for the luxurious new Del Monte Hotel, entrepreneur Samuel Morse leased 37 acres to the city for an airport. This land, deeded to the city in 1937, was the nucleus of today's 600-acre airport.

Condor Airlines initiated service from Monterey in 1936, with two daily round trips to Alameda. Travelers on this route could ask to be dropped off at any airport along the way!

The runways and first hangar were constructed by the WPA and dedicated in 1937. In the same year, veteran flyers Fred Kane and Alton Walker, who had earlier visited Monterey on a barnstorming tour, signed a lease with the city to operate Monterey Peninsula Airways.

Monterey was designated as an airmail stop in the United Airlines system in 1938, and United began passenger and airmail service with two daily flights, to San Francisco and Los Angeles, in a 10-passenger B247.

In 1941, legislation was enacted to authorize the formation of a public airport district that would qualify for federal funds. Since then, the Monterey Airport has been operated by the Monterey Peninsula Airport District, governed by a publicly elected Board of Directors.

During World War II the Navy leased the Airport for a dollar a year as a support and training center for its Pacific Fleet units. The Civil Aviation Agency funded runway expansion, and Navy funds were spent to construct barracks, hangars and a tower, some of which are still in existence.

After the war, Fred Kane, former operator of Monterey Peninsula Airways, returned from military service to become the airport's first manager. He was the only employee; the daily traffic level was 100 passengers. Civilian flights were resumed by United Airlines, with added service by Southwest Airlines in 1947.

Over the years airport facilities have expanded to keep pace with federal requirements and passenger traffic. A new control tower was constructed in 1962, the terminal building was enlarged in 1973, and in 1986 the main runway was extended to 7,600 feet.

The peak year for airline passengers was 1978, when almost 638,000 passengers passed through the airport. This was also the year in which federal deregulation of airlines took place. Since then, scheduled air service at Monterey has experienced considerable adjustment as competition among airlines has given rise to a new cost-awareness.

In 1979 the District was removed from the Monterey County tax rolls and became self-supporting. Since that time the Airport has operated solely on revenues derived from user fees and tenant leases.

In the 1980's, noise control and community compatibility emerged as airport priorities. Expanded programs for security and emergency preparedness have been implemented in the 1990's. Marketing is the most recent focus, with the aim of supporting the local tourism economy and improving air service.

Around the clock runway construction during World War II.

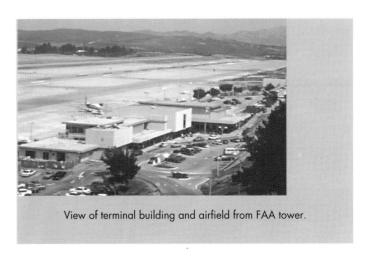

View of terminal building and airfield from FAA tower.

OXNARD AIRPORT

Commuter airlines on ramp at Oxnard airport.

The Oxnard airport was opened in 1934 by the County of Ventura, and consisted of a 3,500-foot dirt runway. The first fixed base operator on the field was Joe Plosser. He owned only two aircraft, but had no housing for them. During the thirties Howard Hughes erected a tent on the airport to shelter his H-1 racer, which he tested from the Oxnard field.

The County of Ventura paved the runway in 1938, and a large hangar (#2) was built by the Works Progress Administration. In 1939 James "Elmo" McLean opened the Oxnard Flying School with two aircraft, a 40hp J-3 Cub and a Kinner two-seater. The U.S. Army Air Corps moved its civilian training program onto the airport in 1940 to establish a primary training base called Mira Loma Flight Academy. Housing was built across the street for the cadets and instructors.

In December 1941 war was declared; all civilian flying was curtailed within 200 miles of the coastline. As a result, Oxnard Flying School moved to Boulder City, Nevada. The Army Air Corps operated the airport until 1944 when it was reassigned to the Navy until the Naval Air Station at Point Mugu could be completed. The Navy moved to NAS Point Mugu in 1945 and Oxnard Flying School returned to the airport, occupying hangar two. The County of Ventura officially took back control of the airport from the federal government in 1948 by receiving a final quitclaim deed. The state of California issued the airport an operating permit in 1949.

The first scheduled airline flights began in 1946 by Southwest Airlines, and later Pacific Airlines, flying Douglas DC-3's to Los Angeles and San Francisco. Pacific Airlines, operating Fokker F-27's, was replaced by Airwest Airlines in 1967 and was later purchased by the Hughes Corporation, becoming Hughes Airwest. The current terminal building opened in 1971 and has been served by commuter airlines such as Cable, Golden West, Wings West and other small short-lived air carriers.

The Federal Aviation Administration built and staffed the air traffic control tower in 1960, and in 1963 Oxnard's single Runway 7-25 was extended from 4,750 feet to its present length of 5,950 feet. Between 1974 and 1976 the runway was upgraded with an ILS and approach lighting, and in July 1992 it was completely rebuilt.

Today, American Eagle and United Express airlines connect over 40,000 passengers annually to Los Angeles International Airport and destinations beyond. With the terminal fully occupied, tenants providing air/ground transportation services, and a new restaurant having been recently opened, the future of Oxnard airport looks bright. On the general aviation side, a new $2 million corporate hangar and office complex is being designed to replace hangar one, lost to a fire in October 1994. This will be the first of several new large hangars slated for future customers of this facility, which has been a Ventura County asset for over 65 years.

SANTA MARIA PUBLIC AIRPORT

The Santa Maria Public Airport is located on the Central Coast of California at the northernmost part of Santa Barbara County. Situated in the Santa Maria Valley, the Airport serves the cities of Santa Maria, Guadalupe, Los Alamos, Casmalia and other surrounding communities.

In the early 1940s, during World War II, the U.S. Army Corps of Engineers constructed what was then known as Santa Maria Army Airfield. In May 1942, the Fourth Air Force began using the field as a training facility for crews of B-25 aircraft. A few years later the B-25 groups left and the facility became a training field for P-38 pilots and ground crews.

In 1946, following the war's end, the County of Santa Barbara acquired the property by means of an interim permit issued by the War Assets Administration. The County retained control of the facility

The Santa Maria Public Airport encompasses approximately 2,600 acres including two active runways for airline, corporate & general aviation use.

Santa Maria Public Airport offers a modern and convenient airline terminal.

until 1949, at which time the City of Santa Maria obtained an undivided one-half interest. This dual ownership/management proved cumbersome to administer. So, in March of 1964 transfer of the Airport to the newly formed Santa Maria Public Airport District, which encompassed an approximate area of 400 square miles, was accomplished.

As prescribed by law, the District was formed by voter approval. The legislation which covered this action was in the form of the California Airport District Act. The District is governed by a five-member Board of Directors who serve four-year terms and are elected at large. The directors entrust the General Manager with the responsibility for the efficient execution of airport policies.

Since the formation of the District, numerous projects have been accomplished including design and construction of Skyway Drive

from Betteravia Road to the Orcutt Expressway; design and construction of the planned industrial park east of Skyway Drive; and construction of the new airport terminal building, Aircraft Rescue and Firefighting station, air traffic control tower, and other facilities adjacent to the primary runway.

Currently, Santa Maria Public Airport is a Certificated FAR Part 139 facility that encompasses approximately 2,600 acres, including two active runways. The Airport provides facilities for three regional airlines enplaning approximately 60,000 passengers annually with service to Los Angeles and Las Vegas. The Airport also serves as home base for over 150 general aviation aircraft.

The future looks bright for the Santa Maria Public Airport District in 1996 and beyond. The Airport District recently completed a Strategic Business Plan and Marketing Plan to promote aviation- and non-aviation-related business. The Marketing Plan revealed that, with jet service, Santa Maria would be the most convenient jet airport for over 420,000 people. In addition, the City of Santa Maria recently approved the Santa Maria Research Park Specific Plan. The Specific Plan utilizes approximately 1,100 acres and will combine light industrial, research, manufacturing, and commercial type land uses around a 27-hole championship-level golf course. A major portion of the project area will also be used for Airport operations and services and a small area of the site is set aside for public uses.

The Santa Maria Public Airport has full community support and is prepared to meet the current and future air transportation needs of the airport service area.

SANTA MONICA AIRPORT

The Santa Monica Airport is the oldest continuously operating airport in Los Angeles County. It was established in 1919, when the city leased a portion of a barley field for aviation use. At that time, the aviation industry was in its infancy. The first users of the field were primarily pilots who learned to fly during World War I. Many of the private pilots who used the field were associated with the motion picture industry.

The Douglas Aircraft Company moved to Santa Monica in 1922 to build military aircraft. In 1924, aircraft manufactured by Douglas were flown on the first "round the world" flight. This event attracted some 50,000 spectators to Clover Field, bringing public attention to the aviation industry and to the airport. In addition to building military aircraft, the Douglas Company developed the "DC" series of civilian airplanes. Designed in 1934, the DC-3 was the first successful mass-produced practical air carrier; it represented a significant technological advance, and was successfully used for both military and commercial applications.

As the United States' entry into the World War became imminent, the Federal Government leased the entire airfield from the City. The current runway was constructed and improved with air traffic control facilities and hangars. The Douglas Company expanded and began an all-out manufacturing effort. At its peak, the Douglas Company employed 44,000 people. As a result of its intense manufacturing activity, Douglas was largely responsible for a significant increase in the demand for housing in the area.

After the end of World War II, the Army returned the Airport to the City. In the late 1940's and early 1950's, as general aviation was still in its formative stages, SMO became a base for significant general aviation activity. In the late 1950's, Douglas shifted its manufacturing emphasis from propeller to jet aircraft. As SMO could not accommodate large jets on its 5,000 foot runway, the center of Douglas' aircraft manufacturing shifted to Long Beach.

During the early and mid sixties, SMO rivaled Van Nuys Airport as the busiest general aviation airport in the nation, reaching a peak of 374,000 operations in 1966. Noise from aircraft using SMO, tolerated previously because of the important role Douglas played in the local economy, grew both in volume and as a source of community annoyance. Through the later sixties and all of the seventies, noise became the prevailing issue for the City, several law suits were filed to determine if the City was liable for damages caused by airport noise and to what extent the City could mitigate airport noise.

In 1982, the United States Department of Justice informed the City Attorney that it intended to file suit against the City for violation of federal law and contracts in the operation of the airport. The city responded that it is obligated to continue operating the airport due to various binding commitments with the United States. Following a series of negotiation meetings between the City and the FAA, the City agreed to plan in good faith for the operation of SMO consistent with the City's legal obligation and environmental goals. With that, in 1983 the City Council authorized preparation to update the Airport Master Plan and a related Noise Study.

In 1983, SMO made numerous improvements to the airport and moved much of the aviation activity from the southside to the northside of the field where a business park was developed buffering many of the homes from noise. Private investment in the northside aviation facilities totalled over $20 million during 1983 - 1990.

Since 1990 over $6 million in federal and local monies have been dedicated to noise and safety improvements for the Santa Monica Airport including: runway overlay, washrack facilities, blast walls, fencing and gates, perimeter road realignment, lighting and signing, paving infield areas, refurbishing rotating beacon, and seal coating and marking existing taxiways and parking aprons.

The Santa Monica Airport offers two full service FBO's, a speciality hangar dedicated for specific maintenance needs, flight schools, three first class restaurants, a pilot supply shop, charter service, conference and meeting facilities, observation decks, world-class museum and airport tours all against a background of airport activity that includes vintage, corporate and recreational aircraft.

The Santa Monica Airport remains one of the busiest single runway airports in the United States with over 208,000 operations in 1994. The proximity of the Santa Monica Airport to the heart of the entertainment industry, Century City, excellent medical facilities, LA's financial district, premier shopping in Beverly Hills and beautiful beaches makes it an attractive airport for both corporate jet operators as well as the general aviation enthusiast.

SHUTT MOEN ASSOCIATES

Founded in 1976 as Hodges & Shutt, *Shutt Moen Associates* is now entering its 20th year of dedicated service to the West Coast airport community. A multi-discipline consulting firm, Shutt Moen Associates offers unsurpassed expertise in the highly specialized fields of airport planning, engineering, and management.

Shutt Moen Associates is a professional corporation registered in the state of California and owned by Michael A. Shutt, P.E. and Lee B. Moen, P.E. The firm's office is located in Santa Rosa, California — adjacent to the Sonoma County Airport.

Our firm's client base reflects the complete spectrum of publicly owned and operated airports — from large metropolitan air carrier airports to small general aviation facilities. Our professional capabilities include the planning and engineering of airports, heliports, hangars, fixed base operator facilities, and aviation fuel storage/dispensing systems. The development of land use compatibility plans for airports is a major element of our airport planning practice. In addition, we provide a wide range of management and operationally oriented consulting services to airport owners and operators.

and commitment is unsurpassed in the industry. Our clients benefit significantly from the continuity and level of teamwork that this stability allows.

Over the past 20 years, *Shutt Moen Associates'* primary corporate focus has remained the same: *providing superior service to our clients.* We are committed to providing the highest quality product, on-time and within budget. One important reason that we have been able to continue to provide this quality service is our aggressive use of integrated computer technologies. With a computer on every desk, we can take a project from planning, through design, to construction with each phase building upon the previous one. As a result, we have a very high percentage of longtime clients — clients who have repeatedly turned to *Shutt Moen Associates* over the years for their airport consulting needs.

At *Shutt Moen Associates*, we are looking forward with great enthusiasm and optimism to the opportunities and challenges of the 21st Century. Please let us know how we can be of service to you and your community's airport.

Our firm's greatest resource is its staff of 20 full-time employees. Through our staff, we offer the synergistic advantage of experienced airport planners, engineers and managers working side by side to produce realistic, readily implementable plans and designs. In addition, our staff reflects an exceptional level of tenure and stability. Five of our key project managers have been with the firm for more than 10 years; four staff members have more than 18 years of service with the firm. We believe that this record of employee tenure

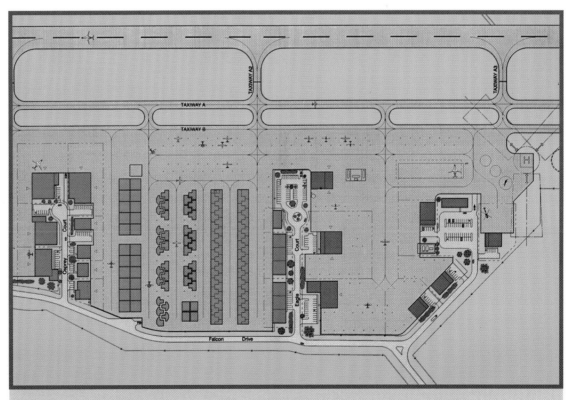

AutoCAD drawings can satisfy engineering needs to support public presentations.

YUBA COUNTY AIRPORT

When World War II was over, Dick Brandt came home to the Yuba-Sutter Area following his military service to find a big airport out in Arboga. The airport had a huge hangar — an ideal place for Brandt to work on airplanes.

Originally built in 1943 by the U.S. Government, the field was used by the Army Air Corps as a grounds air support base. After the war was over, it reverted back to the City of Marysville and the County of Yuba, the entities which jointly owned the land.

Marysville's Mayor, representing the City Council, together with the Yuba County Board of Supervisors, were in charge of the airport. Unfortunately, there was a constant conflict between the two agencies over what was to be done with the airport and who was to pay for it. It was during that time that Brandt confided in and befriended W. T. Ellis, Jr., the chairman of the Board of Supervisors.

Yuba County finally became the sole owner of the airport with Brandt as its manager. It was pretty run-down and needed a lot of maintenance, but the hangar was the jewel that held Brandt's interest. Brandt fixed it up as best he could, and he also helped the airport and the county acquire surplus tractors and other large equipment from the War Assets Administration.

Unfortunately, the huge hangar that attracted Dick Brandt to the airport in the beginning was destroyed by fire on Feb. 23, 1951. With that hangar went a lot of Yuba County history — legendary aviator Jimmy Doolittle's squadron of B-25 bombers trained at the Yuba County Airport for their historical raid on Japan during World War II.

During this time, Dick Brandt was in partnership with his brother, Roger. They, together with Sherman Perkins, became what is known as "Fixed Base Operators" and provided aircraft maintenance and pilot training services for the area. They also converted surplus military trainers into planes which could be used for crop-dusting and spraying.

Eventually the partnership was dissolved and Dick Brandt continued supervising the airport's operations on his own. He and his family lived at what was then called the Alicia Airport (it was later renamed the Yuba County Airport) from 1946 until July 1, 1957. Brandt resigned in 1957 to explore his other interests, but to this date, he continues to have an interest in aviation.

The Yuba County Airport was licensed as an approved airport by the State of California on September 30, 1949. Today Yuba County Airport is a modern aeronautical facility with capabilities to accommodate jet air carriers and freight carriers. It is a well-planned and carefully engineered airport which encompasses 1,000-plus acres — 265 acres of which are designated for fully improved, industrial sites with direct access to modern, sophisticated airport facilities. The airport consists of a 6,006-foot primary runway and a 3,261-foot crosswind runway.

The airport is situated approximately 3 miles south of the city of Marysville; 1.5 miles west of State Highway 70 and 99; and 10 miles from Beale Air Force Base. Yuba County is strategically located in the north central part of California, 125 miles northeast of San Francisco and 125 miles west of Reno, Nevada.

Yuba County Airport offers eight industrial parks encompassing 1,000-plus acres.

Yuba County Airport consists of two runways — a 6,006-foot primary and a 3,261 crosswind.

YUMA INTERNATIONAL AIRPORT

Sprawled under vast uncluttered skies along the lower reaches of the Colorado River, Yuma, Arizona has long been a prime transportation hub. In the last century, tended by the paddlewheeler, the stagecoach and the railcar, the crossing place along the Colorado known as "Yuma Crossing" provided an important gateway to the great westward movement of the American frontier.

Today's gateway, serving a later frontier, is Yuma International Airport (YUM). It offers convenient and uncongested access to the large markets and production areas of the American Pacific Southwest—and beyond—from the world over. Access to Mexico and California via road and rail make YUM an ideal point of entry for international trade.

As Arizona's fourth most active commercial airport, YUM's passenger traffic and air cargo are growing steadily as they provide services to a fast growing population in the region. Over 60 million people live within a one-day delivery service area. Expeditious arrivals and departures are guaranteed since the dry desert climate is ideal for aircraft and cargo operations.

In addition to exemplary environmental factors, Yuma International Airport offers ideal accommodations for all aircraft types and size, including the Boeing 747-400F. In fact, at one time Yuma International Airport was designated as an alternate landing site for the U.S. Space shuttle.

Yuma International Airport is a public commercial airport and a joint use military field. It is operated by the independent Yuma County Airport Authority (YCAA) and the Marine Corps Air Station Yuma. The YCAA is expanding airport capabilities with local investments and grants from the Federal Aviation Administration and the Arizona Department of Transportation. With an integrated Foreign Trade Zone and the development of agricultural air exports, Yuma International Airport is contributing to the regional economic development effort.

"The Yuma County Airport Authority has kept Yuma International Airport on the leading edge of economic development in Southwestern Arizona for the past three decades. Their mandate to their staff to strive for professionalism and excellence in every endeavor and their encouragement to participate in and support AAAE, ACI and other professional groups has fueled the enthusiasm of every member of our staff," says Edwin M. Thurmond, CAE, AAE.

Yuma International Airport is serving the growing demand for air services in the region and is ready to become a part of the worldwide network in the global market place.

The appendix to this book contains the condensed proceedings of the association from the first meetings in 1947, to the latest in 1995. It contains the names of the officers, the various resolutions adopted by the board and the membership, as well as summaries of the issues of the day. The appendix serves as a living document and it is this component of the book that the association has sought to publish every five years. The student of history may find these proceedings helpful in sorting out what may have been important to the association and its membership at the time. The appendix also lists the individuals who have distinguished themselves over the years, including the various awards given by the association every year.

Organizational meeting of CAAE/SWAAE June 27,1947. L to R: G. Abrogast, 1st Vice President; D. Smith, President; C. Meadows, Secretary/Treasurer; F. Bishop, 2nd Vice President *(Courtesy Kern County Department of Airports.)*

California Association of Airport Executives, First Meeting on June 27,1947
(Left to Right front Row:) Woodruff De Silva, Clarence Shy, Leland Apperson, Gordon McKenney, Ed Moore, Bill Nichols, Cecil Meadows
(Left to Right Back Row:) J.B. Douglas, Fred Kane, W.C. Tanner, Marvin Sturgen, Glenn Arbogast,
Max Black, Mary Nelson, L.C. McGillivray, Frank Bishop, Homer Cruize

1948
OFFICERS

President	Donald Smith
1st Vice President	Glen Arbogast
2nd Vice President	Edward Nichols
3rd Vice President	Frank Bishop
Secretary-Treasurer	Cecil C. Meadows

Meeting Sites

Formation Meeting - Stockton Airport, Stockton, 5/5/1947 General Meeting - Kern County Airport, Bakersfield, 6/27/1947 General Meeting and Short Course - Hancock Field, U.S.C., College of Aeronautics, Santa Maria, 8/18-21/1947 Statewide Meeting (closed to all except bonafide airport managers) - Hilton Hotel, Long Beach, 11/14-15/1947 Sectional Meetings - Southern California, Central Valley, Coastal, 1/9-10/1948 General Meeting - Ambassador Hotel, Los Angeles, 4/13/1948 Annual Meeting - Hollywood Roosevelt Hotel, Hollywood, 6/16 18/1948

Major Issues of the Year

CAAE Business and Policies
Charter membership closed June 30, 1948 with thirty-nine charter members.

Aviation Industry Issues
Governor signed into law AB 2684. This Bill created a five-man Commission and a California State Director of Aeronautics. Many airports took advantage of Public Law #289, allowing transfer of maintenance equipment from the War Assets Administration to public airports without cost, excepting freight and handling.

Resolutions
1-48   Petitioned the Aviation Commission of the State of California to submit for passage by the State Legislature proper enabling laws to allow local political subdivisions of the State to adopt enforceable height limit and zoning ordinances to protect Municipal or County Airports.

2-48   Requested the California Aeronautics Commission to conduct a survey of the potential revenue at public airports from additional hangar rentals and to recommended suitable financing Programs in which subdivisions may participate.

3-48   Petitioned the Air Policy Conference to go on record as favoring the continuance of the G.I. Flight Training (Federal Law #346) as long as veterans in sufficient numbers participated.

4-48   Resolved that the CAAE properly air mark their individual airports and that every assistance be given to the Civil Aeronautics Administration, the California Aeronautics Commission, any and all Chambers of Commerce, clubs and organizations to plan, foster, and complete such air marking.

5-48   Petitioned the Congress of the United States to immediately inaugurate a national defense program which would provide young men of school age flight training.

6-48   Petitioned the California Aeronautics Commission to formulate a plan and with every means at its command, instigate a program to construct a landing strip at every city, town, hamlet and recreational area in California.

3-48   Petitioned the Air Policy Conference to go on record as favoring the continuance of the G.I. Flight Training (Federal Law #346) as long as veterans in sufficient numbers participated.

1949
OFFICERS AND
BOARD OF DIRECTORS

President	Cecil C. Meadows
1st Vice President	Woodruff DeSilva
2nd Vice President	Larry Cookman
3rd Vice President	Richard Harding
Secretary-Treasurer	Marvin Sturgen

Directors
Gordon McKenney	Frank Bishop
Wilmer Garrett	Ted Hannah
Edward Nichols	Donald Smith
Vernon Tyler	

Meeting Sites

General Meeting - Hotel California, Fresno, 12/2-3/1948 Annual Meeting - Palace Hotel, San Francisco, 6/23-25/1949

Major Issues of the Year

CAAE Business and Policies
Committees   Legislative-Frank Bishop
Survey-Vern Tyler

This was the first year of annual survey.

Aviation Industry Issues
California Aeronautics Commission adopted State Approval and Permit Regulations for airports. This was opposed by the CAAE and considered the first major defeat of the association.

Resolutions
7-48 Petitioned the California Aeronautics Commission to conduct an air marketing program.

8-48 Requested legal authority for cities and counties to control the heights of buildings and structures in the vicinity of airports.

9-48 Supported the adoption of a state-wide master plan of airports.

10-48 Opposed airport regulations and permit requirements.

Stand on Bills
Favored: AB432 Dealt with liens for airport services, use of landing aids, facilities and the like.

AB1275 Dealt with unclaimed gas tax refunds and directing these funds for use in support of aviation within state.

1950
OFFICERS AND
BOARD OF DIRECTORS

President	Woodruff DeSilva
1st Vice President	Richard Harding
2nd Vice President	Leland Appearson
3rd Vice President	Vernon Tyler
Secretary/Treasurer	Marvin Sturgen

Directors
Cecil Meadows	Frank Bishop
Glenn Denney	William Nichols
James Nissen	Joe Rust
Donald Smith	

Meeting Sites

Board of Directors Meeting - Santa Barbara, 10/10/1949 (To recommend an appointee to the California Aeronautics Commission, Art Schilder was selected. General Meeting - Santa Barbara Airport, 12/8-9/1949 (All western AAAE members and State officials from throughout the west were invited for the purpose of coordination of matters of mutual interest.) Annual Meeting - Hotel U.S. Grant, San Diego, 6/8-9/1950

Major Issues of the year

CAAE Business and Policies

Committees   Legislative-Frank Bishop
               Survey-Vernon Tyler

The CAAE was incorporated June 1, 1950

The Constitution and By-Laws were changed to allow private airport owners and their representatives to become members or associate members of CAAE.

Aviation Industry Issues

Resolutions

1-49   Petitioned the Secretary of Commerce of the U.S. to request funds and reimburse local government agencies for the actual cost of heat, light, and janitor service; for free space on public airports occupied by the CAA and Weather Bureau, and for the rental of any space occupied by such agencies above essential minimums.

2-49   Petitioned the CAA to more clearly define minimum space requirements for the CAA and the Weather Bureau to be provided by municipalities operating a1reports acquired by the Surplus Property Act.

3-49   Requested that the CAA recognize the inadequacies of the present Federal Airway Radio Aids System and to procure monies necessary to augment the present system to reduce instrument approach and take-off delays and to provide aids required for present day traffic control.

4-49   Requested the Secretary of Defense to consider furnishing financial aid for the maintenance of needy surplus airports.

5-49   Petitioned the Honorable Governor of Utah to reconsider his recent removal of the State Director of Aeronautics of Utah.

1951
OFFICERS AND
BOARD OF DIRECTORS

President	Richard Harding
1st Vice President	Marvin Sturgen
2nd Vice President	Vernon Tyler
3rd Vice President	George Deibert
Secretary/Treasurer	Wilmer Garrett

Directors

Woodruff DeSilva	Glenn Arbogast
C.O. Brandt	Glenn Denney
George M. Dixon	Fred J. Kane
Noble Newsom Jr.	Joe Rust

Board of Directors Meeting - Santa Barbara, 10/6/1950 General Meeting - Hotel Oaks, Chico, 12/7-9/1950 Board of Directors Meeting - Bakersfield Inn, 3/9/1951 Annual Meeting - Bakersfield Inn, 6/7-9/1951

Major Issues of the Year

CAAE Business and Policies

Committees   Resolution-William Nichols
               Time and Place-Wilmer Garrett
               Legislative-Don Smlth

Aviation Industry Issues

At this time, due to the war emergency, the CAA was participating (financially) only in projects which had a definite connection with the military

Stand on Bills

Favored:Assembly Bill 1883, continued the refunding of unclaimed aviation gas taxes to the cities and counties for an extended length of time. This Bill was passed. Assembly Bill 2833, provided that an unspecified amount of money be granted to the Regents of the University of California for the establishment of a School of Aviation at the College of Agriculture, Davis, California. Opposed: Assembly Bill 654, continued the refunding of unclaimed aviation gas taxes to the cities and counties for ninety days. Assembly Bill 733, provided that none of the unclaimed aviation gas taxes would be returned to the cities and counties but rather placed in a California Aeronautics fund to be spent by the legislature upon the recommendation of the California Aeronautics Commission. This was opposed on the basis that the California Aeronautics Commission was meant to be an advisory body and that it was trying to gain more control than appropriate.

Assembly Bills 734 and 735, required registration of aircraft with the exception of air carrier and military aircraft and a license fee tax, in lieu of personal property taxation, amounting to two percent of the depreciated list price with the exception of air carrier and military aircraft. AB733, AB734, and AB735 were held in the Legislative Committee on Municipal and County Government indefinitely.

Assembly Bill 2641, made specific the responsibility of the State Aeronautics Commission to supervise and coordinate plans and programs for the utilization of civil aircraft in civil defense.

Assembly Bill 2841, provided for regulation of intrastate air carriers by the Public Utilities Commission.

1952
OFFICERS AND
BOARD OF DIRECTORS

President	Vernon Tyler
1st Vice President	General William Fox
2nd Vice President	Wilmer Garrett
3rd Vice President	Harry Sham
Secretary/Treasurer	W. H. Levings

Directors

Glen Arbogast	C. O. Brandt
Donald Smith	Noble Newsom
Joseph Rust	Clarence Shy
Gordon Stanton	

Meeting Sites

Board of Directors Meeting - 8/10/1951 Board of Directors Meeting 9/14/1951 General Meeting - Club Del Mar, Santa Monica, 12/5-7/1951 Annual Meeting - Hotel Stockton, Stockton, 6/4-6/1952

Major Issues of the Year

CAAE BUSINESS AND POLICIES

Committees   Survey-Glenn Arbogast
               By-Laws-Glenn Arbogast
               Legislative-Donald Smith

The By-Laws were changed to require the election of officers at the annual meeting nearest the first day of each fiscal year and that those so elected would immediately assume office. Changes also called for the President to appoint the Chairman and one member to the Nominating Committee with the other three members being elected by the membership. This was instead of the Directors comprising the Nominating Committee which meant none of them were ever nominated for office.

Aviation Industry Issues

1-52 Commended Vernon Tyler for a job well done and wished him a speedy recovery and stated that his absence was appreciably felt during the Winter 1952 Meeting.

2-52 Requested the League of California Cities to appoint an Aviation Advisory Committee to work with said organization on all matters pertaining to aviation within the State of California.

3-52 Recommended that necessary legislation be enacted to permit airport owners to dedicate their runways and taxiways to counties and or municipalities.

4-52 Extended an invitation to the AAAE to hold its 1953 Convention in Los Angeles.

5-52 Urged the Administrator of the Civil Aeronautics Administration to advise the manufacturers that they must build aircraft which can operate from existing airports, or from airports constructed within the limits of TSO-N6a. This was in response to certain manufacturers of aircraft who spoke glibly of the necessity of extending runway lengths from 12,000 to 15,000 feet to enable the then new jet aircraft to operate safely.

6-52 Recommended that legislation be sought through the Congress of the United States to relieve the communities of the burdensome restrictions of the Surplus Property Act of 1944, allowing the United States Government to take control or possession of various civil airports, so that the network of civil airports of the United States can best continue to serve their highest and best use in the national public interest.

7-52 Adopted certain procedures as recommendations to airport managers to follow pending adoption by the United States Congress of remedial legislation pertaining to military use of civil airports.

8-5 Commended Delos W. Rentzel for his contributions to the aviation industry and expressed appreciation for his recognition of and assistance to airport managers.

9-52 Presented Cecil C. Meadows a plaque in commemoration of his efforts in the aviation field and granted him the first honorary life membership in the CAAE.

10-52 Commended Joseph K. Hicks for the sincere and conscientious manner in which he has performed his duties as Airport Management Consultant and the assistance he has rendered to member airports of the CAAE.

11-52 Opposed an amendment to the Constitution of the State of California which would have added Section 31.5 to Article IV, prohibiting appropriation or expenditure of public money to the California State Chamber of Commerce, any local chamber of commerce, County Supervisor Association, or any other private organization.

12-52 Commended Clarence Shy and Miss Grace Diveley for their work on the 1952 Annual Meeting in Stockton.

13-52 Urged the President and the Congress of the United States to take immediate steps toward the re-establishment of the Civil Aeronautics Board as separate and independent agencies, as provided in the Civil Aeronautics Act of 1938.

14-52 Contested the contemplated ruling of the Wage and Hour Administrator that stated that Whitman Air Park, California was engaged in interstate commerce and must bring the employees of said airport within the minimum wage and maximum hour provisions of the Fair Labor Standards Act of 1938.

15-52 Petitioned the California Aeronautics Commission, with the assistance of the League of California Cities, and the Supervisors Association of California, to devise and submit legislation to be presented to the State of California Legislature calling for airport approach protection allowing helpful local zoning ordinances.

16-52 Urged Congress to enact legislation to place in the Administrator of Civil Aeronautics responsibility and authority for the planning, development and construction of a system of airports adequate for joint use to serve both military and civilian requirements

17-52 Urged the Congress of the United States of America to increase appropriations for civil airports under the Federal Airport Act as authorized by the Congress, and that the level of appropriations necessary to match available funds by municipalities be immediately made available in order to meet the increased needs of civil airports and necessary bases for the military defense of the United States.

18-52 Urged the Congress of the United States to approve S2815, which would amend the Federal Airport Act to permit continued reimbursement to municipalities for damage inflicted on civil airports by military use.

19-52 Urged the Civil Aeronaut board to remove any doubt that the airspace above the airport referenced imaginary surfaces, prescribed in TSO-N18 (April 26, 1950) is navigable air space within the meaning of the Civil Aeronautics Act of 1938.

20-52 Requested that all government agencies concerned with construction near airports to take such action as may be necessary or appropriate to assure the complete coordination between various government agencies and the Air Coordinating Committee, and furthermore to assure that in each case the airport concerned be informed of any proposed Federal construction which may contribute a hazard prior to the time such construction is commenced.

21-52 Urged that all Federal Agencies be required to coordinate their use of the air spac of the United States through proper procedures already available and that proper consideration be given to civil needs.

1953
OFFICERS AND
BOARD OF DIRECTORS

President	Glenn Arbogast
1st Vice President	Wilmer Garrett
2nd Vice President	Joseph Rust
3rd Vice President	Fred Kane
Secretary/Treasurer	Noble Newsom

Directors	
William Nichols	Gordon Stanton
C. O. Brandt	William Levings
H. W. Livermore	Clarence Shy
Donald Smith	Vernon Tyler

Meeting Sites

General Meeting - Riverside, 11/5-7/1952
Annual Meeting - Claremont Hotel, Berkeley, 5/19-20/1953

Major Issues of the Year

CAAE BUSINESS AND POLICIES
Committees   Survey-Clarence Shy
              Convention-Don Martin

Aviation Industry Issues

Resolutions

22-52 Supported elimination or the recapture rights by the Federal Government as applied to airport facilities from Public Law 289.

23-52 Recommended that all or a portion of the gasoline tax on aviation fuels (excluding military aircraft, manufactured air craft, scheduled and non-scheduled airline carriers with Civil Aeronautics Board certificates, and aircraft owned by any politi cal subdivision of the state) be retained by the State Comptrol ler and established as an aeronautics fund to be annually appropriated by the Legislature to the California Aeronautics Commission for the acquisition and development of airports.

24-52 Resolved that adequate legislation should be enacted to allow the Motor Vehicle Department of the State of California to register aircraft at a cost figure of registration and annually assess them on a formula basis comparable to the method of taxing automobiles. These monies would be distributed back to the counties and cities of origination on the basis of the number of aircraft, and such funds would be earmarked and channeled for aviation purposes. This was to eliminate the use of different formulas by different counties.

25-52 Requested that a means be found for providing some funds for the preservation of airports. This was in response to the high rate at which airports were disappearing in the State of California.

26-52 Urged the Governor and the State Legislature of California to retain the California Aeronautics Commission as an independent agency within the state structure of government.

27-52 Proposed a new formula for the distribution of unclaimed aviation gasoline tax refunds and outlined specific uses for such funds.

1954
OFFICERS AND
BOARD OF DIRECTORS

President	William Nichols
1st Vice President	Joseph Rust
2nd Vice President	Clarence Shy
3rd Vice President	Walter Fell
Secretary/Treasurer	James Nissen

Directors
Woodruff DeSilva	Wilmer Garrett
Glenn Arbogast	Fred Kane
James Long	Donald Martin
Donald Smith	Gordon Stanton

Meeting Sites

General Meeting - Apple Valley, 11/5/1953 Annual Meeting - Fresno, 5/6/1954

Major Issues of the Year

CAAE Business and Policies

Committees   Election-James Brians
              By-Laws-Walter Fell
              Resolutions-Wilmer Garrett
              Convention-Noble Newsom

Time and Place-Donald Smith
Survey-Wilmer Garrett

The By-Laws were changed to provide that any and all persons in an industry allied with aviation be included and acceptable as corporate members of the CAAE providing they pay the required fee of $100.00 per year per member for such corporate membership. Changes also allowed that any and all persons elective or appointive that have political and legal jurisdiction over the operation of a public airport be allowed membership under the category of Associate Members without the power to vote.

Aviation Industry Issues

Resolution

1-53 Urged the Department of Commerce of the United States to include in the National Budget for the fiscal year 1954-1955 sufficient funds to assure that airports to be used during any future national emergency be provided with Federal monies to match monies provided by the local political subdivisions to maintain and improve said airports as need dictated. Also urged the Department to make a comprehensive survey of the future uses of civil airports for military purposes in case of a dire national emergency, and that a comprehensive assistance program be initiated to assure that said airports are maintained in such a manner to allow future military use with minimum cost and disruption of civil operations.

2-53 Requested that the Legislature initiate legislation to preclude the payment of taxes by incorporated cities to counties on land owned and used for aviation purposes and that such legislation include the exclusion of privately owned facilities providing that the California Aeronautics Commission has surveyed and found that the operation of said private facilities is in the interest of the public at large and should be exempt.

3-53 Authorized changes in the By-Laws to provide for Corporate Membership for industry and Associate Membership for elected of ficials.

4-53 Commended William Barrls and Noble Newsom for their out standing efforts in providing an orderly agenda and a most suc cessful meeting at Apple Valley.

5-53 Requested the California Congressional Delegation in Congress to demand from the Civil Aeronautics Board a ruling granting additional air services to and throughout the Great State of California.

6-53 Urged the Governor of California to fill the fifth posi tion on the California Aeronautics Commission with a man who will represent the Airports' interest in aviation matters.

7-53 Requested that the Civil Aeronautics Administration con tinue the operation of control towers and landing aids with Civil Aeronautics Administration Funds.

1-54 Urged the Civil Aeronautics Board to grant certificates of convenience and necessity of a longer term during the early stages of any new development for scheduled air service to assist the carrier, airports, and the flying public.

2-54 Urged that sufficient funds be provided to re-inaugurate the TVOR Program.

3-54 Urged Congress to support a measure continuing Federal assistance to major airports.

1955
OFFICERS AND
BOARD OF DIRECTORS

President	James Nissen
1st Vice President	Walter Fell
2nd Vice President	C. O. Brandt
3rd Vice President	Leroy Gregg
Secretary/Treasurer	Fred Taplin

Directors

Woodruff DeSilva	Edward Nichols
William Forshee	Joseph Rust
Donald Martin	James Brians

Meeting Sites

Annual Meeting - Hilton Hotel, Long Beach, 5/18-20/1955

Awards

Outstanding Airport Manager Certificate - James Nissen Outstanding Service Award - Leroy "Pop" Gregg, for his work on behalf of aviation in securing a modification of the Federal Airport Program to make it more realistic in light of current needs.

Major Issues of the Year

CAAE Business and Policies

Committees   Nominations-Gordon Stanton
Membership-Edward Nichols
Resolutions-Wilmer Garrett
Time and Place-James Brians
Awards-Donald Hobbs
Civil Defense Plans-Vernon Tyler
Liaison to University of California
Transportation Division-James Nissen

Decided to have one Annual meeting instead of two to facilitate full attendance. The By-laws were, however, not changed to reflect this decision.

Aviation Industry Issues

A special committee was appointed to assist Frank Duarte of Tracy who was having problems getting Tracy airport in good operating condition due to some long term leases and other problems caused by past City governing bodies. Civil Defense Plans to keep general aviation flying during times of emergency or disaster were firmed up with the two Air Command divisions in charge of the defense of the Pacific Coast area.

Resolutions

1-55   Reaffirmed support for the abolition of the California Aeronautics Commission. allow for more specific spending levels to aid airport construction.

4-55 Opposed the adoption of Section 274 of the United States Revenue and Taxation Codes, which would prohibit aircraft manufacturers from deducting rental fees for any facilities built with general obligation or revenue bonds for tax purposes.

5-55 Opposed the plan of Secretary of Defense Charles Wilson, which provided for no future aircraft plant facilities on the Pacific Coast.

6-55 Accepted the professional membership requirements of the AAAE as an index of the professional qualifications of persons who would enter the field of Airport Management and called for wide publicity of these standards.

7-55 Urged that the Federal Airport Aid Program be returned to its original goals of advancing all phases of aviation, including general aviation and that the annual criteria changes be stopped.

8-55 Urged all concerned to study runway length problems and accelerate research and experimentation on all devices such as jato, arresting gear, barriers, reverse thrust, boundary layer control and other items.

9-55 Urged the Civil Aeronautics Administration to certify and to conduct quarterly flight checks of the aerial navigation facilities and terminal radio ~abilities installed by local s~on sors.

10-55 Supported the AAAE in appointing represent Airport Use Panel Advisory Comm1ttee.

11-55 Supported AB 3388, wnicn should provide for the establish ment of aviation criteria n California State school curriculum.

1956
OFFICERS AND
BOARD OF DIRECTORS

President	Wilmer Garrett
1st Vice President	Walter Fell
2nd Vice President	C. O. Brandt
3rd Vice President	L. B. Gregg
Secretary/Treasurer	Donald Hobbs

Directors

Woodruff DeSilva	Thomas Dardis
James Brians	Vernon Tyler
Harry Sham	Fred Kane

Meeting Sites

Board of Directors Meeting - Paso Robles Inn, Paso Robles, 12/1-2/1956, League Advisory Committee on Aviation Problems - Berkeley,12/14/1955 Special Meeting - Norton Air Force Base, 3/16/1956 Special Meeting - Hamilton Air Force Base, 4/3/1956 Committee on Security Control of Air Traffic Meeting - Norton Air Force Base, 4/20/1956 Annual Meeting - El Cortez Hotel, San Diego, 7/12-15/1956

Major Issues of the Year

CAAE Business and Policies

Committees   Nominating-Glenn Arbogast
Membership and Attendance-Woodruff DeSilva
Resolutions-Fred Kane
Budget/Audit-Donald Hobbs
Awards-James Brians
Time and Place-Vernon Tyler
Constitution and By-Laws-Woodruff DeSilva
Legislation-James Nissen
Civil Defense-Vernon Tyler
Liaison to the University of California
Transportation Division-Thomas Dardis
Representative to the Industry Advisory
Committee to the California
Aeronautics Commission-Cecil Meadows

Decided that the Secretary/Treasurer may serve a two year term and that the Secretary/Treasurer would serve from January to December instead of July to July. It was also decided that the Secretary/Treasurer would be bonded. (Although accepted, these policies were not written 1nto the By-laws until 1958.) The word "Association" was added to section III, Article IV of the By-laws.

Aviation Industry Issues

CAAE supported abolishing the California Aeronautics Commission as it was constituted at the time.

Participants at the Norton AFB and the Hamilton AFB meetings were able to tour the facilities and attend special presentations. They were also able to observe and ask questions about various Air Force aircraft.

Resolutions

1-56   Urged the California Division of Highways and the California Public Works Commission to take immediate steps to coordinate the location of freeways with the owners of nearby airports in order to guarantee the least possible interference to future development of airports.

2-56   Opposed the present method of assessing possessory interests of tenants occupying publicly owned airport property.

3-56   Endorsed legislation that would separate the Civil Aeronautics Administration from the Department of Commerce and establish it as an independent agency.

4-56   Endorsed a statement of policy released by the Airport Operators Council asking the aircraft manufacturers and carrier operators of jet transport aircraft to consider the problem of the airports in their aircraft design and proposed operational procedures.

5-56   Recommended abolishment of Chapter 1800 of the statutes of the State of California, which required Counties to advertise for bids on all leases negotiated by the Counties.

1957 OFFICERS AND BOARD OF DIRECTORS

President	Wilmer Garrett
1st Vice President	Walter Fell
2nd Vice President	C.O. Brandt
3rd Vice President	L.B. Gregg
Secretary/Treasurer	Tom Guiney

Directors

Wanda Branstetter	Joe Marriott
Jack Nystrom	Donald Hobbs
Joe Rust	Norman Coad

Meeting Sites

Board of Directors Meeting - Hotel Claremont, Berkeley, 11/14/56 Board of Directors Meeting - Bakersfield Inn, 2/12-13/1957 Annual Meeting - Hobergs Resort, Clear Lake, 7/9-11/1957

Major Issues of the Year

CAAE Business and Policies

Committees   Membership-Vernon Tyler
Resolution-Fred McElwain
Budget/Audit-C.O. Brandt
Confidential Survey-Wanda Branstetter
Program-Tom Guiney
Air Defense-Donald Hobbs
Legislative-James Nissen Aviation Industry Issues

Resolutions

1-57   Recommended that federal funds be made available the construction of storage hangers either by federal grant or by federal loan from the Small Business Administration.

2-57   Recommended that the Civil Aeronautics Administration promulgate a Technical Standard Order for the marking of runways of all civil airports to indicate to the pilot the remaining length of runway available to him.

3-57   Requested the Airport Use Panel and the Air Space Panel to adhere to the pertinent terms of reference and to assume their full responsibility, acting for their agency in the negotiation and resolution of the problems Involved toward the end that an agreement can be reached and solutions found for said problems and cases.

4-57   Requested that the Secretary of Defense remove flight training activities and such other flight activities as may be possible away from coastal congested areas.

Stand on Bills

Favored: Assembly Bill 456, which added section 107.1 to the Revenue Taxation Code, changing the existing method of assessing possessory interest.

Assembly Bill 457, which added section 1267 to the Code of Civil Procedure, relating to the measure of damages to be paid to the lessee in an eminant domain proceeding taking the leasehold or a fee estate of which the leasehold is a part.

Assembly Bill 458, which added section 107.2 to the Revenue and Taxation Code, relating to nonexclusive licenses and preferential rights to use or possession of tax exempt land, improvements or personal property exempt from taxation.

Senate Bill 366, amended section 21212 of the Public Utilities Code, requiring the California Aeronautics Commission to reimburse members for actual and necessary expenses plus $25 a day for meetings.

Senate Bill 646, added section 21240 to the Public Utilities Code, provided recognition of the fact that the Federal Government regulates and controls the use of airways and nothing in this act gives the Californla Aeronautics Commission any powers to so regulate.

Senate Bill 647, repealed Article 12 of Chapter 1 of Division 5 of the Education Code, and added Article 12 of Chapter 1 of Division 5 with the words "California Aeronautics Commission" deleted, wherever stated and the words "State Board of Education" in their place.

Opposed: Assembly Bill 2612, added section 3486 to the Civil Code, relating to damages resulting from operation of an airport.

Favored: Assembly Bill 456, which added section 107.1 to the Revenue Taxation Code, changing the existing method of assessing possessory interest.

Assembly Bill 457, which added section 1267 to the Code of Civil Procedure, relating to the measure of damages to be paid to the lessee in an eminant domain proceeding taking the leasehold or a fee estate of which the leasehold is a part.

Assembly Bill 458, which added section 107.2 to the Revenue and Taxation Code, relating to nonexclusive licenses and preferential rights to use or possession of tax exempt land, improvements or personal property exempt from taxation.

Senate Bill 366, amended section 21212 of the Public Utilities Code, requiring the California Aeronautics Commission to reimburse members for actual and necessary expenses plus $25 a day for meetings.

Senate Bill 646, added section 21240 to the Public Utilities Code, provided recognition of the fact that the Federal Government regulates and controls the use of airways and nothing in this act gives the Californla Aeronautics

Commission any powers to so regulate.

Senate Bill 647, repealed Article 12 of Chapter 1 of Division 5 of the Education Code, and added Article 12 of Chapter 1 of Division 5 with the words "California Aeronautics Commission" deleted, wherever stated and the words "State Board of Education" in their place.

Opposed: Assembly Bill 2612, added section 3486 to the Civil Code, relating to damages resulting from operation of an airport.

1958
OFFICERS AND
B0ARD OF DIRECTORS

President	Walter Fell
1st Vice President	C.O. Brandt
2nd Vice President	Harry Sham
3rd Vice President	Joe Marrlott
Secretary/Treasurer	James Brians

Directors

Wanda Brandstetter	John Caywood
Woodruff DeSilva	Wilmer Garrett
Harold Messersmith	Tom Guiney
Lew McIntosh	

Meeting Sites

Board of Directors Meeting - :Hacienda Hotel, Fresno, 11/4-6/1957 Board of Directors Meeting - Los Angeles Airport, 1/21/1958 Board of Directors Meeting - Fresno, 4/4/1958 Annual Meeting - Hacienda Hotei, Fresno, 5/4-7/1958

Awards
Airport Manager of the Year - Wilmer Garrett

Major Issues of the Year

CAAE Business and Policies

Committees	
	Nominating-James Nissen
	Membership-Tom Guiney
	Resolution-Joe Marriott
	Annual Survey-William Swain
	Budget/Audit-Robert Wanamaker
	Awards-Joe Rust
	Publicity and Education-Charles Overton
	Time and Place-Johnny Caywood
	Constitution and By-Laws-William Nichols
	Legislation-Wilmer Garrett
	Technical Information-David Zebo
	University of California Coordination-Donald Martin
	Civil Defense-Donald Hobbs
	Placement-Fred Kane
	Airspace-Joe Marrlott
	Liaison with Western Air Defense Force-Donald Hobbs
	AAAE Convention-Wilmer Garrett
	Moffett Changes-James Nissen

The By-Laws were updated to reflect decisions from 1956 allowing the Secretary to serve two terms if desired and that the term of Secretary run from January-Thru December 31.

It was decided to change the By-Laws back to allow for two general meetings each year.

It was decided that closer coordination with NBAA, ALPA, AOC, and other such organizations was lmportant and that at least one CAAE member should attend all of the meetings of these other aviation organizations.

It was decided to give a plaque to the Outstanding Manager of the Year and a gavel to the outgoing President.

Resolutions
6-58 Opposed a part time VFR Restricted Area for afterburner powered departures of high speed aircraft for training purposes at Moffett Field (sought by Navy).

7-58 Requested that the Administrator of the Civil Aeronautics Administration investigate the existing restrictions to the use of the navigable airspace because of special use assignments and reservations which are not being fully utilized. Further, to continue this study in the future.

8-58 Appreciation to the Officers and Directors of the past year.

9-58 Urged the Congress of the United States to immediately adopt and implement Senate Bill 1189, which called for increased Federal participation to seventy-five percent in the acquisition of runway "clear zones".

10-58 Urged the passage of an extension to the Federal Airport Act and a continuance of the present program of airport aid.
11-58 Appreciation and commendation to Wilmer J. Garrett.

1959
OFFICERS AND
BOARD OF DIRECTORS

President	C.O. Brandt
1st Vice President	Joseph Marriott
2nd Vice President	John Caywood
3rd Vice President	James Brians
Secretary/Treasurer	George Cote

Directors

Harold Messersmith	Walter Fell
Woodruff DeSilva	Lew McIntosh
William Partain	Fred Taplin
Tom Guiney	

Meeting Sites

Board of Directors Meeting - Santa Maria, 7/22/1958
General Meeting and Fall Airport Clinic - Arrowhead Springs
Hotel, San Bernadino, 11/5-6/1958 Board of Directors Meeting - Hacienda Hotel, Fresno, 2/4-5/1959 Annual Meeting - Casa Munras Hotel, Monterey, 5/5-7/1959

Major Issues of the Year

Committees	
	Nominating-Joseph Marriott
	Membership-Tom Dardis
	Resolution-Walter Fell
	Budget/Audit-Robert Wanamaker
	Publicity and Education-George Cote
	Awards-Wilmer Garrett
	Annual Survey-Jack Harper
	Convention Program-Fred J. Kane
	Time and Place-John Caywood
	Technical Development-David Zebo
	Constitution and By-Laws-William Nichols
	Legislation-Wilmer Garrett
	Air Traffic Control Advisory-Fred Taplin
	Air Defense Coordinator-George Cote

The first panel discussions were neld at the annual meeting.

Adopted amended By-laws and Constitution. These included previous changes that had not been officially written in prior to this time.

Tour of the 27th Air Defense 3ivision Headquarters, Norton Air Force Base, 11/5-6/1958.

Aviation industry issues

It was decided that purchase or land for clear zones, rather than lease, was the best way to conform tO CAA requirements.

It was agreed that alrline trlp insurance should be provided for Air taxi service.

A motion passed favoring the transfer of the CAA into the Federal Aviation Agency intact.

Resolutions

1-59   Resolved that the CAA circulate a draft of TSO N-13b for industry comment prior to the adoption of any changes in TSO N-13 as other TSO's have in the past. This TSO may force huge expenditures on airport owning communities.

2-59   Opposed the abolition of the California Aeronautics Commission.

3-59   Notified the Administrators of the Federal Housing Author ity, the Veteran's Administration, the Farmer's Home Administra tion and the Federal Aviation Agency that the CAAE vigorously op posed approval of projects in any area near established airports, in violation of the strictest interpretation of the loan provi sions of laws governing the operation of said agencies, and recommended close coordination between these agencies and local airport managers in the early planning stages of such proposed developments.

4-59   Requested that the Administrator of the Federal Aviation Agency take the necessary steps to provide for the issuance of entitlement cards to operators of publicly owned airports which will permit the purchasing of surplus property through properly established channels in a manner similar to that available to the Civil Defense Agency.

5-59   Endorsed the action taken and the resolution enacted by the Board of Airport Commissioners of the City of Los Angeles, to invite the AAAE to hold their annual business meeting during the month of April, 1962, in the City of Los Angeles.

6-59   Appreciation to Senator Stepnen P. Teale.

7-59   Appreciation to Fred J. Kane.

Stand on Bills

Favored: Assembly Bill 268 wnicn imposed a penalty for flying aircraft while under the influence or an intoxicating beverage.

Assembly Bill 1516, regarding financial responsibility of airports.

Assembly Joint Resolution Number 1, which requested the Secretary of Defense of the U.S. to hold public hearings prior to closing, by restricted areas, any area to the public.

1960 OFFICERS AND BOARD OF DIRECTORS

President   Joseph Marriott
1st Vice President   John Caywood

2nd Vice President   James Brians
3rd Vice President   Albert Huber
Secretary/Treasurer   George Cote

Directors
Jack Nystrom   Harry Culver
Dave Zebo   Jack Egan
Fred Kane   C.O. Brandt

Meeting Sites

Board of Directors Meeting - Bakersfield, 7/9/1959 General Meeting and Fall Airport Clinic - Hacienda Hotel, Bakersfield 11/18-19/1959 Annual Meeting - Mission Inn Hotel, Riverside 6/21-23/1960

Major Issues of the Year

CAAE Business and Policies

Committees   Nominating-James Nissen
                Membership-Jack Nystrom
                Resolution-Gordon Stanton
                Budget/Audit-Robert Wanamaker
                Publicity and Education-Fred Taplin
                Constitution and By-Laws-C.O. Brandt
                Awards-Walter Fell
                Convention-Joseph Marriott
                Annual Survey-John Caywood
                Professional Standards-Fred Taplin
                Technical Development-William Richardson
                Legislation-James Nissen
                Air Traffic Control Advisory-Fred Taplin
                Air Defense Coordinators-
                North-Thomas Flaherty
                South-Fred McElwain

Decided that not more than five membership cards be issued to Corporate members for designated representatives.

As a matter of Board Poiicy, regular members who have discontinued active management of an airport would now be permitted to continue as Associate members.

The Secretary was instructed to send newsletters to all cities, counties and airports as a matter of course.

Aviation Industry Issues

Resolutions

1-60   Appreciation for Senator A.S. Mike Monroney and Clair Engle.

2-60   Appreciation to George Cote.

3-60   Appreciation to all Officers and Directors of the CAAE.

4-60   Appreciation to the Convention Committee and Joe Marriott, Director of Airports, Riverside County.

5-60   Appreciation to the vendors and organizations that con tributed to the success of the 14th Annual Convention of the CAAE.

6-60 Appreciation to the County Board of Supervisors of River side County and the City Council of the City of Riverside and the Riverside County Airport Commission.

7-60   Urged the Congress of the United States to act favorably on HR 10895.

8-60   Requested that the California Education Code be amended to make it mandatory to follow the findings and recommendations of the Department of Education and the California Aeronautics Commission with reference to the proposed acquisition of any school site within two miles of an airport boundary.

9-60   Urged the Congress of the United States to enact into law such legislation that would ensure that the revenue derived from the Federal Aviation Fuel Tax would be set into a fund which would provide that an equal amount of money be appropriated for the development and expansion of domestic civil aviation and airport facilities.

10-60   Requested that a representative of the FAA meet with a representative of the CAAE and that the FAA immediately clarify the meaning of the phrase "obligated to furnish", with respect to free space at airports for the United States Weather Bureau.

1961
OFFICERS AND
BOARD OF DIRECTORS

President	John Caywood
1st Vice President	James Brlans
2nd Vice President	Albert Huber
Secretary/Treasurer	Jack Egan

Directors

Joseph Marriott	Fred McElwain
Harry Culver	Robert Gould
Elmer Harmon	Dave Zebo

Board of Directors Meetings - Southgate Bowl, Hayward, 8/3/1960 General Meeting and ITTE Short Course - Hacienda Motel, Fresno, 12/2/1960 Annual Meeting - Lafayette Hotel, Long Beach, 6/14-16/1961

Major Issues of the Year

CAAE Business and Policies

Committees	Nominating-Walter Fell
	Membership-Robert Gould
	Resolution-Robert Wanamaker
	Budget/Audit-Albert Huber
	Awards-Walter Fell
	Public Relations-Walter Fell
	Time and Place-Wilmer Garrett
	Annual Survey-John Croghan
	Constitution and By-Laws-Jack Egan
	Technical Development-David Zebo
	Legislation-Robert Wanamaker
	Air Traffic Control Advisory
	North-Fred Taplin
	South-Woody DeSilva
	Air Defense Coordinating-Fred McElwain

It was decided to eliminate the fall airport clinic in favor of the ITTE University of Californla Course.

Aviation Industry Issues

Resolutions

11-60   Appreciation to the ITTE or University of California for their programming and conduct or the Airport Manager's Short Course on Airport Property Management.

12-60   Appreciation to the Fresno State College and its staff for its hosting the Short Course.

1-61   Petitioned the Congress to adopt the recommendations of the President relative reorganization and streamlining of procedures governing the operations of the Civil Aeronautics Board.

2-61   Requested that the Congress enact in the law HR 6500 and SB 1703 to extend the Federal Airport Aid for a period of five years.

3-61 Appreciation to C. Thomas Dean and Long Beach State College.

4-61   Appreciation to the City of Long Beach for hosting the annual convention.

1962
OFFICERS AND
BOARD OF DIRECTORS

President	James Brians
1st Vice President	Albert Huber
2nd Vice President	Robert Wanamaker
3rd Vice President	Jack Egan
Secretary/Treasurer	Marvin Scott

Directors

John Caywood	Earl Woodly
Tom Raffety	Harry Culver
Fred McElwain	

Meeting Sites

General Meeting and ITTE Short Course Annual Meeting - Ambassador Hotel, Los Angeles, 5/20-24/1962

Major Issues of the Year

CAAE Business and Policies

Committees	Nominating-James Nissen
	Membership-Wallace Robbins
	Resolution-Joseph Marriott
	Budget/Audit-Albert Huber
	Public Relations and Information-Walter Fell
	Awards-Gordon Stanton
	Time and Place-Lovell Hurlbut
	Constitution and By-Laws-Jack Egan
	Annual Survey-James Hunter
	ITTE Short Course-Fred Taplin
	Legislation-Robert Wanamaker
	Technical Development-David Zebo
	Air Defense-Fred McElwain
	Air Traffic Control-North-Fred Taplin
	South-Woodruff DeSilva
	Daily Newsletter-Marvin Scott
	Unrefunded Gas Tax-John Caywood

Aviation Industry Issues

Resolutions

1-62   Endorsed the general provisions of the proposed Federal Aid Airport Act as outlined by the Administrator of the FAA and urged passage of this proposed legislation.

2-62   Urged the Federal Aviation Agency:
   1. To establish a priority for research and development of a solution to produce more adequate air navigational aids for small hub and non-hub communities;

   2. To consider the revision of FAA criteria for the establishment of landing aids at less dense, small hub and non-hub communities:

3.   To study the modification of already existing air navigational aids with a view to lowering minimums at airports with clear approaches.

3-62   Requested that the Civil Aeronautics Board not invoke its "Use it or lose it" policy in determined:

A. That air carrier service has been adequate develop the potential for air travel within the community;

B. That the number of of the importance of community; and any community until it has passengers is a valid mea sure air transportation within the community

C. That the National interest is not adversely affected by the suspension of scheduled service.

4-62   Urged that the standards and recommended practices set forth in the "Proposed National Airport Evaluation System" not be adopted unless the Federal Aviation Agency has the resources and is prepared to under-take the implementation of the entire program as a part of its overall National air navigation facilities.

5-62   Thanks to the Officers, Directors, and Committee Members who so faithfully discharged their duties during the year 1961 1962.

Stand on Bills
Opposed: AB 152, which would have given the Public Utilities Commission regulatory power to issue certificates of convenience and necessity to whol-ly intrastate air carriers. Air Charter operators would be issued a permit upon meeting certain eligibility standards as to financial stability, insur-ance, and experience, etcetera, to be determined by the Public Utilities Commission.

1963
OFFICERS AND
BOARD OF DIRECTORS

President	Albert Huber
1st Vice President	Robert Wanamaker
2nd Vice President	Jack Egan
3rd Vice President	Malcolm Wordell
Secretary/Treasurer	Marvin Scott

Directors

Arthur Johnson	James Brians
John Caywood	Melvin Landon
Dale Fearn	David Zebo
Earl Woodley	Joseph Crotti

Meeting Sites

Board of Directors Meeting - Ambassador Hotel, Los Angeles,
5/24/1962 Board of Directors Meeting - Meadows Field, Bakersfield,
9/12/1962 General Meeting and ITTE Short Course - Hacienda Motel and Fresno State College, Fresno, 1/9-11/1963
Board of Directors Meeting - Fullerton Airport, 3/26/1963
Board of Directors Meeting - Sacramento Municipal Airport,
5/21/1963 Annual Meeting - Mountain Air Hotel, Mount Shasta, 6/19-21/1963

Awards
Airport Manager of the Year - Harry Culver

Aviation Industry Issues

CAAE Business and Policies
Committees   Nominating-James Brians

Membership-Roy Bayless
Resolution-Joseph Marriott
Budget/Audit-Robert Wanamaker
Time and Place-Roy Bayless
Public Relations and Information-James Hunter
Awards-Harry Culver
Annual Survey-John Croghan
Annual Convention-Farold Christensen
Constitution and By-Laws-Joseph Rust
ITTE Short Course-Frank Whitcomb
Technical Development-Donald Hobbs
Legislation-John Caywood
Air Defense-Keiffer Parker
Air Traffic Control
North-James Nissen
South-Arthur Johnson
President's Special-Joseph Crotti

Constitution and By-Laws changed eliminating the office of Third Vice President and establishing the office of Past President.

Decided that the job announcements provided by the CAAE would be limited to Executive Members and not be included in the text of the CAAE Newsletter.

$250 was donated to the R.W.F. "Bob" Schmidt Memorial Fund to the National Foundation for Asthmatic Children.

Aviation Industry Issues

Resolutions
1-63   Reaffirmed previously stated position favoring a two cent per gallon fuel tax and also endorsed whatever further study may be considered nec-essary by the State of California to substantiate airport facility needs.

2-63   Endorsed AB 1771, the Aircraft Financial Responsibility Act, or a like substitute, to ensure that all aircraft operators in the State of California will be uniformly financially responsible for damages; however, opposed any bill that would provide for State registration of aircraft, licensing of pilots, or investigation of aircraft accidents for determination of cause by any State Agency.

3-63   Thanks to Mr. Christensen, the City of Mount Shasta, the County of Siskiyou, and others who assisted in making the 16th annual meeting of the CAAE a pleasant and successful event.

4-63   Thanks to Mr. Huber and the County of Kern.

5-63   Endorsed the petitions of NANAC, AAC, and AAAE, and requested the Administration of the Federal Aviation Agency to cause the subject report prepared by the firm of Bolt, Berenek, and Newman to be printed and used as an internal FAA document, available to public use airport owning agencies upon request.

6-63   Recommended that the County of Los Angele purchase and operate the Compton Airport as a publicly owned and operated facility to continue serving the public need.

7-63 Expressed highest esteem of Donald B. Smith in recognition of his forty years in the profession of airport management.

8-63   Opposed SB 88, which would have prohibited the granting of exclu-sive rights for the sale of aviation fuel on former military surplus airports.
9-63   Appreciation to Assemblyman John Willianson for his work on behalf of the CAAE.

Stand on Bills

Favored: General concept of SB 1279, which allowed for a two cent tax of aviation fuel for use at publicly operated airports and eliminated such aircraft from the motor vehicle fuel license tax. Certain exemptions for private airports were included.

AB 1494, which was an amendment to PUC Codes relating to accounting funds, eliminating the "Air Development Fund" and providing for deposit in a "Special Aviation Fund" of the State, allocated for acquisition and development of airports.

SB 891, which exempted aircraft dealers from payment of personal property tax on aircraft held for sale. CAAE recommended that a provision be inserted applying this to new aircraft only.

Support was also given for any legislation requiring financial responsibility for aircraft operators along the same lines as that required for motor vehicles in California. Such legislation had previously been opposed by the CAAE.

Opposed: AB 2482, which required that the public agency owning an airport pass an ordinance requiring compulsory liability insurance in order to be eligible for the $2,500 State Airport Assistance Fund.

1964
OFFICERS AND
BOARD OF DIRECTORS

President	Robert Wanamaker
President Elect	Jack Egan
1st Vice President	Malcolm Wordell
2nd Vice President	Marvin Scott
Secretary/Treasurer	Roy Bayless

Directors	
Albert Huber	Farold Christensen
Robert Gould	Frank Witcomb
Arthur Johnson	Melvin Landon
David Zebo	Joseph Crotti

Meeting Sites

General Meeting and ITTE Short Course - Hacienda Motel, Fresno, 1/7/1964 Annual Meeting - Miramar Hotel, Santa Monica, 6/17-19/1964

Major Issues of the Year

CAAE Business and Policies

Committees   Nominating-James Brians
Membership-George Cote
Resolution-Norman Coad
Budget/Audit-Walter Fell
Time and Place-Budd Peaslee
Convention and Program-Clyde Fitzgerald
Technical Development-Wallace Robbins
Salary Survey-Jack Egan
Legislation-Nicholas Dallas
ITTE Short Course-William Partain
Records-Roy Bayless
Ethics-Delmar Canady

Ethics committee was first organized to develop a Code of Ethics for the Association.

Aviation Industry Issues

Resolutions

1-64   Commended the work of State Senator Randolph Collier as Chairman and his Senate Committee on Transportation and Public Utilities, and State Assemblyman Thomas C. Carrell as Chairman and his Assembly Committee on Transportation and Commerce.

2-64   Recommended that all airline and general aviation airports open for public use should have guide signs marking access routes and entrances.

3-64   Commended Clyde V. Fitzgerald and the members of the Program Committee for the success of the Annual Meeting.

1965
OFFICERS AND
BOARD OF DIRECTORS

President	Jack Egan
President Elect	Malcolm Wordell
1st Vice President	Marvin Scott
2nd Vice President	Roy Bayless
Secretary/Treasurer	Harry Culver

Directors	
Robert Wanamaker	Robert Sheker
Athur Johnson	Frank Witcomb
Joseph Crotti	Robert Gould
Charles Overton	Farold Christensen
Melvin Landon	David Zebo

General Meeting and ITTE Short Course - Hacienda Hotel and Fresno State College, Fresno, 1/13-15/1965 Board of Directors and Aviation Legislation Meeting - MansionInn, Sacramento, 4/9-10/1965 Annual Meeting - Edgewater Inn Garden Motel, Oakland, 6/22 25/1965

Awards

Airport Manager of the Year - David Zebo, for his direction of airport resources to help with the floods in Humbolt County. Certificate given to Senator Collier for furthering Aviation Legislation.

Major Issues of the Year

CAAE Business and Policies

Committees   Nominating-C.O. Brandt
Membership-Lovell Hurlbut
Resolution-Robert Wanamaker
Budget/Audit-Dale Fearn
Awards-Walter Fell
Education-Malcolm Wordell
Convention Manual-Clyde Fitzgerald
Constitution and By-Laws-Melvin Landon
Survey-Delmar Canady
Technical Development-Wallace Robbins
Legislative-Arthur Johnson
Highway Sign-Marvin Scott

Decided to support freeway signs for all publicly owned, general aviation airports. Signs were previously provided for those airports with scheduled airlines only.

1966
OFFICERS AND
BOARD OF DIRECTORS

President	Malcolm Wordell
President Elect	Marvin Scott
1st Vice President	Roy Bayless
Secretary/Treasurer	Glenn Plymate

Directors
Delmar Canady   Joseph Crotti
Jack Egan   David Zebo
Robert Sheker   Farold Christensen
Harry Culver   Charles Overton

Meeting Sites

General Meeting and ITTE Short Course - U.C. Berkeley, Richmond
Field Station, 1/12-14/1966 Annual Meeting -Las Casitas Garden Hotel,
Santa Catalina Island, 6/21-24/1966

Awards
Airport Manager of the Year - Delmar Canady

Major Issues of the Year

CAAE Business and Policies
Committees   Membership-Lovell Hurlbut
               Resolution-Robert Wanamaker
               Budget/Audit-Dale Fearn
               Time and Place-Fred Kane
               Public Relations-Robert Hamilton
               Awards-Walter Fell
               Confidential Survey-Delmar Canady
               Education-Fred Taplin
               Constitution and By-Laws-Melvin Landon
               Convention Manual-Clyde Fitzgerald
               ITTE Short Course-Frank Witcomb
               Ethics-Delmar Canady
               Legislation-Arthur Johnson
               Technical Development-John Meacham
               Air Space Utilization
               North-Frank Witcomb
               South-Richard Kessler

A committee was formed to dispose of CAAE's obsolete records.

The second design for a lapel pin, with wings, was approved.

Aviation Industry Issues
Opposed Federal Aid to Airports Program fund cut, proposed by Lyndon B.
Johnson. The funds were saved.

Recognition was given to Congressman Don Clausen for the help he gave
the CAAE in the campaign to retain full Federal Aid to Airports Program.

Approval was given for the formation of a Federal Transportation
Department.

Support was given for providing highway signs for heliports.

Resolutions
1-66 Urged the Congress of the United States to promptly proceed with
the consideration of legislation to extend the Federal Aid to Airports
Program, allowing for a five-year program funded at $150,000,000
annually.

2-66 Urged the Senate to enact the necessary legislation to direct the
Federal Aviation Agency to obligate the amount of $71,000,000 for the
fiscal year 1967 Federal Aid to Airports Program.

3-66 Requested that the Federal Government
    1. Recognize public uae airports;

    2. Recognize airports as vital to the national economy
    and business in general for the movement of goods and

people rapidly and efficiently; and

    3. Establish a priority which will ensure that safety,
    operation, expansion, and overall efficiency be allotted to
    public use airports.

4-66 Commended the FAA and GSA for their outstanding efforts in
assisting public airports to obtain essential surplus properties.

5-66 Endorsed and recommended to the Senate and House of
Representatives of the United States that Section 1673(b) of Public Law 89-
358 be amended to provide that a course in flight training may be obtained
from any FAA Approved Flight School.

6-66 Recommended to the FAA that the criteria for these installations be as
follows:
    1. Under no circumstances shall an arresting cable permanently
    located above the runway surface be permitted within the
    runway operational area of any airport serving civil aviation;

    2. All arresting gear shall be located in the overrun area;

    3. All such installations shall be adequately identified both day
    and night; and

    4. All such installations shall be in accordance with the part 77
    obstructions criteria, and no waiver shall be granted as in the case of
    navigational aids.

8-66 Recommended that the priority system for FAAP expenditures be
revised to take into account all passengers using the airports, whether in
general aviation or scheduled air carrier aircraft, and also take into
account the cost of each project with respect to the benefits to be obtained
therefrom.

9-66 Appreciation to the City of Avalon, Santa Catalina Island, and
Robert and Mrs. D. Sheker (Conference Chairman).

1967 OFFICERS AND BOARD OF DIRECTORS

President   Marvin Scott
President Elect   Roy Bayless
1st Vice President   Arthur Johnson
2nd Vice President   Dave Zebo
Secretary/Treasurer   William Barnard

Directors
Malcolm Wordell   Farold Christensen
Joseph Crotti   Robert Hamiliton
Lovell Hurlbut   Elmer Harmon
Delmar Canady   Frank Whitcomb

Meeting Sites

General Meeting - Asilomar, Pacific Grove, 1/17-19/1967
Annual Meeting - El Dorado Hotel, Sacramento, 6/27-30/1967

Awards
Airport Manager of the Year - Harry Sham

Ma jor Issues of the Year

CAAE Business and Policies
Committees   Ethics-Dave Zebo
               Nominating-Wilmer Garrett

Membership-Melvin Landon
Budget/Audit-William Barnard
ITTE Short Course-Walter Gilfillian
Promotion and Publicity-Frank Witcomb
Awards-Walter Fell
Time and Place-Jack Harper
Resolution-Jack Egan
Legislation-Arthur Johnson
Insignias-Roy Bayless
Highway Signs-Joe Crotti
Technical-Raymond Foreaker
Constitution and By-Laws-Roy Bayless
Education-Jack Tippie
Master Airport Plan-Glenn Plymate
Public Relations-Robert Hamilton

A Code of Ethics was presented and accepted.

An organization of managers from the Los Angeles Basin was recognized as a sub-organization of the CAAE.

It was agreed all members would receive a lapel pin with the CAAE insignia on it.

Aviation Industry Issues

A motion was made to send a resolution to the California Airport Department urging the development of a new Master Plan and to update existing Master Plans.

1968
OFFICERS AND
BOARD OF DIRECTORS

President	Roy Bayless
President Elect	David Zebo
1st Vice President	Harry Culver
2nd Vice President	Glenn Plymate
Secretary/Treasurer	Delmar Canady

Directors	
Reginald Schmitz	Elmer Harmon
Frank Whitcomb	Robert Hamilton
Marvin Scott	Robert Bresnahan
Norman Coad	John Meacham

Meeting Sites

General Meeting - Asilomar, Pacific Grove, 1/18/1968 Annual Meeting - Palm Springs, 6/20-21/1968

Awards

Airport Manager of the Year   William Barnard

Major Issues of the Year

CAAE Business and Policies

Committees   Ethics-Walter Fell
Nominating- Marvin Scott
Membership-Lovell Hurlbut
Budget/Audit-Harry Culver
ITTE Short Course-James Brians
Public Relations-Robert Hamilton
Awards-Walter Fell
Time and Place-Robert Hamilton
Conference-Delmar Canady
Conference Manual-Robert Sheker
Legislation-Wilmer Garrett

Constitution and By-Laws-Melvin Landon
Technical-David Zebo
Highway Signs-Raymond Foreaker
Insignias-Roy Bayless
Salary Survey- John Croghan
State Master Plan of Airports-Glenn Plymate
Past President Pins-Wallace Robbins

Changes in the By-Laws were made to clarify membership classifications. The wording, "within the State of California" was added to Executive Membership to make for a true California association. The wording, "affiliated with a public or private corporation" and "or who is otherwise interested in aviation" were deleted from the associate membership, as it was felt that these statements permitted almost anyone to join as an Associate Member.

It was decided that future salary surveys would contract a professional survey firm to establish weight factors, but the actual work would still be accomplished by the CAAE.

It was decided that sites for summer conferences would be made two years in advance.

Aviation Industry Issues
CAAE supported the recommendation that an outside firm be retained to prepare a new state Master Plan of Airports.

Resolutions
1-68   Appreciation to President Bayless for his fine performance in office.

2-68   Appreciation to the City of Palm Springs for hosting the 1968 convention.

3-68   Issued a statement to the President and Congress of the United States regarding CAB's "monopoly" of commercial helicopter operations. This resolution failed to pass the membership.

1969
OFFICERS AND
BOARD OF DIRECTORS

President	David Zebo
President Elect	Harry Culver
1st Vice President	Glenn Plymate
2nd Vice President	Delmar Canady
Secretary/Treasurer	Norman Coad

Directors	
Richard Kessler	James Hunter
Bill Barnard	Mel Landon
Robert Bresnahan	James Mc Call
Reg Schmitz	Roy Bayless

Meeting Sites

ITTE Short Course - The Alisal, Solvang, 1/22-24/1969
Board of Directors - Oakland International Airport, 4/9/1969
Annual Meeting - Eureka Inn, Eureka, 6/24-27/1969

Awards
Airport Manager of the Year - Edwin Thurmond

Major Issues of the Year

Aviation Industry Issues

Resolutions

1-69   Memorial for Ben J. Audette.

2-69   Memorial for Norman Larson.

3-69   Appreciation for David Zebo.

4-69   Appreciation for Farold Christensen and William Barnard.

1970
OFFICERS AND
BOARD OF DIRECTORS

President	Harry Culver
President Elect	Glenn Plymate
1st Vice President	Delmar Canady
2nd Vice President	Norman Coad
Secretary/Treasurer	Lovell Hurlbut

Directors

William Barnard	Dave Zebo
James Hunter	Melvin Landon
Nicholas Dallas	Edwin Thurmond
Robert Sheker	Herbert Thayer

Meeting Sites

Board of Directors Meeting - Hawthorne Airport, 11/6/1969

Board of Directors Meeting - Asilomar, Pacific Grove, 1/6/1970

General Meeting - Asilomar, Pacific Grove, 1/7/1970

Board of Directors Meeting - Lindberg Field, San Diego, 5/7/1970

Annual Meeting - Bahia Hotel, San Diego, 7/7-10/1970

Awards

Airport Manager of the Year - Marvin Scott Scholarship Award - Robert F. Wilson, $300 plus two year Junior membership awarded.

Major Issues of the Year

CAAE Business and Policies

Committees	
	Nominating-James Hunter
	Budget and Audit-Robert Sheker
	Audit-Raymond Foreaker
	ITTE Short Course-James Brians
	Publicity-Glenn Plymate
	Resolution-Walter Fell
	Conference-Delmar Canady
	Constitution and By-Laws-Walter Fell
	Legislation-William Barnard
	Public Relations-Glenn Plymate
	Technical-Harry Culver
	Scholarship-David Zebo
	Highway Signs-Raymond Foreaker
	Insignias-Roy Bayless
	Rates and Charges Survey-Albert Huber

This was the first year of the CAAE Scholarship. It was noted that the CAAE was getting publicity at the national level for the scholarship award.

The By-Laws were changed to add a seventh class of membership:

Executive Affiliate. This was for those members who could not meet Executive requirements solely because of geographic location. This class was given one vote in all matters except those pertaining to California legislation. The By-Laws were further changed to require that all officers and directors be Executive members except for one which may be an Executive Affiliate member.

1971
OFFICERS AND
BOARD OF DIRECTORS

President	Glenn Plymate
President Elect	Delmar Canady
1st Vice President	Norman Coad
2nd Vice President	Lovell Hurlbut
Secretary/Treasurer	Edwin Thurmond

Directors

Harry Culver	Jack Tippie
Merrill Day	Nicholas Dallas
James McCall	Robert Sheker
Herbert Thayer	Jack Harper

Meeting Sites

Board of Directors Meeting - South Lake Tahoe Airport, 10/1/1970

General Meeting - Asilomar, Pacific Grove, 1/5-6/1971

Board of Directors Meeting - Ontario Airport, 4/22/1971

Annual Meeting - Tahoe-Sands Motel, South Lake Tahoe,7/13-16/1971

Awards

Airport Manager of the Year - John Dickenson Scholarship Award - Stanley Huddle, given in recognition of Reuben H. Fleet. $300 plus a Junior membership awarded.

Major Issues of the Year

CAAE Business and Policies

Committees	
	Nominating-David Zebo
	Membership-Raymond Farlin
	Budget/Audit-Herbert Thayer
	ITTE Short Course-William Partain
	Publicity-John Dickenson
	Awards-Marvin Scott
	Time and Place-Harry Culver
	Resolution-Walter Fell
	Conference-Mark Smith
	Legislation-Delmar Canady
	Brochure-James Hunter
	Noise Standards-Robert Bresnahan
	Salary Survey-John Croghan
	Environmental Quality-Wilmer Garrett
	Airport Certification-Robert Young
	Aims-Reginald Schmitz

The CAAE rejected an invitation to become a Regional Chapter Affiliate with the AAAE.

Francis Torr won a drawing for a color television set. This was used to boost attendance at meetings.

Aviation Industry Issues

Supported two bills in the U.S. House and Senate pertaining to retro-fitting engines on jet powered transport aircraft.

Resolutions

1-71   Urged the FAA to adopt Federal noise standards; and urged the State to postpone any noise standards until Federal standards are in effect.

2-71   Urged the implementation of the Airport and Airways Development Act for funding of $280 million .

3-71   Urged State, County, and City officials to urge Congress for the adoption of the Airport and Airways Development Act.

1972
OFFICERS AND
BOARD OF DIRECTORS

President	Delmar Canady
President Elect	Norman Coad
1st Vice President	Lovell Hurlbut
2nd Vice President	Edwin Thurmond
Secretary/Treasurer	John Croghan

Directors

Robert Bresnahan	Jack Tippie
John Dickenson	Nicholas Ford
William Partain	James McCall
Robert Young	Jack Harper

Meeting Sites

Board of Directors Meeting - Ramada Inn, Riverside, 11/3/1971
General Meeting - Asilomar, Pacific Grove, 1/26/1972
Annual Meeting - Bakersfield Inn, Bakersfield, 7/11-14/1972

Award s

Airport Manager of the Year - Roy Bayless Scholarship Award - John Costas, $500 plus basic expenses to attend CAAE meeting.

Major Issues of the Year

CAAE Business and Policies

Committees	
	Nominating-Harry Culver
	Membership-Jack Harper
	Budget/Audit-Merrill Day
	ITTE Short Course-William Partain
	Publicity-Robert Bresnahan
	Awards-John Dickenson
	Resolution-Nicholas Dallas
	Conference-William Drum
	Aims-Reginold Schmitz
	Legislation-Al Huber
	Airport Certification-Robert Young
	Salary Survey-Robert Sheker
	Noise Standards-Robert Bresnahan
	Environmental Quality-Gordon Reddall
	Highway Signs-James Hunter
	Hucksters-Harry Culver

It was decided that all past and future CAAE Presidents receive a plaque involving a gavel and a bronze replica of the Association's insignia .

It was agreed to not charge new members for their pins.

The Code of Ethics was rewritten.

Aviation Industry Issues
Support was given for tax relief to private-public airports.

Resolutions
1-72 Unqualified gratitude to the Chairman and Board of Supervisors, and the Mayor and City Council of Bakersfield and Kern County.

2-79 Appreciation to Bill Drum and his Conference Committee, especially Reg Smith, for the success of the conference.

3-79 Sincere gratitude to Delmar L. Canady for a most successful and outstanding year.

4-79 Urged the Department of Transportation and the Federal Aviation Administration to accelerate the research and development program of the Microwave Landing System for installation not later than July 1, 1974.

1973
OFFICERS AND
BOARD OF DIRECTORS

President	Norman Coad
President Elect	Lovell Hurlbut
1st Vice President	Edwin Thurmond
2nd Vice President	John Croghan
Secretary/Treasurer	James Hunter

Directors

Delmar Canady	John Dickenson
Nicholas Ford	William Partain
Robert Goodman	Robert Young
Richard Smith	Frances Torr

Meeting Sites

General Meeting - Asilomar, Pacific Grove, 1/17/1973
Board of Directors Meeting - Airport Marina Hotel, Fresno, 4/24/1973 - Annual Meeting - Oakland Airport, 8/17-21/1973

Awards
Airport Manager of the Year - Robert Bresnahan Scholarship Award - Dennis Farmer

Ma jor Issues of the Year

CAAE Business and Policies
Committees

Nominating-Harry Culver
Audit-John Croghan
ITTE Short Course-James Brians
Conference-Wilmer Garrett
Legislation-Delmar Canady
Scholarship-David Zebo

It was decided that at all CAAE meetings the President would appoint at least one Sergeant of Arms to monitor and control behavior.

The Legislative Committee was reorganized to participate, represent CAAE, and propose and submit legislation in Sacramento.

1974
OFFICERS AND
BOARD OF DIRECTORS

President	Lovell Hurlbut
President Elect	Edwin Thurmond
1st Vice President	John Croghan
2nd Vice President	James Hunter
Secretary/Treasurer	John Dickenson

Directors

Maurice MacDonald	Norman Coad
Raymond Farlin	Robert Gould
Richard Smith	Robert Goodman
Robert Young	Frances Torr

Board of Directors Meeting - San Diego Airport, 11/2/1973
General Meeting - Asilomar, Pacific Grove, 1/22-23/1974
Board of Directors Meeting - San Jose Airport, 3/7/1974
Annual Meeting - Sheraton Hotel, Universal City, 7/15-18/1974

Awards
Airport Manager of the Year - Nicholas Dallas

Major Issues of the Year

CAAE Business and Policies

Committees   Ethics-James Mummert
Nominating-Norman Coad
Membership-Jack Tippie
Budget/Audit-John Croghan
ITTE Short Course-James Hunter
Awards-Edwin Thurmond
Time and Place-John Croghan
Conference-John Dickenson
Salary Survey-Marvin Scott
Legislation-Delmar Canady
Airport Certification-Jack Harper
Noise Standards-Wallace Berry
Airport Manager Certification-Roy Bayless
Association Improvement-Roy Bayless
Management Qualifications-Robert Young
Professional Development-Robert Young
Sergeant of Arms-Raymond Farlin

The Scholarship Award was defunct; it was revived in 1976.

Curriculum was being devised to offer an Airport Manager Certificate or AA degree from participating colleges.

Aviation Industry Issues
Opposition was stated to the adoption of a State law prohibiting coin operated toilets in airport terminals.

Resolutions
1-74   Commended Past President Lovell Hurlbut for his leadership during his term of Presidency.

2-74   Commended the 1974 Conference Chairman, John Dickenson, for the outstanding success of the conference.

3-74   Urged that an aggressive research and development program be pursued to reduce aircraft engine noise.

4-74   Commended the 1974 Co-Chairmen, Bill Brodek, for the out standing success of the conference.

1975
OFFICERS AND
BOARD OF DIRECTORS

President	Edwin Thurmond
President Elect	John Croghan
1st Vice President	James Hunter
2nd Vice President	John Dickenson
Secretary/Treasurer	Richard Smith

Directors

Maurice MacDonald	Lovell Hurlbut
Robert Gould	David Cole
Ronald Chandler	Robert Young
James Mummert	Paul Gaines

Meeting Sites

Board of Directors Meeting - San Jose Airport, 9/18/1974
Board of Directors Meeting - Sacramento Metro Airport, 12/17/1974
General Meeting - Asilomar, Pacific Grove, 1/14-15/1975

Board of Directors Meeting - Orange County Airport, 3/21/1975
Board of Directors Meeting - San Jose Airport, 5/29/1975
Annual Meeting - Buchanan Field, Concord, 7/14/1975

Awards
Airport Manager of the Year - Nicholas Ford President's Special Award - John Dickenson

Major Issues of the Year

CAAE Business and Policies

Committees   Ethics-James Mummert
Nominating-William Farlin
Membership-Jack Tippie
Budget/Audit-Raymond Farlin
ITTE Short Course-James Hunter
Publicity-Frances Torr
Awards-Nicholas Dallas
Time and Place-George Edmondson
Resolution-Nicholas Dallas
Conference-Marvin Scott
Conference Manual-John Dickenson
Legislation-Delmar Canady
Salary Survey-Marvin Scott
Noise Standards-Wallace Berry
Airport Certification-Jack Harper
Airport Security-Ralph Tonseth
Aims-Raymond Farlin
Professional Development-Robert Young
Hucksters-John Dickenson
Security-Ralph Tonseth
Finance/Investment-Paul Gaines
Blue Ribbon-Robert Young

Kent Stacey was hired for legislative bill following, for ten months for $1000.

This was the first year for the Blue Ribbon Committee, created to develop long range goals for the CAAE.

The Association agreed to reciprocate corporate memberships at no cost to either organization.

A standard press release format was developed for each member to send to his local media.

For legislative purposes, the CAAE classified all airports as Air Carrier, Provisional, or General Aviation.

Support was given to amend existing legislation to allow all Air Carrier airports to have their own police department.

Opposition was stated to the FAA soliciting the public to ask for increased security at General Aviation Airports in an FAA publication.

1976
OFFICERS AND
BOARD OF DIRECTORS

President	John Croghan
President Elect	James Hunter
1st Vice President	John Dickenson
2nd Vice President	Richard Smith
Secretary/Treasurer	Maurice MacDonald

Directors

Edwin Thurmond	Vernon Ackerman
Jack Tippie	William Brodek
Ronald Chandler	James Mc Call
James Mummert	Paul Gains

Meeting Sites

Board of Directors Meeting - Hollywood-Burbank Airport,10/16/1975
General Meeting - Asilomar, Pacific Grove,1/13-15/1976
Annual Meeting - Town and Country Hotel, San Diego, 5/16-19/1976

Awards

Airport Manager of the Year - Robert Goodman
Wanamaker Award - Carl G. Hand
Scholarship Award - Randall Julian, Award made at San Jose State
University, Department of Aeronautics

Major Issues of the Year

CAAE Business and Policies

Committees   Ethics-James Mc Call
               Nominating-John Dickenson
               Membership-Jack Tippie
               Budget/Audit-Richard Smith
               ITTE Short Course-Nicholas Ford
               Publicity-Robert Whitehair
               Awards-Nicholas Ford
               Time and Place-Vernon Ackerman
               Resolution-Nicholas Dallas
               Conference-Lovell Hurlbut
               Conference Manual-Marvin Scott
               Legislation-Delmar Canady
               Salary Survey-James Mummert
               Noise Standards-Wallace Berry
               Hucksters-Stephen Schmitt
               Aims-James Harper
               Airport Certification-Ronald Chandler
               Association Improvement-James Hunter
               Professional Development-Robert Young
               Security-Ralph Tonseth
               Credentials-John Dickenson
               Airport Aid Programs-Richard Smith
               CalTrans Plan Evaluation-Edwin Thurmond

This was the first year for the Wanamaker Award, given in honor of Robert Wanamaker.

Unanimous approval was given to the affiliation of the AAAE and the CAAE.

Aviation Industry Issues

The Association recommended public acquisition of the Hollywood Burbank Airport and for the continued operation of the facility as an airport.

Opposition was stated to the closing of the Southern California office of the California Division of Aeronautics.

1977
OFFICERS AND
BOARD OF DIRECTORS

President	James Hunter
President Elect	John Dickenson
Past President	John Croghan
1st Vice President	Richard Smith

Secretary/Treasurer	Delmar Canady

Directors

Maurice MacDonald	John Croghan
VernonAckerman	Jack Tippie
William Brodek	James Mc Call
Ralph Tonseth	Frances Torr

Meeting Sites

Board of Directors Meeting - Ontario Airport, 7/23/1976 General Meeting - Asilomar, Pacific Grove, 1/4-5/1977 Board of Directors Meeting - Stockton, 3/25/1977 Annual Meeting - Stockton, 7/18-21/1977

Awards

Airport Manager of the Year - Stephen Schmitt
Wanamaker Award - David Hatfield
Scholarship Award - John Griffen

Major Issues of the Year

CAAE Business and Policies

Committees   Nominating-John Croghan
               Membership-Jack Tippie
               Publicity and Awards-William Brodek
               Time and Place-James Mc Call
               Resolution-Richard Mettler
               Conference-Ralph Tonseth
               Legislation-Delmar Canady
               Credentials-John Dickenson
               Airport Security-Richard Smith
               Airport Aid Programs-Richard Smith
               Cal-Trans Plan Evaluation-James Mummert
               Scholarship-Pat Farlin

The Scholarship Award was now being funded by an anonymous donor it was decided that the Association would not match the $250 would send the winner to the Asilomar conference.

Changes in the By-Laws were made to remove the offices of First and Second Vice President and add the office of Past President. The office of First Vice President was retained this year to allow Richard Smith to remain in the chain of office. The Secretary/Treasurer was made a permanent office with Delmar Canady currently serving. It was also decided that the President and President Elect must be Certified Executive members. This was the first year of certification with eight members being given the title "Certified airport Executive".

1978
OFFICERS AND
BOARD OF DIRECTORS

President	John Dickenson
President Elect	Richard Smith
Past President	James Hunter
Secretary/Treasurer	Delmar Canady

Directors

Maurice MacDonald	James Hunter
James Mc Call	Jack Tippie
William Brodek	Ralph Tonseth
James Mummert	Frances Torr
Raul Regalado	

Meeting Sites

Board of Directors Meeting - San. Jose, 9/14/1977 Board of Directors

Meeting - Ontario, 12/1/1977 General Meeting - Asilomar, Pacific Grove, 1/17-18/1978 Board of Directors Meeting - Santa Ana, 4/14/1978 Annual Meeting - Santa Ana, 7/16-18/1978

Awards
Airport Manager of the Year - Wallace Berry
Wanamaker Award - Thomas Leonard
Scholarship Award - Danilo Simich

Major Issues of the Year

CAAE Business and Policies
Committees   Ethics-Richard Smith
             Nominating-James Hunter
             Membership-Jack Tippie
             ITS Short Course-James Mummert
             Publicity and Awards-William Brodek
             Time and Place-Vernon Ackerman
             Resolution-Clifton Moore
             Conference-Robert Bresnahan
             Legislation-Delmar Canady
             Noise Standards-William Berry
             Security-Richard Smith
             Credentials-Frances Torr
             Cal-Trans Plan Evaluation-Ralph Tonseth
             Finance/Investment-Raul Regaldo
             State Aeronautics-Ralph Tonseth
             Out of State Affairs-Richard Smith
             Scholarship-Pat Farlin

The CAAE became the Southwest Chapter of the AAAE and now encompasses the States of California, Arizona, Nevada, and Utah.

Due to the large number of Executive Emeritus members, it was decided to charge them a token fee for newsletters and other services.

Aviation Industry Issues
Opposition was declared to the FAA's request that their personnel be given free access to airport operating areas.

ITTE initials were changed to ITS (Institute of Transportation Studies).

Resolutions
1-78   Authorized and directed the Secretary of the CAAE to issue the routine resolutions concerning the hosting of the 1978 Conference.

2-78   Support for HR-8729 (the Anderson Noise Reduction Act).

3-78   Support for the use of annual allocation funds for maintenance of airport capitol improvements.

4-78   Offered cooperation and support with the newly formed California Transportation Commission.

1979
OFFICERS AND
BOARD OF DIRECTORS

President	Richard Smith
President Elect	Frances Torr
Past President	John Dickenson
Secretary/Treasurer	Delmar Canady

Directors	
Everett Julkowski	John Dickenson
Jack Tippie	William Brodek
James Mc Call	Delmar Canady
James Mummert	Raul Regalado

Meeting Sites

Board of Directors Meeting - Stockton, 10/13/1978
General Meeting - Asilomar, Pacific Grove,1/2-4/1979
Board of Directors Meeting - Ontario, 3/16/1979
Annual Meeting - San Jose, 7/16-19/1979

Awards
Airport Manager of the Year - William Brodek
Scholarship Award - Robert Grave

Major Issues of the Year

CAAE Business and Policies
Committees   Ethics-Frances Torr
             Nominating-John Dickenson
             Membership-Jack Tippie
             ITS Short Course-William Partain
             Public Relations-Donald Flynn
             Publicity and Awards-William Brodek
             Time and Place-James Mc Call
             Resolution-Clifton Moore
             Conference-Richard Harper
             Legislation-Delmar Canady
             Noise Standards-Wallace Berry
             Security-Ralph Tonseth
             Credentials-James Mummert
             Finance/Investment-Raul Regalado
             State Aeronautics-Everett Julkowski
             CFR Training Course-Robert Mandeville
             Historical-Walter Fell
             Scholarship-Pat Farlin

This was the first year of the Crash, Fire and Rescue (CFR) Training Course Committee. The first School was held in 1980.

The CAAE was appointed as a member organization to the Aviation Technical Advisory Committee of the California Transportation Commission.

The By-Laws were amended to provide for absentee ballots in the election of officers.

It was decided that ad hoc committees would be formed any time an airport was in danger of being closed.

Aviation Industry Issues
A letter was written to the California Transportation Commission to remove aviation from the State Transportation Improvement Plan process as it is not an effective tool for aviation planning.

Resolutions
1-79   Appreciation to the City of San Jose and the Airports Department.

2-79   Support for the nomination of Edwin Thurmond to serve as Secretary/Treasurer, and higher offices, in the AAAE.

3-79   Appreciation to R.C. Smith for his service as President of the CAAE.

4-79   Recommended that the California Transportation Commission keep the CAAP funds separate from other transportation funds.

5-79   Urged the California Transportation Commission to adopt a policy supporting continued direct contact between local projects' sponsors and the Federal Government, and opposing channeling of Federal funds through the State; further, urged a timely adoption of a Comprehensive State Airport Systems Plan.

6-79 Recommended that the California Transportation Commission adopt a unified state-wide improvement plan based upon local or regional plans and priorities.

7-79 Reaffirmed support of the CAAE for the orderly reduction of aircraft noise as expressed in and required by FAR Part 36, and opposing federal legislation that might permit escape from the requirements of FAR Part 36.

1980
OFFICERS AND
BOARD OF DIRECTORS

President	Francis Torr
President Elect	Raul Regalado
Past President	Richard Smith
Secretary/Treasurer	James Hunter

Directors

William Critchfield	Everett Julkowski
Clifton Moore	Jack Tippie
Donald Flynn	William Brodek

Meeting Sites

Board of Directors Meeting - San Jose, 10/5/1979
ITS Short Course - Asilomar, Pacific Grove, 1/8-10/1980
Board of Directors Meeting -
John Wayne Airport,Santa Ana, 4/11/1980
Annual Meeting - Hyatt House Hotel, Los Angeles, 7/20-24/1980

Awards

Airport Manager of the Year - William Critchfield
Wanamaker Award - Walter Gillfillan
President's Award - Jack Tippie
Scholarship Award - Caron Garfield

Ma jor Issues of the Year

CAAE Business and Policies

Committees Membership-Jack Tippie
Finance-Everett Julkowski
Awards-William Brodek
Public Relations-Donald Flynn
Conference-Clifton Moore
ITS Short Course-Donald Flynn
Ethics-Raul Regalado
Historical-William Brodek
Scholarship-Raymond Farlin
Legislation-Everett Julkowski
Credentials-Richard Smith
Certification-William Critchfield
Noise-William Critchfield
CFR Training Course-Robert Mandeville
State Technical Advisory Committee Representative
Richard Smith
Bill Following Service-James Mummert
STIP-Richard Smith

The By-Laws were changed to allow for a standing Public Relations Committee.

The first Reno CFR School was held .

1981
OFFICERS AND
BOARD OF DIRECTORS

President	Raul Regalado
President Elect	James Mummert
Past President	Francis Torr
Secretary/Treasurer	James Hunter

Directors

William Critchfield	Delmar Canady
Ralph Tonseth	Donald Flynn
Jack Tippie	Robert Mandeville

Meeting Sites

Board of Directors Meeting - San Jose, 10/17/1980
ITS Short Course - Asilomar, Pacific Grove, 1/13-16/1981
Board of Directors Meeting - Los Angeles International Airport, 3/20/1981
Board of Directors Meeting - Sacramento Metropolitan Airport, 5/29/1981
Annual Meeting - Wood Lake Inn, Sacramento, 7/6-9/1981

Awards

Airport Manager of the Year - James Mc Call
Wanamaker Award - General William Fox (Retired)
President's Award - Jack Ewald
President's Award - Barbara Hunter
Scholarship Award - David Scott

Major Issues of the Year

CAAE Business and Policies

Committees Nominating-Francis Torr
Membership-Jack Tippie
Resolution-Delmar Canady
Finance-Ralph Tonseth
Conference-Kenneth Joule
ITS Short Course-James Mummert
Publicity and Awards-Donald Flynn
Credentials-William Crichfield
Ethics-James Mummert
Legislation-Delmar Canady
Scholarship-Charles Foster
Noise-William Critchfield
Reference Library-Howard Corbin
Historical-Robert Mandeville
State Technical Advisory Committee Representative
Richard Smith
CFR Training Course-Robert Mandeville
AAAE Accreditation-Richard Smith
State Liaison-Arizona: Edwin Thurmond;
Utah: Robert Mandeville;
Nevada; Thomas Greer;
California: Francis Torr
Security Training Course-John Dickenson
Special CAAE Name Change-Wilmer Garrett

It was decided to no longer pursue the reconciliation of the C.A.E. program with the A.A.E. program and to continue the C.A.E. program separately.

The Credentials Committee was directed to be further charged with the requirement to continue to upgrade and reinforce the criteria for certification, subject to the Board of Directors' approval.

The newly formed Arizona Airport Managers Association was recognized and it was decided that it posed no conflict with the CAAE.

Section I of the By-laws was changed to read: "Only Executive Members who are Certified Airport Executives of the CAAE shall hold elective office in CAAE. Article IV - Committees was also changed to specify membership status required for the various standing committees.

Aviation Industry Issues

The Board voted to support the LAX Security Conference, a possible new program.

Supported the effort to have legislation introduced to have the California Aeronautics Division removed from Caltrans. The CAA concurred with this decision.

Resolutions

1-81   Opposition to state block grants of ADAP funds.

2-81   Supported continuation of the previous ADAP program.

Stand on Bills

Opposed: AB 379, which required all airports serving passengers to provide suitable means to safeguard arriving baggage so only the owner thereof may remove baggage from the passenger terminal area.

1982
OFFICERS AND
BOARD OF DIRECTORS

President	James Mummert
President Elect	Jack Tippie
Past President	Raul Regalado
Secretary/Treasurer	James Hunter

Directors	
Robert Mandeville	Robert Tonseth
Thomas Greer	Raymond Burdick
Richard Smith	Robert Quincey

Meeting Sites

Board of Directors Meeting - Sky Harbor International Airport, Pheonix, 9/4/1981
Board of Directors Meeting - Los Angeles International Airport, 10/30/1981
ITS Short Course - Asilomar, Pacific Grove, 1/12/1982
Board of Directors Meeting - San Jose, 3/12/1982
Annual Meeting - Harrah's Hotel, Reno, 7/11-15/1982

Awards

Airport Manager of the Year - Clifford Moore Scholarship Award - Janet Namiko Chilcote

Major Issues of the Year

CAAE Business and Policies

Committees   Nominating-Raul Regalado
Membership-Quincey
Resolutions-Delmar Canady
Finance-Ralph Tonseth
Conference-Robert Mandeville
ITS Conference-Raymond Burdick
Publicity and Awards-Thomas Greer
Scholarship-Charles Foster
Credentials-Richard Smith
Historical-Robert Mandeville
Reference Library-Howard Corbin
Ethics-Jack Tippie
Legislation-Delmar Canady

CFR Training Course-Robert Mandeville
AAAE Accreditation-Richard Smith
Security Training Course-James Mummert
State Technical Advisory Committee Representative
Richard Smith
State Liaison-Nevada: Robert Mandeville, Arizona: Robert Bresnahan, California: Richard Smith

Decided that the President would be the Chapter Representative on the AAAE Nominating Committee.

Decided that the Southwest Chapter would decline to nominate anyone in 1982 to go thru the AAAE chairs-but instead would have a nomination in 1985.

Article II, Section II of the By-Laws was changed to include: "A nominee for the appropriate AAAE office or Member of the AAAE Board of Directors shall be elected at the Annual Winter Meeting." Article II, Section III was changed to require the Nominating Committee "to select eligible members as nominees for the appropriate AAAE office or member of the AAAE Board of Directors which will be due to be elected at the next succeeding Annual Winter Meeting."

Aviation Industry Issues

Objection was raised to the loss of 2.7 million dollars from the Special Aviation Funds to the State General Fund.

Stand on Bills

Favored: AB 2707, which called for the creation of a California Aeronautics Board. The Board would be responsible for all functions of the Aeronautics Division and the Division would be removed from the Transportation Department.

Opposed: AB 2708, which called for the Aeronautics Division to develop and submit to the Transportation Department a plan for local air service within California.

1983
OFFICERS AND
BOARD OF DIRECTORS

President	Jack Tippie
President Elect	Ralph Tonseth
Past President	James Mummert
Secretary/Treasurer	James Hunter

Directors	
Robert Mandeville	Raymond Burdick
Thomas Greer	Chris Kunze
Robert Quincey	Richard Smith

Meeting Sites

Board of Directors Meeting - Salt Lake City, 10/29/1982
ITS Short Course - Asilomar, Pacific Grove, 1/11-14/1983
Board of Directors Meeting - Los Angeles, 4/8/1983
Annual Meeting - RMS Queen Mary, Long Beach, 7/12-16/1983

Awards

Airport Manager of the Year - Howard Corbin
Wanamaker Award - Herman Bliss
President's Award - Robert Mandeville
Scholarship Award - John Rogers

Major Issues of the Year

CAAE Business and Policies

Committees   Nominating-James Mummert
Membership-Robert Quincey
Resolutions-Phil Lock
Finance-Robert Mandeville
Publicity-Thomas Greer/Kenneth Joule
Conference-Chris Kunze
ITS Conference-Raymond Burdick
Awards-Thomas Greer/Kenneth Joule
Credentials-Richard Smith
Scholarship-Charles Foster
Ethics-Ralph Tonseth
Historical-Richard Peacock/Robert Mandeville
Legislation-Delmar Canady
CFR Training Course-Robert Mandeville/Tony Capucci
AAAE Accreditation-Richard Smith
Sponsors and Exhibitors-Jack Ewald/Kenneth Keats
State Liaison-Nevada: Robert Mandeville;
California: Ralph Tonseth; Utah: ThomasGreer;
Arizona: James Mummert
State Technical Advisory Committee Representative
Francis Torr

The Crash, Fire, and Rescue Training Course was accredited by the International Civil Aviation Organization.

The normal source of $250 for the scholarship award was not available and the Board approved $250 from the CAAE for the scholarship.

1984
OFFICERS AND
BOARD OF DIRECTORS

President	Ralph Tonseth
President Elect	Raymond Burdick
Past President	Jack Tippie
Secretary/Treasurer	David Andrews

Directors

Robert Quincey	Raymond Farlin
Donald Bua	Robert Brydon
Chris Kunze	Phil Lock

Meeting Sites

Board of Directors Meeting - Reno, 8/31/1983
Board of Directors Meeting - Los Angeles, 11/18/1983
ITS Short Course - Asilomar, Pacific Grove, 1/10-12/1984
Board of Directors Meeting - Fresno, 3/30/1984
Board of Directors Meeting - Ontario, 5/11/1984
Annual Meeting - Red Lion Inn, Ontario, 7/8-12/1984

Awards
Scholarship Award - Fred von Zabern

Major Issues of the Year

CAAE Business and Policies

Committees   Nominating-Jack Tippie
Membership-Chris Kunze
Resolution-Phil Lock
Finance-Robert Mandeville
Publicity-Donald Bua
Awards-Robert Brydon
Conference-Mike Di Girolamo/Robert Quincey
ITS Conference-Raymond Burdick
Ethics-Raymond Burdick

Credentials-Phil Lock
Reference Library-Howard Corbin
Historical-Richard Peacock
Scholarship-Charles Foster
Legislation-Harold Wight
CFR Training Course-Ralph Tonseth
AAAE Accreditation-Richard Smith
STIP-Mike Merrey
State Technical Advisory Committee Representative
Richard Smith
State Liaison-California: Richard Smith; Nevada: Raymond
Farlin; Arizona: James Mummert; Utah: Thomas Greer

Article I, Section IV of the By-Laws was changed, deleting: "Each member of the Board shall be the Chairman of one of the standing committees of the CAAE." The purpose of the revision was to delete the reference in Article I that standing committees shall be chaired only by Board members. Article I was also amended to read: "The standing committees will be chaired as appointed by the President, annually, and their functions will be:" This was done to make Article I consistent with the change to Article IV approved by the membership in 1981.

The Board approved the award of $200 to CAAE members acquiring AAAE Executive status.

CAAE donated $100 in seed money to the newly formed Southeast Chapter of the AAAE.

Aviation Industry Issues
CAAE objection to the name change from Stockton Metropolitan Airport to Stockton-Modesto Regional Airport was stated. This decision was reached after the Mayor of Modesto objected to the change in a letter to the CAAE.

Resolutions
1-84   Stated that fueling safety is a national problem equally applicable at all airports and enjoined the Federal Aviation Administration to consider the licensing of aircraft fuelers with the same control and supervision now directed to pilots and aviation mechanics.

2-84   Condemned the "Jarvis IV" initiative as a deterrent to productive airport management. This ballot initiative would endanger the revenue producing capability of the airports in California.

3-84   Urged passage of AB 3521, which would return the 2.7 million dollars taken from the Special Aeronautics Fund.

4-84   Appreciation to Mark Mispagel, member of the California division of Aeronautics, for his contribution to the CAAE and the entire aviation community.

5-84 Commended Michael Di Girolamo and the entire Conference Committee for the success of the 1984 Annual Conference.

6-84   Commended Dennis Sannes, General Manager, Thunderbird Red Lion Inn, and his entire staff for a job "WELL DONE."

1985
OFFICERS AND
BOARD OF DIRECTORS

President	Raymond Burdick
President Elect	Robert Quincey
Past President	Ralph Tonseth
Secretary/Treasurer	David Andrews

Directors
Raymond Farlin
Phil Lock
Howard Corbin

Robert Brydon
Donald Bua
Denis Horn

Meeting Sites

Board of Directors Meeting - Los Angeles, 10/26/84
ITS Short Course - Asilomarr Pacific Grove, 1/22-25/1985
Board of Directors Meeting - Concord, 5/3/1985
Annual Meeting - Concord, 7/14-18/1985

Awards
Airport Manager of the Year - William Partain
President's Award - Thomas Leonard
Scholarship Award - Kristi McKenney

Major Issues of the Year

CAAE Business and Policies

Committees   Nominating-Ralph Tonseth
              Membership-Denis Horn
              Resolution-Hal Bostic
              Finance-Raymond Farlin
              Publicity and Awards-Donald Bua
              Conference-Harold Wight
              ITS Conference-Robert Brydon
              Awards-Richard Smith
              Credentials-Phil Lock
              Historical-Howard Corbin
              Ethics-Robert Quincey
              Scholarship-Charles Foster
              Reference Library-Howard Corbin
              Legislation-Harold Wight
              CFR Training Course-Richard Peacock
              AAAE Accreditation-Dick Traill
              STIP-Michael Merrey State Technical Advisory Committee
              Representative Richard Smith
              State Liasion-Arizona: James Mummert; Utah: Bern Case;
              Nevada: Raymond Farlin; California: Richard Smith;
              Mexico: Jack Tippie
              Constitution and By-Laws Review-Delmar Canady

Robert Quincey resigned from the office of President Elect in anticipation of retiring in August, 1985. Phil Lock was elected President Elect and Michael Merrey was elected Director to fill Phil Lock's vacancy in May 1985.

It was decided to retain the Airport Manager of the Year Award but not issue it every year.

Decided against the CAAE joining the CAC.

Aviation Industry Issues

Resolutions

1-85 Enjoined the State Director of Parks and Recreation to retain the two airstrips within Henry Coe State Park, Stanislaus County, California. Both were later closed, one because it was located in a wilderness area and the second because the expense of bringing it up to standards to make it safe for public use was cost prohibitive.

2-85 Urged Congress and the Administration to continue tax exempt financing for airport development without new restrictions .

3-85 Appreciation and heartfelt thanks to Contra Costa County for the use of Concord as the site of the 1985 Annual Conference.

4-85 Commended Hal Wight, his staff, and the entire Conference Committee for a job "WELL DONE."

5-85 Commended Scott Seymore and his entire staff for a job "WELL DONE" and extended heartfelt thanks for the use of their excellent facilities for the 1985 Annual Conference.

6-85 Appreciation to Ray Burdick for his administration of the organization during his term of office.

7-85 Appreciation to Bill Shea, FAA Associate Administrator for Airports, for his contribution and support of the Association and the entire aviation community.

8-85 Endorsed any and all efforts by the Congress of the United States to enact legislation to protect the airport improvement trust funds for the users entitled to its benefits. This was to insure that these funds would not be used by Congress to help achieve a balanced budget.

9-85 Supported the changes to the STIP recommended earlier by the CAAE and recommended timely implementation by the State of California.

1985-86
OFFICERS AND
BOARD OF DIRECTORS

President   Phil Lock
President Elect   Tom Greer
Past President   Ray Burdick
Secretary/Treasurer   Dave Andrews (Jul-Feb)
                                      Del Canady (Mar-Jun)

Directors
Pat Farlin   Howard Corbin
Denis Horn   Bern Case
Donna Murray   Mike Merrey

Meeting Sites

Board of Directors meeting - 11/1/85 - Ontario, California ITS Short Course, Board of Directors and
General Membership - 1/14-17/86 - Asilomar, Pacific Grove Board of Directors - 4/18/86 - Reno, Nevada Annual Conference , Board of Directors and General Membership - 7/13-17/86 - Sparks, Nevada

Awards
Airport Manager of the Year - Hal Wight
President's Award - Bob Bloom,
FAA Wanamaker Award - none

Committee Chairpersons

Standing Committees:

Ethics - Tom Greer   Conference - Verne Troup
Historical - Howard Corbin   Finance - Pat Farlin
Nominating - Ray Burdick   Credentials - Bern Case
Membership - Donna Murray   Publicity and Awards - Mike Merrey
ITS Conference - Hal Bostic & Joan Castaneda

Special Committees;

Resolutions - Hal Bostic   State Tech - R. C. Smith
AAAE Accred - Dick Traill   Scholarship - ChuckFoster
State Liaison:Arizona - Donna Murray   Nevada - Pat Farlin
Mexico - Jack Tippie   Calif. - R. C. Smith   Utah - Bern Case
Construction & by Law Review - Ray Burdick, Del Canady

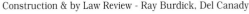

President Phil Lock stated that his goal for the year was a substantial increase in the number of members of the organization, and he tasked each member to recruit one additional member.

Organization Concerns and Action

During the year the CAAE/SWAAAE came into the computer age. The Secretary/Treasurer, Dave Andrews, advised that the workload for the Secretary was getting to be too much for a part time volunteer to handle. He recommended that computer equipment be purchased and used for the job of record keeping. He further recommended that a study be made of the alternatives to the present way the Secretary/Treasurer position is filled and functions. As a result of the extensive workload now encompassed in the duties of the Secretary/Treasure.

Dave Andrews tendered his resignation.

The Board of Directors appropriated money to purchase a new computer and other related office equipment. A committee was appointed to study the alternatives. Del Canady was appointed to the position of Secretary/Treasurer, instructed to purchase the new equipment and to start putting the organization records on the computer.

Under the direction of Howard Corbin, CAE, compilation of the history of CAAE was commenced and finished. Credits for the vast amount of work are listed in the front of the book, "History of the CAAE".

In accordance with recommendations made by the CAAE. The funding criteria and priorities for projects in the Aviation Segment of the State Transportation Improvement Plan were changed, and new criteria and priorities were adopted.

For the past several years a topic for informal discussions among members has been the relationship of responsibilities, priorities and services performed by the organization as an instrument of CAAE vis-a-vis the Southwest Chapter of CAAE. The discussions have centered around whether the interests of both the CAAE and Southwest Chapter of AAAE might better be served by two separate but closely related organizations. A committee to study the entire situation and report back to the organization was appointed and consisted of: Denis Horn (Calif), Chairman: Michael Klein (Ariz); Tim Phillips (Utah); Robert Esperance (Nevada)j R. C. Smith (Calif); Ray Burdick (Calif); and Dick Traill (Ariz). The committee was tasked to report back to the Board and &eneral Membership when the report was completed. Upon completion of the study and report, the general membership voted to make no changes in the organizational structure of CAAE/SWAAAE at this time.

Efforts have been underway to revive the Crash/Fire/Rescue School that had been held in prior years at Reno, Nev. The stringent regulations of the Air Quality Management laws seem to preclude any open fires for such training in the State of California.

During the year the following resolutions were adopted:

85-1 urges Congress not to enact laws which would discontinue tax exempt bonding availability for airports.

85-2 expressed thanks to Contra Costa County for hosting the 39th Annual Conference of CAAE/SWAAAE.

85-3 commends and thanks Hal Wight for being host of the 39th Annual Conference.

85-4 expresses thanks and appreciation to staff of the Concord Airport Hilton Hotel for the fine work done in connection with the 39th Annual Conference.

85-5 expresses praise and thanks to Ray Burdick for the fine work performed during his tenure as President during 1985-86.

85-6 expresses thanks and appreciation to Bill Shea, upon his resignation from the FAA, for his support of the aviation industry and the CAAE/SWAAAE.

85-7 encourages Congress to resist any efforts to appropriate money from the Aviation Trust Fund for uses other than those intended.

85-8 requests and encourages the State Division of Aeronautics to adopt changes in the prioritization of aviation projects in connection with the State Transportation Improvement Plan.

1986-87 OFFICERS AND BOARD OF DIRECTORS

President	Tom Greer
President Elect	Denis Horn
Past President	Phil Lock
Secretary/Treasurer	Del Canady

Directors

Pat Farlin	Howard Corbin
Hal Wight	Jim Chappell
Donna Murray	Mike Merrey

Meeting Sites

Board of Directors Meeting - 10/29/86 - Burbank, California ITS Short Course, Board of Directors and General Membership - 1/14-17/87 - Asilomar, Pacific Grove Board of Directors - 4/22/87 - Santa Maria, Calif. Annual Conference , Board of Directors and General Membership - 7/13-16/87 - Santa Maria, Calif.

Awards

Airport Manager of the Year - David E. Andrews
President's Award - Phil Lock
Wanamaker Award - none
Scholarship ($250) - John C. Olson, San Jose State College

Committee Chairpersons

Standing Committees:

Ethics - Denis Horn	Conference - Dan Hoback
Historical - Mike Merrey	Finance - Pat Farlin
Nominating - Phil Lock	Credentials - Hal Wight
Membership - Donna Murray	ITS Conference - Joan Castaneda
Publicity and Awards - Howard Corbin	

Special Committees:

Resolutions - Ray Burdick	State Tech - R. C. Smith
AAAE Accred - Dick Traill	Scholarship - Chuck Foster
State Liaison: Arizona - Donna Murray	Calif. - R.C. Smith
Nevada - Pat Farlin	Utah: Tim Phillips
Mexico - Jack Tippie	Legislation - Jim Chappell
CAAE/SWAAAE Organization - Denis Horn	Ref Library - Howard Corbin
CFR Training - Denis Horn	STIP - Ron Karge, Mike Merrey

During this year the Association added two new sections to the Membership Directory. One new section lists all Corporate Members according to types of services/products they sell. The other new section lists all airports represented by a member in the Association.

The Association, for the first time, allowed a conference chairman to obligate the Association funds to contract for services and products to stage the Annual Summer Conference.

A new display board was purchased for the use of the Association in displaying its activities and officers roster at various public gatherings.

Completed a year long study and discussion regarding the relationship between the organizational and membership functions of the Association when acting as the CAAE vis a vis the SW Chapter of AAAE.

The Association decided to change the location of the Winter Conference from Asilomar to some alternate location in the Monterey Peninsula area, probably a hotel.

RESOLUTIONS ADOPTED WERE:

1-86 To honor and thank Vern Troup for his efforts as Chairman of the 1986 Annual Summer Conference.

2-86 To thank Washoe County Airport Authority for hosting the 1986 Annual Summer Conference in Sparks, Nevada.

3-86 To thank the Mayor of Sparks, Nevada, for the hospitality of his City during the 1986 Annual Summer Conference.

4-86 To thank the Nugget Hotel and its outstanding staff for excellent service during the 1986 Annual Summer Conference.

5-86 To Phil Lock as an expression of appreciation on behalf of the Association for the outstanding job he had done as President of the Association during 1986-87.

1987-88
OFFICERS AND
BOARD OF DIRECTORS

President	Denis R. Horn
President Elect	R. "Pat"Farlin
Past President	Tom Greer
Secretary/Treasurer	Del Canady (July-October)
Executive Director/Secty.	Victoria Collins (Nov.-June)

Directors

G. Hardy Acree	Ray Beeninga
Hal Wight	Jim Chappell
Mary Rose Loney	Donna Murray
Vern Troup	

Meeting Sites

Board of Directors Meeting - 10/30/87 - Ontario-California ITS Short Course, Board of Directors and General Membership - 1/12-15/88 - Monterey, Calif. Board of Directors - 4/22/88 - Oakland, Calif. Annual Conference , Board of Directors and General Membership - 7/10-14/88 - Oakland, Calif.

Awards

Airport Manager of the Year - Thomas E. Greer
President's Award - Ray Burdick
Wanamaker Award - John L. Pfeifer
Scholarship ($1,000) - Julio Cesar Morales, San Jose State University

Committee Chairpersons

Standing Committees:

Ethics - Pat Farlin	Conference - Chuck Foster
Historical-	Finance - Pat Farlin
Publicity - Phil Lock	Nominating - Phil Lock
Credentials - Hal Wight	Membership - Donna Murray
ITS Conference - Bruce Mosley	Awards - Dave Andrews

Special Committees:

Resolutions-	Legislation - Jim Chappell
State Tech - R. C. Smith	AAAE Accred - Dick Traill
Scholarship - Chuck Foster	Ref Library - Howard Corbin
CFR Training - Denis Horn	State Liaison; Arizona - Donna Murray
Calif. - R. C. Smith	Nevada - Pat Farlin
Utah - Tim Phillips	Mexico - Jack Tippie
Negotiate Exec. Dir. Contract - Tom Greer	
Specialty Conference - Mary Rose Loney and Hal Wight	

President Horn's goals for the Association for 1987-88 are;

a. Determine what Association may be able to do to help cure growing disparity between airspace and airport demands and capacity of system to meet those demands.

b. Continue examining organizational relationship between CAAE and SWAAAE at any time substantial portion of membership desires to further discuss the matter.

c. Explore ways for Corporate and Associate members to take a more active role in the Association.

d. Explore expansion of the Scholarship Awards program.

During the year 1987-88 the organization of the Association was changed in accordance with revised By-Laws approved by the members of the Association. The changes include adding one additional Director to the Board of Directors, hiring a regular, paid Executive Director on contract for one year at a time and deleting the office of Secretary/Treasurer. The Executive Director will have no vote on the Board of Directors. Victoria Collins was selected to be the Executive Director of the Association effective November 1, 1987.

Effective July 1, 1988, the dues and initiation fees were raised to $50 per year for Executive and Associate members and $60 per year for Corporate members. The initiation fee was raised to $20.

This was the year the Annual Winter Conference was moved from Asilomar, after many years in that location, and was held in a hotel in Monterey, California.

The Association was active in contributing to the formation and adoption of a "Ground Access Policy" by the California Transportation Commission. Rather than require airports arbitrarily to spend vast sums on roadway improvements that might not necessarily benefit the particular airport, the policy is a simple declaration of the case-by-case negotiation procedure looking at the benefit to accrue to the airport concerned.

This year the Association commenced holding "Specialty Conferences" on timely subjects of immediate interest in airport management. Topics of fiscal, regulatory or technical subjects will be scheduled. The conferences may be held as often as three or four times per year in the future and at various locations. The conferences are expected to become a source of additional revenue for the Association.

Resolutions approved by the association during the year were:

1-87 To Dan Hoback and conference committee for an outstanding job in planning and staging the 1987 Summer Conference.

2-87 To Santa Maria Airport District Authority for hosting the 1987 Summer Conference.

3-87 To Santa Maria Airport Hilton Hotel and its staff for fine cooperation and courtesy exhibited during the 1987 Conference.

4-87 In support of Assembly Bill 276 in the State of California Legislature which would increase state grants to airports from $5000 to $10,000 per year.

5-87 and 6-87 To the FAA urging the creation of "fly quietly" sections in aircraft flight manuals to instruct pilots how to operate their individual aircraft more quietly in urban environments. Resolutions were identical in wording and varied only in the headings depending on which states the resolutions were sent from.

1-88 To Del and Ginny Canady for outstanding service to the Association while acting as Secretary/Treasurer.

2-88 To put the Association on record as being in favor of the provisions proposed in California State Senator Rogers' Bill concerning the use of Sales and Use Tax revenue for airport projects.

3-88 To Ray Burdick in appreciation of the service he had rendered to the Association upon his retirement from the airport management profession.

1988-89
OFFICERS AND
BOARD OF DIRECTORS

President	R. "Pat" Farlin (July 1988 - Jan. 1989)
President	Hal Wight (Jan. 1989 - June 1989)
President Elect	Hal Wight (July 1988 - Jan. 1989)
President Elect	Donna Murray (Jan. 1989 - June 1989)
Past President	Denis R. Horn
Executive Director/Secretary	Victoria Collins

Directors

G. Hardy Acree	Ray Beeninga
N. Bertholf	Jim Chappell
Philip A. Lock	Mary Rose Loney
Donna M. Murray (7/88 - 1/89)	Hank Dittmar (1/89 - 6/89)
Barry S. Craig *	

President R "Pat" Farlin resigned his office in January 1989 due to leaving the airport management profession and going into private industry. President Elect, Hal Wight, succeeded to the office of the President. As he was resigning, "Pat" Farlin appointed Donna Murray to the office of President Elect and Hank Dittmar to fill Donna Murray's position on the Board of Directors until the next regular election of officers.

*For the first time, a corporate representative, elected by the Corporate Members, sits with the Board of Directors as an advisory member but without a vote.

Meeting Sites

Board of Directors Meeting - 10/14/88 - Las Vegas, Nevada ITS Short Course, Board of Directors and General Membership - 1/10-13/89 - Monterey, Calif. Board of Directors - 4/28/89 - Riverside, California Annual Conference ,Board of Directors and General Membership - 7/9-13/89 - Riverside, Calif.

Awards
Airport Manager of the Year - Ralph Tonseth
President's Award - Jack Kemmerly, 5tate Director of Aviation
Wanamaker Award - Tim Merwyn (SCAG)

Committee Chairpersons

Standing Committees:

Ethics - Hal Wight	Conference - Murray Bywater
Historical - Del Canady	Awards - Dutch Bertholf
Resolutions - Kim Wirht	Scholarship - Denis Horn and Mary Rose Loney

Time and Place - Hal Wight	Accreditation - Dick Traill
Gen. Aviation - Ray Beeninga	Specialty Workshops - Mary Rose Loney

President Farlin's goals for the Association for 1988-89 are:

a. Continue examining the expansion of the Scholarship Award Program.

b. Continue the feasibility study of the Association being the sole sponsor of the winter conference.

c. Further development of the "specialty conferences" to meet the educational and training needs of airport professional managers in the Southwest region.

d. Development of a program that will identify General Aviation airports on the verge of closure and recommend solutions for the problems that plague those airports.

e. Build and strengthen our Association throughout the Southwest Region.

The Federal Aviation Administration is considering channeling federal aviation grant funds through selected states during a trial period. California is one of the states being considered. In this state, however, the prioritization and selection of projects would be the extent of state participation. The CAAE/SWAAAE has been asked by the state to support the trial program in this state. After extensive study and discussion, CAAE/SWAAAE took a position in favor of the trial process. The Association will be engaging in development of the new project rating matrix.

A critical look has been taken by the Association relative to conduct of the midwinter conference by the University of California (ITS). The Association has decided to solicit bids from various educational institutions for staging the 1990 Winter Conference, with CAAE/SWAAAE acting as consultant . The University of California (ITS) will be given the first right of refusal to stage the conference at or below the lowest bid price.

At future Summer Conferences, Executive Emeritus Members will be afforded reduced registration fees.

With the final auditing of the Summer Conference financial records, it is noted that for the first time in many years the Conference has failed to generate any profit for the Associations treasury.

A change in the By-Laws of the Association has created two new classes of memberships. They are "Participating" for government, college or airport commission members, and "Student" for those engaged in the study of airport management or a related field at any accredited university or college.

Financial support by the Corporate Members has enabled the Association to start granting two $1000 scholarships per year, starting in 1990. A single $1000 scholarship was awarded this year to Jennifer Donohue who is interning at San Francisco International Airport.

The Association suffered a net loss of twenty members during the year.

SPECIALTY CONFERENCES (WORKSHOPS) CONDUCTED DURING THIS YEAR:
Disadvantaged Business Enterprises - 11/10-88 - San Jose, California.
Pavement Maintenance Program - 1/10/89 - Monterey, Calif.

RESOLUTIONS APPROVED BY THE ASSOCIATION DURING THE YEAR WERE;
Resolution 1-88 -- to Del Canady for outstanding service to the Association as Secretary/Treasurer.

Resolution 2-88 -- to put the Association on record in support of SB263 (Rogers) relative to Sales & Use Tax Revenue and Airport Projects.

There was no record of Resolution 3-88 as to its subject matter or adoption.

Resolution 4-88 -- to Denis Horn for a job "well done" during the term of his Presidency.

Resolution 5-88 -- to Walter Abernathy and the Port of Oakland for their outstanding contribution to the success of the 42nd Annual Summer Conference.

Resolution 6-88 -- to Chuck Foster and the entire Conference Committee for their "entrepreneurial approach" in developing the 1988 Summer Conference.

Resolution 7-88 -- to the Claremont Hotel and Tennis Club staff for providing the ambience and service so deeply appreciated by the conference attendees.

1989-90
OFFICERS AND
BOARD OF DIRECTORS

President	Hal Wight
President Elect	Donna Murray (7/89-4/90)
President Elect	Neilson Bertholf (4/90-6/90)
Past President	Denis Horn
Executive Director/Secretary	Hal Bostic

Directors

G. Hardy Acree (7/89-1/90)	Jim Chappell
Hank Dittmar (7/89-1/90)	Philip A. Lock
Ray Beeninga	Dan Hoback
Bob Trimborn (1/90-7/90)	Bob Esperance (1/90-7/90)
Barry S. Craig *	

* Special Corporate Representative (non voting)

During the year, Donna Murray, President Elect, and Directors G. Hardy Acree and Hank Dittmar resigned from their employment and their offices in the Association. They were replaced by Neilson Bertholf, Bob Trimborn and Bob Esperance, respectively.

Meeting Sites

Special Board of Directors Meeting - 7/10/89 - Riverside, California.
Board of Directors Meeting - 10/20/89 - Oakland, California
Winter Conference, Board of Directors and General Membership 1/16-19/90 - Monterey, Calif.
Board of Directors - 4/20/90 - Tucson, Arizona
Annual Conference , Board of Directors and
General Membership - 7/16-19/90 - Tucson, Arizona

Awards

Airport Manager of the Year - Charles W. Foster
President's Award - Henry E. Dittmar
Wanamaker Award - Joseph Irvine
*Aviation Excellence Award - Joseph L. Pietrowski
Scholarships ($1,000) - Matthew Tager, San Jose State University
Ann Richart, Embry Riddle University

*The "Aviation Excellence Award" was established this year. Joseph Pietrowski is the first recipient. The award will be given each year to the person, other than an airport manager, who has been selected for outstanding achievement in aviation management.

Committee Chairpersons

Standing Committees:

Ethics - Donna Murray	Conference - Walter A. Burg
Historical - Del Canady	ITS Conference - Hank Dittmar
Awards - Dutch Bertholf	Resolutions - Leonard Peterson
Scholarship - Denis Horn	Nominating - Denis Horn
Credentials - Jim Chappell	Membership/ Publicity - Phil Lock
Legislative - Rob Leonard	Time and Place - Donna Murray
Accreditation - Hardy Acree	Gen. Aviation - Ray Beeninga
Specialty Conferences - Allen Smoot	Channelization and Stip - Hardy Acree
Aviation Awareness - Dan Hoback	Intern Programs - Denis Horn

President Hal Wight has set as one of his goals for the year the involvement of more members in the matters of the Association, including serving on committees.

SPECIALTY CONFERENCES (WORKSHOPS) CONDUCTED DURING THIS YEAR:

Construction Management - 11/6/89 - Ontario, California Earthquake Preparedness and Response for Airports 1/16/90 - Monterey, California

RESOLUTIONS APPROVED BY THE ASSOCIATION DURING THE YEAR WERE:

Resolution 1-89 -- to put the Association on record in support of the FAA being established as an independent agency rather than a part of the Transportation Department of the United States.

Resolution 2-89 -- in favor of using Aviation Improvement Project Funds to purchase fire trucks for Sacramento Metro Airport to be used in a CFR Training Facility.

Resolution 3-89 -- to commend the Conference Committee

Resolution 4-89 -- to commend the Ontario Airport Guides and to thank Mike Di Girolamo for making them available.

Resolution 5-89 -- commending the Riverside Sheraton Hotel.

Resolution 6-89 -- commending the Riverside Visitors and Convention Bureau and Marriott Catering.

Resolution 7-89 -- commending Victoria Collins for her contributions to the Association.

By policy decision, the organization this year authorized emergency action on urgent legislative matters in California to be taken by a committee composed of the President, President Elect and Legislative Committee Chairperson.

For some time, membership in the Association from the State of Utah has been almost non-existent. Many eligible members from Utah have felt that they had more in commom with the Northwest Chapter of AAAE than with the CAAE/SWAAAE. By action of the AAAE Board of Directors, Utah will remain in the Southwest Chapter area of AAAE, but AAAE members in Utah will be allowed to join either the Northwest or Southwest Chapters of AAAE. Thus, CAAE/SWAAAE still includes the State of Utah within its boundaries, officially.

Beginning this year, corporate advertising was accepted for publication in the "AIRPORTS WEST" newsletter, for a stated fee.

1990-91
OFFICERS AND
BOARD OF DIRERCTORS

President	Neilson Bertholf
President Elect	Jim Chappell

Past President   Hal Wight
Executive Director/Secretary   Hal Bostic

Directors
Ray Beeninga   Joan Castaneda
Barclay Dick   Bob Esperance
Dan Hoback   Phil Lock
Rod Murphy   Jim Harris *

* During this year the By-Laws were amended to include on the Board of Directors, as a voting member, a corporate representative elected only by the vote of other corporate members.

Meeting Sites

Board of Directors Meeting - lO/26/90 Phoenix, Arizona
Winter Conference, Board of Directors and and General Membership 1/8-11/91 - Monterey, Calif.
Board of Directors - 4/5/91 - Modesto, California
Annual Conference , Board of Directors and
General Membership - 7/14-18/91 - Modesto, California

Committee Chairpersons

Standing Committees:

Ethics - Jim Chappell   Conference - Howard Cook
Historical - Del Canady   Monterey Conference-Dave Andrews
Nominating - Hal Wight   Credentials - Rod Murphy
Membership/ Publicity Phil Lock   Legislative - Rob Leonard
Awards - Bob Esperance   Time and Place - Jim Chappell
Aviation Awareness - Dan Hoback   Accreditation - Bruce Mosley
Scholarships   Barclay Dick   Gen. Aviation - Joan Castaneda
Specialty Conferences - Bob Trimborn

SPECIALTY CONFERENCES (WORKSHOPS) CONDUCTED DURING THIS YEAR

Managing Helicopter Activity at Your Airport 7/14/90 - Tucson, Arizona
Hazardous Materials - 1/8/91 - Monterey Calif.

President Bertholf stated his goals for the year as being:

1. Improvement of the financial state of the organization
2. Increased membership in the organization
3. Improved relations with the individual state chapters
4. Promotion of AAAE Accreditation by individual members
5. Promotion of awards programs and increased nominations
6. Development of a "specialty conference" on general aviation

Awards

Airport Manager of the Year - Robert P. Olislagers
President's Award - David E. Andrews
Wanamaker Award - Don Smith, Commissioner, Petaluma
Aviation Excellence Award - Joe Potts, Airport Authority of Washoe County
Scholarships ($1,000) - Kelly Howat and Chris Melville

RESOLUTIONS APPROVED BY THE ASSOCIATION DURING THE YEAR WERE:

90-1 a resolution commending Christine Eberhard for her efforts on the successful "Helicopter" Specialty Conference.

90-2 a resolution commending the staff of Loew's Ventana Canyon Resort.

90-3 a resolution commending the Conference Committee.

Effective this year, a new schedule of dues and initiation fees were established. Annual dues are now $60 for Executive, Participating and Associate members with an initiation fee of $30. For Corporate memberships, annual dues are $70, and the initiation fee is $35. Student membership dues remain at $15, with the same amount for initiation. Retired membership dues remain at one-half the amount for Executive members -- $30 -- with no initiation fee.

Corporate membership annual dues contain a $5 allocation, established by voluntary recommendation of the corporate members, to help support the annual scholarship awards.

There are now two $1000 scholarship awards given annually at the Winter Conference in Monterey.

A fee was instituted this year for publishing Job Opportunities and Business Opportunities in "AIRPORTS WEST".

1991-1992 OFFICERS AND BOARD OF DIRECTORS

President   Jim Chappell
President Elect   Rodney Murphy
Past President   Neilson (Dutch) Bertholf, Jr.
Executive Director/Secretary   Hal Bostic
* Corporate Director   Robert Olislagers

Meeting Sites
Directors
Bob Esperance   Phil Lock (7/91 - 10/91)
Jim Monger (10/91 -6-92)   Bruce Mosley
Joan Castaneda   Barclay Dick
Robert Trimborn   Jim Harris *

General Aviation Conference, Board of Directors Meeting - 10/9-11/91 - San Diego, California
Winter Conference, Board of Directors and General Membership -1/8-10/92 - Monterey, Calif.
Board of Directors - 4l24l92 - Burbank, California
Annual Conference, Board of Directors and General Membership - 7/12-16/92 - Burbank California

Committee Chairpersons

Ethics - Rodney Murphy   Conference Tom Greer
Historical - Hal Bostic   Monterey Conference - David Andrews
Awards - Bob Esperance   Scholarships - Barclay Dick
Corporate Liaison - Jim Harris   Intern - Barclay Dick
General Aviation - Joan Castaneda   Nominating - Neilson Bertholf, Jr.
Credentials - Robert Olislagers   Membership/Publicity - Phil Lock
Legislative - Brian Raber   Time and Place - Rodney Murphy
Speciality Conferences - Bob Trimborn   Resolutions - Phil Lock
Association Structural Review- Howard Cook
Aviation Awareness - Robert Trimborn

SPECIALITY CONFERENCES (WORKSHOPS) CONDUCTED DURING THE YEAR:
Developing and Negotiating Airport Lease Agreements January 7, 1992 at Monterey, California
California Storm Water Compliance Workshop
January 23, 1992 - Los Angeles
January 24, 1992 - San Francisco

Awards
Airport Manager of the Year - Ray L. Beeninga
President's Award - Phil Lock

Wanamaker Award - Spyridon N "Speedy" Sideris
Aviation Excellence Award - Gloria Vasques

RESOLUTIONS APPROVED BY THE ASSOCIATION DURING THE YEAR WERE:

92-1 a resolution recognizing Robert Olislagers for the development of the First Annual G.A. conference.

92-2 a resolution commending the Corporate membership for their support in the success of the Association and conferences.

92-3 a resolution supporting AAAE amendment to the By-Laws to create three at-large seats on the Board of Director to achieve the goals of diversity and executive service.

92-4 a resolution commending the staff of the Burbank Airport Hilton for supporting the Summer Conference. a resolution commending Warner Bros for hosting a wonderful reception, at the Summer Conference.

92-6 a resolution thanking Robert Garcia and the Burbank-Glendale-Pasadena Airport Authority for hosting the Summer Conference.

92-7 a resolution commending the Summer Conference Committee.

92-8 a resolution recognizing Phil Lock for his years of service to the organization.

1992-93
OFFICERS AND
BOARD OF DIRECTORS

President	Rodney Murphy
President Elect	Barclay Dick
Past President	Jim Chappell
Executive Director/Secretary	Hal Bostic

Directors	
Howard Cook	Bruce Mosley
James Bennett	Robert Trimborn
Robert Esperance	Robert Olislagers
Jim Monger	Jim Harris *

*Corporate Director

Meeting Sites

General Aviation Conference, Board of Directors Meeting - 9/30-10/2/92 - San Diego, California
Winter Conference, Board of Directors and General Membership -116-8193 - Monterey, Calif.
Board of Directors - 412193 - Sparks, Nevada
Annual Conference, Board of Directors and General Membership - 7118-22193 - Reno, Nevada

Committee Chairpersons

Ethics - Barclay Dick	Conference - Robert White/Robert Esperance
Historical - Hal Bostic	Publicity - Hal Bostic
Legislative - Krys Bart	Awards - Robert Esperance
John Kinney	Scholarships - Mark Myers
Student Airport Manager Committee	Scott Gray
Conference Program Coordinator	Robert Olislagers
Association Structural Review	Bruce Mosley
Nominating - Jim Chappell	Credentials - Robert Olislagers
Membership - Jim Monger	Monterey Conference - Dave Andrews
Intern - Mark Myers	Time and Place - Barclay Dick
Aviation Awareness - John Minkler	Speciality Conferences - Bob Trimborn

Resolutions - Phil Lock - Tracy Williams   Corporate Liaison - Jim Harris
G.A. Conference - Joan Castanea

SPECIALTY CONFERENCES (WORKSHOPS) CONDUCTED DURING THIS YEAR:

Airport Land Use Planning, July 7, 1993, Reno, Nevada

Awards
Airport Manager of the Year - Doyle C. Ruff
President's Award - Robert Trimborn
Wanamaker Award - Jay C. White
Aviation Excellence Award - Robert L. Becker
Scholarships ($1,000) - Pushpa Nair and Christy Burriesci

RESOLUTIONS APPROVED BY THE ASSOCIATION DURING THE YEAR WERE:

93-1 a resolution expressing appreciation to the University of California for many years of service and efforts in the promotion of extension education and airport development.

93-2 a resolution commending the Summer Conference Committee.

93-3 a resolution commending the staff of John Ascuaga's Nugget for supporting the Summer Conference.

POLICY DECISIONS

The Board adopted a policy whereby members serving as off1cers or Directors of AAAE shall also serve as members of SWAAAE/CAAE Board in a non-voting, advisory capacity.

92-2 The Board adopted a policy at its regular meeting September 30, 1992 charging the nomination committee to be mindful to provide for diversity in the make-up of the Officers and Board of Directors.

92-3 The Board modified the requirements for Executive membership in the Association

Arizona State University in cooperation with SWAAAE/CAAE will present the Airport Management Short Course in Monterey beginning January 1994.

1993-1994
OFFICERS AND
BOARD OF DIRECTORS

President	Barclay Dick
President Elect	Bruce Mosley
Past President	Rodney Murphy
Executive Director/Secretary	Hal Bostic
Corporate Director-	

Directors	
Howard Cook	Krys Bart
James Bennett	Robert Trimborn
Margaret Purdue	Ted Anderson
Jim Monger	Jim Harris *

General Aviation Conference, Board of Directors Meeting - 9/25-26/93 - San Diego, California Winter Conference, Board of Directors and General Membership -1/5-7/94 - Monterey, Calif. Board of Directors - 418194 - Sacramento, California Annual Conference, Board of Directors and General Membership - 7/17-21/94 - Sacramento, Calif.

Committee Chairpersons

Ethics - Bruce Mosley
Conference - Bruce Mosley
Historical - Hal Bostic
Monterey Conference - James Bennett, Dave Andrews
Awards - John Kinney
Scholarships - Mark Myers
Resolutions - Tracy Williams
Nominating - Rodney Murphy
Credentials - Ted Anderson
Membership - Jim Monger
Publicity - Hal Bostic
Legislative - Krys Bart
Time and Place - Bruce Mosley
Speciality Conferences - Bob Trimborn - Howard Cook
Conference Program Coordinator - Robert Olislagers
Corporate Liaison - Jim Harris
Intern - Mark Myers
G. A. Conference - Joan Castaneda
Student Airport Manager Committee By-Laws- Rodney Murphy, Scott Gray

Awards

Airport Manager of the Year - John Swizer
President's Award - Hal Bostic
Wanamaker Award - Jack Kemmerly
Aviation Excellence Award - Krys Bart
Scholarships ($1,000) - Regina Donnelly and Amy Corathers

RESOLUTIONS APPROVED BY THE ASSOCIATION DURING THE YEAR WERE:

94-1 a resolution recognizing Jack Kemmerly for service to aviation and the Association.

94-2 a resolution against an amendment to S.1491, Airport Improvement program authorization.

94-3 a resolution in honor of James Magnus "Jim" Nissen.

94-4 a resolution recognizing the contribution of Delmar Canady, E.E. has made to the Association.

94-5 a resolution in honor of Joseph R. "Joe" Crotti A.A.E.

94-6 a resolution commending the Summer Conference Committee.

94-7 a resolution commending the staff of the Radisson Hotel for support of the Summer Conference.

94-8 a resolution recognizing Barclay Dick for an outstanding job and his leadership as president.

January 5,1994 the members of the Association voted to change the name to Southwest Chapter of the American Association of Airport Executives.

1994-1995 OFFICERS AND BOARD OF DIRECTORS

President	Bruce Mosley
President Elect	Robert Olislagers
Past President	Barclay Dick
Executive Director/Secretary	Hal Bostic

Directors

Brent Shiner	Krys Bart

James Bennett	Robert Trimborn
Randall Berg	Margaret Purdue
Tracy Williams	Jim Harris*
*Corporate Director	

Meeting Sites

General Aviation Conference, Board of Directors Meeting - 10/12-14/94 - San Diego, California Winter Conference, Board of Directors and General Membership -1/18-20/95 - Monterey, Calif. Board of Directors - 4/17-20/95 Long Beach, California Annual Conference, Board of Directors and General Membership - 7/16-20/95 - Long Beach, Calif.

Committee Chairpersons

Ethics - Robert Olislagers
Conference - Chris Kunze
Historical - Hal Bostic
Monterey Conference - James Bennett
Awards - John Kinney
Scholarships - Mark Myers
Corporate Liaison - Jim Harris
Intern - Krys Bart
Association Structural Review - Howard Cook
Finance - Robert Olislagers
Diversity - Krys Bart, Tracy Williams
AAE Oral Board Training Program - Randall Berg
Nominating - Barclay Dick
Credentials - Brent Shiner
Membership/Publicity - Margaret Purdue
Legislative - Robert Wiswell
Time and Place - Robert Olislagers
Speciality Conferences - Bob Trimborn
Resolutions - Tracy Williams
Student Airport Management - Scott Gray, Tara Tighe
Conference Program Coordinator - Robert Trimborn

Awards

Airport Manager of the Year - Robert N. Broadbent
President's Award - Laurence Gesell
Wanamaker Award - Sylvia L. Paoli, Judge Pro. Tem.
Aviation Excellence Award - Robert R. Erickson
Scholarships ($1,000) - Jeffrey Johnson

RESOLUTIONS APPROVED BY THE ASSOCIATION DURING THE YEAR WERE:

95-1 a resolution commending the Summer Conference Committee.

95-2 a resolution recognizing Bruce Mosley for his leadership with class and style as president of SWAAAE.

The membership adopted a new logo for the association that reflects representation for the four state area.

CHAPTER 1

1. The precise date of the first flight is subject of some debate. John's brother James first recalled the date of August 28, 1883, while in his 70s and many of Montgomery's supporters have accepted this date as given. However, evidence suggests that the flight took place in 1884. This is in part based on a newspaper article in 1909 which placed the flight sometime in 1884; and a 1928 letter by John's brother Richard, which also placed the flight in 1884.

2. Scott, Mary L. *San Diego: Air Capital of the West.* 1991. The San Diego Aerospace Museum. Page 9.

3. Crouch, Tom D. *A Dream of Wings: Americans and the Airplane, 1875-1905.* 1989. The Smithsonian Press. Pages 26, 27.

4. It was not until 1942 that the Smithsonian Institution would recognize the Wright Brothers' place in history, having bestowed that honor to its former secretary, S.P. Langley and his aerodrome.

5. Chanute, Octave. *Progress in Flying Machines.* 1894. Reprinted by Lorenz & Herweg, Publishers, Long Beach, CA. 1976. Pages 248, 249.

6. Montgomery, Richard J., to Secretary (Walcott) of the Smithsonian Institution, dated March 22, 1928. Smithsonian Institution Archives. Record Unit 46. Office of the Secretary, 1925-1949 (Charles D. Walcott, Charles G. Abot, Alexander Wetmore) Box 111.

Note: Dr. Tom D. Crouch, Chairman of the Aeronautics Department at the National Air and Space Museum, is the only historian who identifies 1884 as the year in which the flight took place in his book *A Dream of Wings,* originally his Ph.D. dissertation. Although the date is not referenced, Dr. Crouch was able to identify its sources some 20 years after the fact.

CHAPTER 2

1. Harris, Sherwood. *The First to Fly.* Simon and Shuster. New York. 1970. Page 67.

2. Ibid. Page 73.

3. Gibbs-Smith, Charles H. *The World's First Aeroplane Flights.* Her Majesty's Stationary Office. London. 1965. Page 20.

4. Harris, Sherwood. *The First to Fly.* Simon and Shuster. New York. 1970. Page 109.

5. Doolittle, James H. *I Could Never Be So Lucky Again: An Autobiography of Jimmy Doolittle.* with Glines, Carroll, V. Shiffer Military/Aviation History. Atglen, Pennsylvania. 1995. Page 25, 26.

6. Harris, Sherwood. *The First To Fly.* Simon and Shuster. New York, 1970. Page 256, 257.

7. Lebow, Eileen F. *Cal Rodgers And The Vin Fiz.* Smithsonian Institution Press. Washington, 1989. Page 193.

8. Ibid. Page 194.

9. Ibid. Page 195, 196.

10. Ibid. Page 197.

11. Ibid. Page 204.

12. On April 3, 1912 Cal Rodgers was killed in the Wright B Flyer, the back up to the *Vin Fiz,* not more than a few hundred feet from the place where he rolled his wheels in the Pacific following his historic flight.

CHAPTER 3

1. *History of Modesto.* (Author unknown) 1970. Page 72 .

2. Ibid. Page 72.

3. Karsner, Douglas George. "Leaving on a Jet Plane: Commercial Aviation, Airports and Post-Industrial American Society, 1933-1970" Ph.D. Dissertation, Temple University 1993. UMI Dissertation Services, Ann Arbor, Michigan, 1995. Page 1.

4. Glines, Carroll V. *Airmail: How It All Began.* Tab Aero Books, Blue Ridge Summit, PA. 1990. Page 34.

5. *Airport Construction and Management* magazine. June, 1929. Page 18.

6. Ibid. Page 34.

7. Ibid. Page 38, 39.

8. Ibid. Page 40.

9. Ibid. Page 43.

10. Ibid. Page 60.

11. Glines, Carroll V. *Airmail: How It All Began.* Tab Aero, Blue Ridge Summit, Pennsylvania. 1990. Page 69, 70.

CHAPTER 4

1. Komons, Nick A. *Bonfires To Beacons: Federal Civil Aviation under the Air Commerce Act, 1926-1938.* Smithsonian Institution Press, Washington, D.C. 1989. Page 35.

2. Ibid. Page 35.

3. Ibid. Page 36.

4. Ibid. Page 84.

5. Ibid. Page 85.

6. Ibid. Page 86.

7. Smith, Henry Ladd. *Airways: The History of Commercial Aviation in the United States.* The Smithsonion Institution Press, Washington, D.C., 1991 Page 104.

8. Douglas, Deborah G. *From Airships to Airbus: The History of Civil and Commercial Aviation. Infrastructure and Environment.* Vol. I, William M. Leary, Ed. Smithsonian Institution Press, Washington, D.C., 1992. Page 58.

9. Ibid. Page 60.

10. Greif, Martin. *The Airport Book.* The Main Street Press. New York, 1979. Page 43.

11. Douglas, Deborah G., *From Airship to Airbus.* Page 60.

12. Scott, Mary L. *San Diego: Air Capital of the West.* The Donning Company, Virginia Beach, VA, 1991.

13. Underwood, John . *Madcaps, Millionaires and "Mose".* Heritage Press, Glendale, CA. 1984, Page 45.

14. Wells, Alexander T. *Airport Management and Administration.* TAB Books/McGraw Hill, Blue Ridge.

14. Komons, Nick A . *Bonfires To Beacons: Federal Civil Aviation under the Air Commerce Act. 1926-1938.* Smithsonian Institution Press, Washington, D.C. 1989. Page 35.

14 Ibid. Page 35.

14. Ibid. Page 36.

14. Ibid. Page 84.

14. Ibid. Page 85.

14. Ibid. Page 86.

14. Smith, Henry Ladd. *Airways: The History of Commercial Aviation in the United States.* The Smithsonion Institution Press, Washington, D.C., 1991 Page 104.

14. Douglas, Deborah G. *From Airships to Airbus: The History of Civil and Commercial Aviation. Infrastructure and Environment.* Vol. I, William M. Leary, Eds. Smithsonian Institution Press, Washington, D.C., 1992. Page 58.

14. Ibid. Page 60.

14. Greif, Martin. *The Airport Book.* The Main Street Press. New York, 1979. Page 43.

14. Douglas, Deborah G. *From Airship to Airbus.* Page 60.

14. Scott, Mary L. *San Diego: Air Capital of the West.* The Donning Company, Virginia Beach, VA, 1991.

14. Underwood, John. *Madcaps, Millionaires and "Mose".* Heritage Press, Glendale, CA. 1984, Page 45.

14. Wells, Alexander T. *Airport Management and Administration.* TAB Books/McGraw Hill, Blue Ridge Summit, PA 1992, Page 8.

CHAPTER 5

1. Shumpeter, Joseph H. *History of Economic Analysis.* Oxford University Press, New York. 1976. Page 1175.

2. Douglas, Deborah G. "Airports as Systems and Systems of Airports: Airports and Urban Development in American before World War II". *From Airships to Airbus: The History of Civil and Commercial Aviation.* William M. Leary, Ed., Vol. I Infrastructure and Environment. Smithsonian Institution Press, Washington D.C. 1992. Page 67.

3. Ibid. Page 75.

4. Ibid. Page 78.

5. Ovington, Earle. "The Saucer Airport". *Airport and Construction Management* magazine, June 1929. Page 18.

6. Ibid. Page 18.

7. Waterman, Waldo D. "Nine Kinds of Airports." *Airport Construction Management* magazine. 1929. Page 12.

8. Ibid. Page 13.

9. Probert, Richard J. "Where To Put Your Airport." *Airport Construction and Management* magazine. April 1929. Page 6.

10. Reed, Thomas R. "How's the Weather?" *Airport Construction and Management* magazine. 1929. Page 12.

11. Wells, Alexander T. *Airport Planning and Management.* TAB Books-McGraw-Hill Publishing Co., New York 1992. Page 10.

CHAPTER 6

1. Smith, Henry Ladd. *Airways; The History of Commercial Aviation in the United States.* The Smithsonian Institution Press, Washington, D.C., 1991. Page 342.

2. Ibid. Page 344.

3. Wells, Alexander T. *Airport Planning and Management.* TAB Books. McGraw Hill Publishing Co., New York 1992. Pages 10, 11.

4. Ibid. Page 13.

5. "Pancho." Video produced and narrated by Dr. Jim Young, USAF Historian, Edwards AFB., for the Flight Test Historical Foundation.

6. Greiff, Martin. *The Airport Book.* 1979. The Main Street Press, Clinton, New Jersey. Page 142.